ANCIENT FUTURE

ANCIENT FUTURE

The Teachings and Prophetic Wisdom of the
Seven Hermetic Laws of Ancient Egypt

By

Wayne B. Chandler

Black Classic Press
1999

ISBN-13 978-1-57478-001-7 ISBN-10 1-57478-001-8

Library of Congress Cataloging In Publication # 96–85977

Photos reprinted with permission from Penguin Putnam,
Inc., Thames and Hudson Ltd, and What's A Face
Productions. Other photos and illustrations are from the
author's private collection unless otherwise noted.

Front cover:
Amenhemet II, Pharoah of the 12th Dynasty of Egypt

Cover design by Akosua B. Reedy,
Dez-Tech Information Services & IFA Typesetting
Atlanta, GA
Text design by
BCP Digital Printing

Dedication

I dedicate this book to my mother Helen R. Chandler and to my brother Brian E. Chandler. Their undying support, confidence, and love have allowed miraculous events to occur in my life. I also dedicate this book to my spirits on the wind, who watch over me and have touched the deepest part of my soul.

Contact Information

For more information or to contact the author directly about lectures and other programs, send e-mail to the following address:waynebchandler@gmail.com

Preface

Along the time line of human life, we find periods of light, characterized by great spiritual and technological achievement, considered by many to be *golden ages.* Just as prominent on the timeline are periods of the disintegration of civilization brought about by dissension, greed, war, and malice. These are frequently known as the *dark ages.* We find that it is during these times of dire disharmony that the greatest of Earth's heroes have walked among humans, leading people from the murky darkness into the light. Many of these beings — individuals such as Buddha, Jesus, Isis, Ishtar, Muhammad, and Krishna — are considered saviors of humanity due to the magnitude of influence and change they caused during their terms on Earth. These early heroes are often confused with gods.

Though we live forward, we are forever looking backward; the present is viewed as ever intolerable, full of pangs and neuroses. I grew up hearing "tomorrow will be better, like the good old days." From this chronic contradiction, the hero arises — a model of the past bound to the present to create the future. Such a hero is the entity historically identified as the Egyptian god Tehuti, known to ancient Greeks and contemporary scholars as Thoth or Hermes.

Ancient Future, though it briefly explores the man, is more concerned with the philosophical and scientific axioms engendered by Tehuti/Hermes and their impact on the human race, both past and present. The written work of Tehuti has come to be known as the Hermetic philosophy and is considered by many to be among the most important precepts expressed in the last five thousand years.

Ancient Future comprehensively examines the Hermetic principles of Tehuti, creating a link between antiquity and the future. Winston Churchill was perhaps the most famous to state the truism, "The farther back we look, the further forward we'll be able to see."

It has been five thousand years since the great civilizations of China, India, Kush, Southern Arabia, Mesopotamia, Sumeria, and Egypt were eminent. Those laws found in the Hermetic philosophy comprised the scientific, spiritual, and moral fabric of these ancient empires, bequeathing to them a wisdom we have yet to discover in our current period. Though these axioms are still evident in fragmented form in many of the historical texts left to us, the understanding that constituted the vision of our ancestors is long forgotten. Under the dark shadow cast over our current epoch, we have forgotten who we are, where we have been, and more importantly, where we are heading.

Thus, *Ancient Future* is an overview of the Hermetic philosophy, a road map to reacquaint all members of the human race with its unremitting challenge. It is presented with the specific mission of reaching those who are the heirs of its principles and whose ancestors were the guardians of time long before the darkness of our age. This book is not a story of contributions, but a testimony to the people of the first world order, who, research shows, were the inhabitants of Egypt and Kush in Africa, India in South Asia, Brigantia in Europe, Sumeria and Mesopotamia in West Asia, and China in East Asia. These were the people who laid the very foundation of Earth's first civilizations.

Modern people have fallen prey to a reductionist view of history. We have compromised our impetus to learn, to seek our own truth rather than being told by others what that truth is. We constrict our reality, thereby losing opportunities to learn and benefit from systems of mental, moral, and spiritual resolution currently attributed to older, erudite cultures of the world — cultures that lit the way for younger nations. Without a holistic view of life, we relinquish to others the fruits of the "tree of knowledge." The greatest of these fruits are the seven principles of Tehuti/Hermes, which originated in ancient Egypt and were carried into all continents, and remain evident in those places in forms as various as Taoism in China, Jainism in India, and Buddhism in Japan (by way of India). All civilizations have benefited, directly or indirectly, from the knowledge that results from an understanding of the Hermetic philosophy.

Our incessant attempts to intellectualize the accomplishments of our ancestors, without truly understanding them as spiritually dynamic beings, has created a dilemma for the descendants of these great cultures. Our exclusively intellectual methods of learning will never be able to comprehend the kind of philosophy that incorporates both intellect and spirituality. The fact is that the great ancient race from which Tehuti/Hermes came was made up of beings very different from ourselves. They were giants, spiritually as well as intellectually. They created wonders that cannot be duplicated by modern science, which has yet to fully comprehend them. Our cultural indoctrination allows us to experience only that which is tangible and perceptible, which unfortunately comprises but one facet of our multidimensional reality. The seven axioms of Hermetic philosophy were innate in Tehuti's contemporaries, molding and shaping their consciousness, and allowing them insight into the fundamental reality that eludes most of humankind in this age. Thus the seven axioms are doorways through time into a distant past that, when understood and applied, can help prepare us for the future.

Ancient Future represents two decades of collecting material on Hermetic thought. When I began my reading and research on this subject, I had no intention of publishing it; this information was for my edification and growth. I have been able to apply these axioms — mentalism, correspondence, vibration, polarity, gender, rhythm, and causation — to general and specific events in my own life, thereby experiencing the transformative, constructive, and lucid force they have to offer. These axioms of ancient Egypt are a practical guide to obtaining clarity of perception and of imparting this perception to every facet of life: social, political, psychological, spiritual, and metaphysical. The wonder of the Hermetic philosophy is that its message is not only eternal but transformative, regardless of the capacity in which it is being used. Therefore its principles may be applied to science, medicine, technology, or history and the results will be a clear, comprehensive vision of the dynamics inherent in the specific area of study. My goal in *Ancient Future* is to present these ancient laws to a contemporary readership in a focused, practical, and comprehensive fashion.

I study these laws not just for their intellectual value as an historical phenomenon; I have opened myself to witness their manifestation in my life, in contemporary world situations, and in the larger flows and cycles of history. I present them here not so that they can be claimed by one set of people as their own, but so that they can be seen as the basic universal laws that guide all life. They are the axioms of the peculiar human journey. Awareness of these laws allows us the opportunity to recognize and rise above the mundane games of our lives, the divisions that have been constructed for us and those that we have created for ourselves that compartmentalize us by race, class, sex, theology, and a plethora of other categories and identities. In fact, knowledge of these laws makes apparent that in the universe, all things, people, and events are interrelated and interdependent. This interdependence becomes clear when we apply the Hermetic principles to human history. In order to understand any one event in history, it is necessary to back up and broaden our view to get a clear vision of how that event fits into the larger scheme of human interaction. It soon becomes clear that events have repercussions even thousands of years later, and events on one continent have effects in seemingly distant places.

Ancient Future celebrates the wisdom of those ancient civilizations that did not disassociate the philosophical, spiritual, and material realms of life. This book is an attempt to recreate this holistic experience in hopes that a synthesized view of life will become the perspective of the twenty-first century.

Acknowledgments

In one's endeavor to achieve, no matter what the achievement, one must acknowledge the assistance given by those who helped bring to fruition their project, their truth, their dream. The development of this book has been no exception and I would like to thank those who invested time and energy, directly and indirectly, knowingly and unknowingly, to help this book become a reality.

First, I would like to thank Kathryn Barrett-Gaines and the Duke University School of Cultural Anthropology for significant data used in this book. Barrett-Gaines' assistance was invaluable in this undertaking. I would also like to thank Dr. Ivan Van Sertima of Rutgers University, who brought me on board with an elite group of scholars, which for ten years allowed me to research, write, and lecture, transforming my view of history into a more constructive and holistic perspective. His guidance and trust opened a doorway through which I walked and never looked back. The influence of my friend and colleague, Runoko Rashidi, cannot go without mention. Partaking of Rashidi's expertise in the area of ancient and contemporary Asian civilization and culture influenced my vision of history greatly. I would also like to thank historian and author Dr. James Brunson, who stands alone in his research and contributions regarding the impact of the African presence in Asian antiquity. I must also thank author James Granger for pertinent and valuable comments on the text. I would like to extend my thanks and appreciation to graphic artist, David Kennedy. Mr. Kennedy supplied all of the geometric drawings for the first chapter in part two of this book and those of the grid in chapter six. Without his assistance to create on paper what was in the cosmos and ancient doctrines, there would have been countless individuals wondering what in the world I was trying to articulate. I also send a sincere thanks to David "Oggie" Ogburn, the photographer of the "stars" who humbled himself enough to help me develop most of the photos in this book. Though it was quite an undertaking (developing pictures of statues, rocks, sculptures, and bas reliefs can be frustrating for someone used to developing Sade Adu, Cher, or Tina Turner), Oggie came through like a champion. I would also like to thank V. Hap Smith, my uncle, for providing me with much-needed sanctuary, solitude, and advice while I made revisions to the manuscript and my life. While I'm on the subject of revisions, I must thank Michelle L. Watts of the Shaker Heights Ohio Public Library.

I have been fortunate in having great artistic, philosophical, and spiritual minds in my life. These individuals have helped tremendously by providing me spiritual sustenance as food for thought, thus helping define my reality. I send a special thanks to my friend A. Mati Klarwein, probably the greatest artist on the Earth today. His artwork adorned the album covers of Santana's *Abraxas* and Miles Davis' *Bitches Brew*. Mati taught me that perfection does exist, but outside of time. I also extend thanks to Dick Gregory for his wisdom and assistance. I would also like to thank Swami Satchidananda, Sri Cliff Hardy, and my yoga instructor, John Schumacher for insights, training and dialogue on what constitutes a more meaningful expression of life. I must also thank Karl "with a K" Sawyer, who initiated me into the realm of spiritual revelation, Jane DeAngeli for her assistance and heart-felt wisdom, Dr. Michael Frost for insights and refinement of my regenerative practices, and Dr. Jennifer Ann Fletcher for reinitiating me in the path of natural healing.

I would also like to thank the LIGHT WARRIORS, those children of tomorrow's dawn, whom I have had the pleasure of knowing. I am grateful to my spiritual brothers James "Pete" Jackson, Nana Kwaku Sakyi and Michael, Silas Ashley, Greg White, and Waymond Scott. Also Rashida Tutashinda, Sharon Butcher, Deollo and Thadeus, Kilindi Iyi, Aswan Boudroux, Marie Bouman and Silas Smith, Karina Vogt, Tamara, Emmanuel Jennings, Joan Kelly, Denise LeCompte, Leigh Donlan, Judy Pradier, Russel, Carol Harshaw, Dr. Lynn Locklear, Mimi Vreeland, Akosua, Tony Matthews, Charles "Bliss" Tolbert, Hasib, Ana Paula, and numerous other great individuals, like my homie Karen DeVaughn, that I have encountered along the way whose names I have not forgotten but for whom space does not allow honorable mention.

Finally, I would like to thank my friend and former business partner Mr. Gaynell Catherine, "the picture takin' man." We accomplished some great things and one day, maybe the next time around, we'll get it back together. Thank you all for your encouragement, support, and friendship.

Foreword

Late one morning, fourteen years ago, I received a phone call from someone I had never met. He informed me that he had done research on the Olmec civilization and had discovered some startling photographs. Calls such as these are common in my life, and somewhat tiresome at times because these anonymous callers rarely deliver on their promises. About a week later, I received in the mail a photographic contact sheet with images of giant Africoid stone heads from ancient America. Although most of these images were familiar to me, I found on the sheet an extraordinary photo of an indisputably African face with Ethiopian-style braids dangling from behind its head. I reached for my pen to begin a letter to the sender, but before I could finish, the phone rang. The caller and the sender was Wayne Chandler. I invited him to write for the *Journal of African Civilizations,* and throughout the next decade, Chandler submitted photographs that were like windows on forgotten and obscure periods of history.

Much like his photos, Chandler's writing style has a dramatic quality rare in academia. His *Journal* essays fascinated us with the exploits of Hannibal and the invasion of southern Europe by the medieval Moors and the mysteries of Egypt's Old Kingdom and its stupendous pyramids. His information was well researched, ran counter to the views of the academic establishment, and was presented in a style that made it fascinating to academic and lay audiences alike.

In "The Jewel in the Lotus: The Ethiopian Influence in the Indus Valley Civilization" (1985), Chandler's talents as both a photographer and writer are showcased. Chandler's photography not only brings to vivid life the African faces of these ancient times, but his dramatic narrative conveys a sense of the modernity of these cities, some of which blend both early Ethiopian and Asiatic influences. We learn of the creation of a central sewage system — bathrooms with drains that carry waste to the sewers under the main streets, every house with its own private well, a great public bath with carefully made floors that empty into the underground sewers, the bath water changing at regular intervals. Chandler even evokes the dust of passing traffic on the thirty-foot wide streets.

The Moors, according to Chandler, generated a resurgence of activity in the arts and sciences, influenced embryonic nations like

Spain and France and even older nations like China and India, but who were they? I think Chandler has made a more serious attempt to deal with this complex question than most other researchers "The Moor: Light of Europe's Dark Age" (1986). The identity of the Moors is a matter of great importance; and while the African element is the major element, the Moors do not have a single-stranded identity. They are worth the most serious and balanced analysis since they were to make a major contribution to the European renaissance which lifted parts of Europe from the Dark Ages.

In "Hannibal: Nemesis of Rome" (1988), Chandler challenges the accepted myth that the great African general Hannibal was European. Hannibal was the scourge of Rome for fifteen years. His tactical feats awed the military strategists of many different lands and centuries. He single handedly put his nation on the world's historical map. Without his exploits, argues Chandler, Carthage would be unknown save to a few erudite scholars. But who was Hannibal? Chandler provides images of an ancient coin with an African head on one side and Surus, the favorite elephant of Hannibal, on the other. Surus was among the last elephants to survive the march across the Alps. Hannibal mounted this elephant and no other. Why would any artist laboriously carve out the head of an insignificant *mahout* (elephant rider) on the front of a coin that commemorated the general's mount? It is difficult not to conclude that this is an image of the general himself, whose epic march across the Alps was captured wonderfully in Chandler's narrative.

In his study of the Pyramid Age of Egypt "Of Gods and Men: Egypt's Old Kingdom" (1989), Chandler raises questions about the chronology of Egypt. He highlights the extraordinary accomplishments of the early Pharaohs and touched upon the moral code and character of the Egyptian state, exploding myths about slaves as the mainstay of the working force. His approach has been important to students of Egyptian history because it emphasizes that technical accomplishments, however impressive, do not in themselves constitute civilization. Chandler argues that, to the early Egyptian, civilization was the humanization of the human and that the building of an ethical code of human conduct was just as important as the building of a pyramid. The law that ordered them to honor the dead and give bread to the hungry, water to the thirsty, and clothing to the naked, reveals one of the finest qualities of old Egyptian character: pity towards the unfortunate.

Ancient Egyptian science startles us even to this day. Scholars have expounded all sorts of improbable theories to explain how the early Egyptians built the pyramids. Chandler exposes the folly of these still generally accepted assumptions, pointing out how the Japanese experiment in 1979 has humbled and astounded us all. The Japanese eventually resorted to twentieth-century technology which still fell short of the results achieved by the ancient Egyptians. The early Egyptian engineers aligned the stones within 1/1000 of an inch of mathematical perfection, a perfection achieved today only by jewelers cutting gems under microscope. Chandler's introduction to the Pyramid Age is accompanied by a remarkable gallery of African faces. He points to the progressive intermixture over the centuries between the indigenous Africans and the other races that came into the Nile Valley, but he holds (and here his photographic evidence is the best argument) that the dominant ruling figures of the age were indeed African.

In most of his contributions to the *Journal of African Civilizations*, Chandler presents new and provocative information on subjects that were previously regarded as closed. I believe it is his broad immersion in several disciplines that allows him to approach history in an unorthodox manner. He embraces many elements — the religious, philosophical, and scientific — of these ancient empires. In *Ancient Future*, he has blended all his skills and interests to tell a remarkable and original story. Twelve years ago, I was introduced to a promising young scholar who became part of a team working to revise the way African history is told and taught. I am proud to see him finding his own unique voice in this work, a vision of hope born through an understanding of the need for unity and peace between the races of man on the brink of a new millennium.

—Ivan Van Sertima, 1999

Contents

Part I: An Introduction to the Seven Hermetic Axioms of Tehuti

The African Concept of Mythology, The History of Thoth/Hermes and his Philosophy, Poimandres: The Spiritual Vision of Hermes, The Significance of The Number Seven, The Seven Hermetic Axioms of Thoth

Part II: A Comprehensive Analysis of the Seven Hermetic Axioms of Tehuti

Chapter 1. The Principle of Mentalism and the Concept of the All or God   41

The Divine in Western Civilization, The Ancient Religious Model, The Crusades and the Inquisition, The Western Concept of God, The African Concept of the Divine, The Hermetic Explanation of the All or God, The Definition of Spirit, The Divine Mind — The Mental Universe, Time: Linear versus Cyclic Reality, Meditation, Sacred Geometry

Chapter 2. The Principle of Correspondence   69

The "Star of David" or the Egyptian Star of Creation, The Nature of Correspondence, The Three Great Planes of Correspondence, The Impact of Correspondence on Our Lives, The Establishment of Mind on All Planes of Existence, The Relation of the Mind to Correspondence

Part I:

AN INTRODUCTION TO THE SEVEN HERMETIC AXIOMS OF TEHUTI

Introduction

"The Principles of Truth are Seven; he who knows this, understandingly, possesses the Magic Key before whose touch all the doors of the Temple fly open." – Kybalion

Before the dawn of the present era was a period known to the ancient historian as *antediluvian,* or "world before the flood." Much of what the Western world knows of this period comes through biblical tradition. A passage from Genesis 6:4 — "there were giants in the earth in those days and also after that when the sons of God came in unto the daughters of men, and they bear children to them, the same became mighty men which were of old, men of renown" — speaks of this era, which predated the great flood associated in the biblical tradition with Noah. This and several other biblical phrases allude to the fact that the races of the Earth during this age were truly omnipotent, or God-like in every way. Mythological tradition holds that during this antediluvian period was born the great Egyptian sage Tehuti or Thoth. Tehuti, known to the Greeks as Hermes/Thoth, became the principle law-giver of Egypt, or in the tongue of the Africans of that land, Kmt (pronounced Kemet). His axioms provided humanity with a comprehensive analysis of the nature of creation and of the universe. Throughout the text of this book, the names Tehuti, Thoth, and Hermes are used interchangeably.

Western civilization considers most accounts of what transpired during this period to be pure mythology. And because Western influence dominates the present, we have fallen prey to a superficial, linear approach to investigative research. This perspective on ancient history has left a substantial void in our vast ancestral cultural legacy, much of which is located in what we now call *myth.*

The outset of the twenty-first century demands a redefinition of much of our present terminology. Such a redefinition will, in time, allow for a much broader historical perspective than is presently employed by traditional historians. The term *myth* as understood through a Eurocentric perspective connotes fantasy and fable in the realm of the surreal; however, in antiquity, mythology was an ancient mode of thinking. It was founded on

natural facts, still verifiable phenomena, and was not then, nor
is it now, a mechanism based on an irrational perspective. Mythology is the repository of our most ancient science, and when
myth is examined within the context of an ancient cultural belief
system, it becomes a dynamic vehicle for the transmission of
truth:

> The importance of mythology is, of course, that it is a form of
> documentation which transcends the human record as much as
> it states truth rather than fact. Myth can be considered a form of
> reasoning and record keeping by providing an implicit guide
> for bringing about the fulfillment of the truth it proclaims. It
> connects the invisible order with the visible order . . . thought
> reflected in myth is inseparable from the laws of nature. . . . As
> a reflection of the thought and experience of a people, the
> analytical value of myth is that it serves as a measure and/or
> reflection of the human possibilities, PROBABILITIES, and
> potentialities of a people.[1]

Thus, an examination of the origin, development, and contributions of an entity such as Tehuti from the African myth perspective makes the incomprehensible comprehensible, and
allows a true understanding of what would have been lost as
historic ephemera. Discussion on the historical reality of Tehuti
is subject to the nature of the present state of the study of history.
So regardless of fact, fiction, documentation, or myth, my particular examination of Tehuti consists of what little testimony
exists on his actual life, his own account of the divine revelation
of his seven basic axioms, and a study of these illuminated laws
of the universe and the higher message therein.

Tehuti is the personification of universal wisdom and truth.
Egyptian tradition holds that he imparted this truth first to the
old race, the Kushites, who would later be identified by the
Greeks as the Ethiopians. The Greeks, who considered Tehuti or
Thoth "the Scribe of the Gods," would also change his name to
Hermes, or more accurately *Hermes Mercurius Trismegistus,*
which means "the thrice-great," "the great-great," "the greatest-
great," and "master of masters." With the spread of Western influence, this appellation remained globally intact and Tehuti's
teachings have become known as the Hermetic philosophy.

The writings of Tehuti/Hermes have been known to the West
since the fifth century B.C.E. (Before the Current or Christian
Era). Some of the more popular translations have been those of
Hargrave Jennings (1884), a reprint of Everhard's English ver-

sion; the Greek text of C. Parthey Berolins (1854); a German edition by J. Scheible (1855); and the earliest Latin edition of Marsilius Ficinus (1471). It was long assumed that the earliest translation from the Egyptian text was done in Arabic during the conquest and occupation of Egypt by the Moors in the ninth century C.E. (Current or Christian Era), but many fragments contained in the *Liber Hermetis*, a Latin translation of Greek origin, are traceable to the third or fourth century B.C.E. The West presently acknowledges Walter Scott and Andre-Jean Festugiere as the contemporary experts on *Hermetica*: it was they who distinguished the "popular" occultist or secret writings attributed to Tehuti/Hermes from the so-called learned or philosophical treatises, the latter being more prominent in most modern translations of the *Hermetica*. The problem with these recent translations that have flooded the West is that they have been little more than an exercise in academia. Esteemed more for the period in which they were originally written than for their content, the writings of Hermetic Philosophy gave way to the overt mundane skepticism that presently saturates the field of Western academia. It has always been in vogue for Western academicians to stand on the periphery of what they examine, believing somehow that they may osmotically engender the experience without actual involvement. This has been the modus operandi from the outset of Greek civilization to our present period. It is interesting to note the acknowledgment of this pattern regarding the Western mindset of the ancient Greeks by Imhotep (known to the Greeks as *Asclepius*), student of Tehuti/Hermes: "For the Greeks have empty speeches . . . that are energetic only in what they demonstrate, and this is the philosophy of the Greeks, an inane foolosophy of speeches. We [the Egyptians], by contrast, use not speeches but sounds that are full of action."[2] This examination uses the conventional or "philosophical" writings as well as "popular" and rare nontraditional sources in Hermetic academia to unveil the truths therein.

The Hermetic teachings are found in all lands among all religions, but are never identified with any particular creed or religious sect, thus rising above them all. These ancient mystery systems were imparted to India and Persia by their indigenous inhabitants but degenerated with the influx of the Aryans and Indo-Iranians. In time they were lost, a result of the merging of theology and philosophy when teachers became pagan priests who aspired for power amidst religious superstition, cults, and creeds.

Extreme Greek interest in the Hermetic Philosophy led to the separation, and eventually the removal, of these axioms and perspectives from the larger body of Egyptian science and thought, and finally to their placement in the Greek philosophical tradition. So thorough was the transfiguration of Tehuti to Thoth/Hermes that many students and some scholars of Egyptian history are unaware that the Hermetic Philosophy is arguably the world's oldest doctrine, originating not in Greece, but on the African continent.

In regard to Hermes, history has provided several suppositions, much legend, and many myths. Hermes has been associated with many of the early sages and prophets such as Cadmus and Enoch, the latter identified as the "Second Messenger of God." Syrian philosopher Iamblichus averred that Hermes was the author of 20,000 books; the Egyptian priest/historian Manetho increased that number to more than 36,000. Because of the astounding number of books attributed to Hermes, some believe that he was an array of various personalities or an entire secret society dedicated to the evolution of the human race.

According to records retained by Syncellus (a Byzantine monk of the ninth century C.E.), which he believed were written a thousand years earlier by Mer-en-Jehuti (Manetho), the Egyptian high priest of Sebynnetos, there were two gods named Hermes. The first was Tehuti/Thoth, whose legacy extends to the very dawn of African civilization. It was he who originally carved on *stelae* (pillars) in hieroglyphics what became the sacred writings for the Anu, the "old race." The second Thoth, who became Hermes Trismegistus, was the son of Agathodaimon, who seems to have ruled during the time of Imhotep (called Asclepius by the Greeks), ca. 2700 B.C.E. Syncellus, quoting a portion of text written by Manetho and addressed to Ptolemy II Philadelphus (282–229 B.C.E.), stated,

> Manetho knew stelae in the land of Seiria. . . . inscribed in the sacred tongue in hieroglyphic letters by Thoth, the first Hermes, and translated after the flood from the sacred tongue into the Greek language . . . and set down in books by the son of Agathodaimon, the second Hermes, father of Tat, in the sanctuaries of the temples of Egypt; [Manetho] dedicated [them] to . . . Ptolemy . . . writing thus: " . . since you seek to know what will come to be in the cosmos, I shall present to you

the sacred books that I have learned about, written by our
ancestor, Hermes Trismegistus. . ." This is what he says about
the translation of the books written by the second Hermes.[3]

If indeed this information is historically accurate, it would explain much of what has become the dilemma of Tehuti/Hermes
and his immense literary undertaking. There are other accounts
that can be categorized as legend or myth that enunciate the
ability of Tehuti/Hermes to survive such an ample accomplish-
ment. It is the nature of legend that its many parts support one
another, and so it is with the legend of Hermes. Though he is
given credit for an astounding number of published works, he
is also reported to have lived 300 years, which would easily allow for such a prolific literary undertaking.

Certainly most would find this life expectancy of three centuries totally incomprehensible. Biblical references to people living to advanced age are often interpreted as symbolic simply
because they are considered impossible to achieve. In the book
of Genesis, chapters 23–25, the Bible states that Abraham and
Sarah had their son, Isaac, when they were both around a hundred years old, and after Sarah's death at 127 years, Abraham fa-
thered six more sons before his own death at age 175. The
question remains — how could people have lived to such ages in
antiquity but barely survive to a meager seventy years in the
present time? While Tehuti still walked the Earth with human
beings, he entrusted to his most esteemed disciples and chosen
successors his sacred book. The Book of Tehuti/Hermes contained information that explained the process of biological regeneration, which allowed the various biochemical and
physiological systems in the human body to undergo physical
and mental restoration. This axiom was based on the premise
that all of the soft tissue systems within the human body are subject to this process of revitalization every seven months, and the
more fundamental or substantial tissue systems every seven
years. The secret to attaining this level of physical mastery was
said to be the result of various breathing techniques. The work
also contained the secret process by which the regeneration of
humanity was to be accomplished.

According to legend, the Book of Tehuti was kept in a golden
box in the inner sanctuary of a temple dedicated to Tehuti. In order to protect it from the encroaching Christian traditions and
the resulting decay of the mysteries, the highest initiate of what
came to be known as the *Hermetic Arcanum* took the Book of

Tehuti to an undisclosed location in another land, and it was lost to the world. According to Hermetic tradition, this book still exists and continues to lead Hermetic disciples of the present age into the presence of the immortals. The traditions of vital regeneration and other methods contained in the book are still practiced in India and China.

Using the aforementioned concepts of biological regeneration, one doctor, Deepak Chopra, is revolutionizing the way science and the medical establishment perceive the aging process. South Asian by birth, Dr. Chopra taught at Tufts University and Boston University Schools of Medicine before becoming chief of staff at New England Memorial Hospital. Seeing the shortcomings of Western medicine, Dr. Chopra has combined the ancient Indian tradition of Ayurvedic medicine with Western science, achieving remarkable results. Through unfailing example, Chopra has begun to prove that within the human biological framework exists the possibility of immortality: "The new paradigm tells us that life is a process of constant transformation, not decline, and therefore is full of potential for unlimited growth."[4] With the success of Dr. Chopra's research, even staunch adherents to the old paradigm concur that automatic biological degeneration is not programmed into our bodies, and that human life is more resilient than previously imagined.

Using genetics and pioneering new avenues in cytology, Dr. Chopra has asserted that "humans have the capacity to think about being immortal." Information obtained from radioactive isotope studies demonstrates that ninety-eight percent of all the atoms in the body are replaced in less than one year. Research shows that the liver has the potential to regenerate every six weeks, the skin renews once a month, the stomach lining changes every five days, and our skeleton can renew itself once every three months. Dr. Chopra's findings indicate that every two years we replace our entire body, down to the last atom.[5] Deepak Chopra's findings corroborate the ancient traditions of longevity recorded by Tehuti/Hermes in his many writings.

Of the forty-two fragmentary writings believed to have come from the stylus of Hermes only two remain: *The Emerald Tablet* and *The Divine Pymander*. The loss of the balance of his works was a great tragedy to the philosophic world. In his *Stromata*, Clement of Alexandria made repeated reference to these forty-two Hermetic works, which were housed in the magnificent

Egyptian Library of Alexandria, so named after Alexander the Great. In the years following the inevitable demise of the once glorious Egyptian civilization, the Romans, and later the Christians, engaged in an ongoing campaign to nullify the Egyptians as a cultural and philosophical force. The unwavering treachery of the Romans and Christians culminated in one of the most diabolic and nefarious acts in all of history. Because the very hub of Egyptian culture was inextricably connected to these ancient doctrines of Tehuti, in the year 389 A.D., Emperor Theodosius, a Christian, gave the order for the burning of the great Library of Alexandria, knowing that the only way to insure the collapse of a culture was the total obliteration of its history. Tradition holds that the volumes of the Hermetic Philosophy that managed to escape the fire were buried in the desert and their location was known only to a few initiates of the secret societies. Whatever the nature of the being that is known as Tehuti/Hermes, humanity unequivocally owes to him the very foundations of all scientific and philosophical traditions, for his philosophies have impacted upon every civilization.[6]

An appropriate introduction to a discussion of the various axioms that constitute the present Hermetic Philosophy is an examination of the legend/myth of the vision that bequeathed to Tehuti/Hermes the mysteries of the universe and creation. The *Divine Pymander* of Hermes Mercurius Trismegistus is one of the earliest of the Hermetic writings extant. Though it is not in its original form, having been restructured during the first centuries of the Christian period and incorrectly translated several times since, this work still contains several of the original concepts of the Hermetic doctrine. The *Divine Pymander* consists of seventeen fragmentary writings, which were collected and put forth as one work. The second book of *Pymander* is known as *Poimandres* (the vision) and is the most famous of the Hermetic fragments because it has endured virtually unchanged through the ages.

Poimandres: The Vision of Hermes

*"Within each aspiration dwells the certainty
of its own fulfillment." – W.B.C.*

*Hermes, in search for divine truth, found himself seeking solitude
in a rocky and desolate place. He came to a place of rest and gave
himself over to meditation. Following the secret instructions of the
Temple, he gradually freed his higher consciousness from the
bondage of his bodily senses; and, thus released, his divine nature
revealed to him the mysteries of the transcendental spheres. As this
process of unfoldment began to climax, Hermes beheld a figure
which seemed awe-inspiring and beyond approach. It was the Great
Dragon, with wings stretching across the sky and light streaming
in all directions from its body. The Great Dragon called Hermes by
name, and asked him why he thus meditated upon the World
Mystery. Immensely humbled by this spectacle, Hermes prostrated
himself before the Dragon, beseeching it to reveal its identity. The
great creature answered that it was Poimandres, the Mind of the
Universe, the Creative Intelligence, and the Absolute Emperor of
all things. Hermes then besought Poimandres to disclose unto him
the nature of the universe. The Great Dragon nodded its
magnificent head and its form immediately changed.*

*Where the Dragon had stood was now a glorious and pulsating
radiance. Then Hermes heard the voice of Poimandres but his form
was not revealed. "I, thy God, am the Light and the Mind which
were before substance was divided from spirit and darkness from
Light. And the Word which appeared as a pillar of flame out of the
darkness is the Son of God, born of the mystery of the Mind. The
name of that Word is Reason. Reason is the offspring of Thought
and Reason shall divide the Light from the darkness and establish
Truth in the midst of the waters. Understand, O Hermes, and
meditate deeply upon the mystery. So it is that Divine Light that
dwells in the midst of mortal darkness, and ignorance cannot divide
them. The union of the World and the Mind produces that mystery
which is called life. . . . Learn deeply of the Mind and its mystery,
for therein lies the secret of immortality."*

*The Dragon again revealed its form to Hermes, and for a long
time the two looked steadfastly one upon the other, eye to eye, so that
Hermes trembled before the gaze of Poimandres. At the Word of the
Dragon, the heavens opened and the innumerable Light Powers
were revealed. . . . Hermes beheld the spirits of the stars, the*

celestials controlling the universe. . . . Hermes realized that the sight which he beheld was revealed to him only because Poimandres had spoken a Word. The Word was Reason, and by the Reason of the Word invisible things were made manifest. The darkness below, receiving the hammer of the Word, was fashioned into an orderly universe. The elements separated into strata and each brought forth living creatures. The Supreme Being–the Mind–manifested male and female, and they brought forth the Word; and the Word suspended between Light and darkness, was delivered of another Mind called the Workman, the Master-Builder, or the Maker of Things. "In this manner it was accomplished, O Hermes: The Word moving like a breath through space called forth the Fire by the friction of its motion. Therefore, the Fire is called the Son of Striving. The Son of Striving thus formed the Seven Governors, the Spirits of the Planets, whose orbits bounded the world; and the Seven Governors controlled the world by the mysterious power called Destiny. Then the downward-turned and unreasoning elements brought forth creatures without Reason. Substance could not bestow Reason, for Reason had ascended out of it. The air produced flying things and the waters things that swam. The earth conceived strange four-footed and creeping beasts, dragons, composite demons, and grotesque monsters. Then the Father–the Supreme Mind–, being Light and Life, fashioned a glorious Universal Man in its own image, not an earthly man but a heavenly Man dwelling in the Light of God. The Supreme Mind loved the Man it had fashioned and delivered to Him the control of the creations. Man, too, willed to make things, and his Father gave permission. The Seven Governors [Planets], of whose powers He partook, rejoiced and each gave the Man a share of its own nature.

The Man longed to pierce the circumference of the circles and understand the mystery of Him who sat upon the Eternal Fire. Having already all power, He stooped down and peeped through the seven Harmonies and, breaking through the strength of the circles, made Himself manifest to Nature stretched out below. The Man, looking into the depths, smiled, for he beheld a shadow upon the earth and a likeness mirrored in the waters, which shadow and likeness were a reflection of Himself. The Man fell in love with his own shadow and desired to descend into it. Coincident with the desire, that divine or intelligent aspect of Man united itself with the unreasoning image or shape. Nature, beholding the descent, wrapped herself about the Man whom she loved, and the two were mingled. For this reason Man is a composite. Within him is the Sky Man, immortal and beautiful; without is Nature, mortal and destructible. Thus suffering is the result of the Immortal Man's falling in love with his shadow and giving up Reality to dwell in the darkness of illusion; for being immortal, man has the power of the Seven Governors–also the Life, the Light, and the Word–; but being mortal, he is controlled by the rings of the Governors–Fate or Destiny.

Of the Immortal man it should be said that He is hermaphrodite, or male and female, and eternally watchful. He neither slumbers nor sleeps, and is governed by a Father also both male and female, and ever watchful. Such is the mystery kept hidden to this day; for Nature, being mingled in marriage with the Sky Man, brought forth a wonder most wonderful – seven men, all bisexual, male and female, and upright of stature, each one exemplifying the natures of the Seven Governors. These, O Hermes, are the seven races, species, and wheels. After this manner were the seven men generated. Earth was the female element and water the male element, and from the fire and ether they received their spirits, and Nature produced bodies after the species and shapes of men. They reproduced themselves out of themselves, for each was male and female. But at the end of the period the knot of Destiny was untied by the will of God and the bond of all things was loosened. Then all living creatures, including man, which had been hermaphroditical, were separated, the males being set apart by themselves and the females likewise, according to the dictates of Reason."

Then God spoke the Holy Word within the soul of all things saying: "Increase and multiply in multitudes, all you, my creatures and workmanships. Let him that is endowed with Mind know himself to be immortal and that the cause of death is the love of the body; and let him learn all things that are, for he who has recognized himself enters into the state of Good."

And when God had said this, Providence, with the aid of the Seven Governors and Harmony, brought the sexes together . . . He, who through the error of attachment loves his body, abides wandering in darkness, sensible and suffering the things of death; but he who realizes that the body is but the tomb of his soul, rises to immortality.

Then Hermes desired to know why men should be deprived of immortality for the sin of ignorance alone. The Great Dragon answered: "To the ignorant the body is supreme and they are incapable of realizing the immortality that is within them. Knowing only the body which is subject to death, they believe in death because they worship that substance which is the cause and reality of death."

Hermes bowed his head in thankfulness to the Great Dragon who had taught him so much, and begged to hear more concerning the ultimate of the human soul. So Poimandres resumed: "At death the material body of man is returned to the elements from which it came, and the invisible divine man ascends to the source from whence he came, namely the Eight Spheres. The senses, feelings, desires, and body passions return to their source, namely the Seven Governors, whose natures in the lower man destroy but in the invisible spiritual man give life. After the lower nature has returned to the brutishness, the higher struggles to regain its spiritual estate. It ascends the Seven Rings upon which sit the Seven Governors and returns to each their lower powers in this manner: Upon the first ring sits the Moon, and to it is returned the ability to increase and diminish. Upon the second ring sits Mercury, and to it are returned machinations, deceit, and craftiness. Upon the third ring sits Venus, and to it are returned the lusts and passions. Upon the fourth ring sits the Sun, and to this Lord are returned ambitions. Upon the fifth ring sits Mars, and to it are returned rashness and profane boldness. Upon the sixth ring sits Jupiter, and to it are returned the sense of accumulation and riches. And upon the seventh ring sits Saturn, at the Gate of Chaos, and to it are returned falsehood and evil plotting. Then being naked of all the accumulations of the Seven Rings, the soul comes to the Eighth Sphere, namely, the ring of the fixed stars. Here, freed of all illusion, it dwells in the Light which only pure spirit may understand.

The path to immortality is hard, and only a few find it. The rest await the Great Day when the wheels of the universe shall be stopped and the immortal sparks shall escape from the sheaths of substance. Woe unto those who wait, for they must return again, unconscious and unknowing. Blessed art thou, O Son of Light, to whom of all men, I Poimandres the Light of The World, have revealed myself. I order you to go forth, to become as a guide to those who wander in darkness, that they may be saved by my Mind in you. Establish my Mysteries and they shall not fail from this earth."

Hermes heard and replied, The sleep of the body is the sober watchfulness of the mind and the shutting of my eyes reveals the true light. My silence is filled with budding life and hope, and is full of good, for this is the faithful account of what I received from my true mind, that is Poimandres, The Great Dragon, The Lord of The Word, through whom I became inspired with the truth.[7]

The Vision of Hermes is significant in several ways. Theologians will invariably discover that many Hermetic precepts appear in — and obviously influenced — the Christian Bible, which appeared several centuries later. Orientalists familiar with the symbolic iconography of China and India will discover the origin of the Dragon in Chinese mythology and culture, not to mention the philosophical profundities inherent in the Yogic, Hindu, Jaina, and Buddhist traditions of South Asia.

The Vision of Hermes, like so many of the Hermetic writings, is an allegorical exposition of great philosophic and mystic truths. The intention here is to unravel, or in the words of the ancients, "to lift the Veil of Isis," to expose the practical and fundamental function of the axioms therein.

The great Hermetic principles or laws that have been left to us are seven in number. Seven is not an arbitrary figure, but a powerful and extremely significant symbol of divine or universal cohesiveness that permeates the core of our very existence. The following observations illustrate this point:

> 1. There are **Seven Days** in a week and **Fifty-two Weeks** in a year (5 + 2 = 7). In the Christian Bible, the Earth was created in six days and on the **Seventh Day** God rested.
>
> 2. Some psychologists have stated that **Age Seven** is the **Age of Reason**; twice that, **Fourteen,** is **Puberty**; thrice that, **Twenty-one,** is **Maturation.**
>
> 3. There are **Seven Cardinal Colors** in the solar spectrum — violet, indigo, blue, green, yellow, orange, red — from which all other colors are derived.
>
> 4. There are **Seven Key Notes** in the musical scale.
>
> 5. There are **Seven Continents**, as there are **Seven Seas**. Originally, there were believed to be **Seven Planets,** called the **Seven Governors** by the ancients, also referred to as the **Seven Angels** in Revelations in the Christian Bible.
>
> 6. There are **Seven Holes** that lead into the human body — ears, nostrils, mouth, anus, and vaginal or penile orifices. The human brain, heart, eye, and ear are each divided into **Seven Parts**. The skin has **Seven Layers**.

7. There are **Seven Virtues** — faith, hope, charity, strength, prudence, temperance, and justice — and **Seven Deadly Sins** — pride, avarice, luxury, wrath, idleness, gluttony, envy.

It is not by chance that so many components of human life are connected to expressions of seven. The ancients held that seven was the most spiritually inclined of all the numbers, therefore it is befitting that there are seven Hermetic Axioms.

The Hermetic Axioms of Tehuti/Hermes

1. The Principle of Mentalism

"The All is Mind; The Universe is Mental."[8]

This principle embodies the truth that the All or God is Mind. It explains that the All is the substantial reality underlying all the visible manifestations and appearances that we categorize as the material universe: matter, energy, and all that is apparent to our material senses. This entity, the All, is pure spirit, which is unknowable and undefinable, but is regarded in the most ancient traditions as a universal, infinite, living mind. Human beings, in futile attempts to describe the All, attribute to it characteristics that fall within the realm of what is comfortable and comprehensible. This is theology: the assigning of human qualities to the Supreme in order to comprehend the incomprehensible. Thus, the All is always depicted as a man — God, the Father — and is actually given a personality. In reality this axiom explains that the universe is a mental creation of the All; that is to say, the All is everything and everything is the All. This principle also explains the true nature of energy, power, and matter, and how these are subordinate to the mastery of the mind.

2. The Principle of Correspondence

"As above, so below; as below, so above."[9]

This axiom explicates the constant correspondence that exists between the various planes of life, whether recognized or not. When we perceive our solar system, vast and mystifying, with the Sun at its center and the planets in orbit around the Sun, we may acknowledge the same patterns on a much smaller scale: the atom, with the nucleus at its core, and the protons, electrons, and neutrons, which, like the planets, orbit around the nucleus.

The understanding of this law provides a key to unlocking the enigma of the multidimensional reality in which we exist mentally, materially, and spiritually.

3. The Principle of Vibration

"Nothing rests; everything moves; everything vibrates."[10]

This principle embodies the truth that everything is in constant motion. Whether this motion is perceivable is irrelevant, for this law affirms that everything vibrates, and that nothing is ever at rest. Modern science may now attest to this fact, but it should be kept in mind that this fact was known thousands of years ago in ancient Kmt (Egypt) and India. The higher the vibration, the higher the form or entity that exists within that particular frequency. Therefore, the vibrational connection between some of the grosser forms of matter, such as a rock, and a human being, is very great. Spirit has the highest vibrational frequency, vibrating at such a phenomenal speed that it seems to be at rest, just as a rapidly moving wheel seems to be motionless. It is said that those practitioners of the Hermetic teachings who are able to grasp this principle will be able to, with the appropriate formulas, control their own mental vibrations as well as those of others. Or, as stated by one of the old masters, "He who understands the Principle of Vibration, has grasped the scepter of power."[11]

4. The Principle of Polarity

"Everything is dual; everything has poles; everything has its pair of opposites; like and unlike are the same; opposites are identical in nature, but different in degree; extremes meet; all truths are but half-truths; all paradoxes may be reconciled."[12]

This law exemplifies the truth that for every extreme there is another equally as valid, and that the extremes thus opposed may have the effect of balancing each other. There are two sides to everything, and every truth may also be false. Humans experience this duality throughout life. For example, a woman who lives by a particular reality may find that a year later she has matured, grown, and her perspectives have changed, thus invalidating her prior truth or reality. Hermes stated that everything is divided into opposites; however, these opposites are identical in their nature, differing only in their degree. To illustrate, hot and cold are the same thing — temperature. They simply occupy different places on the temperate scale. The same may be seen with short and tall, light and dark, or large and small, all of which reflect opposite extremes of the same scale. One commonly experienced duality is love and hate. These are two mental states that reflect opposing degrees of emotion, and often fade into and out of one another to such a degree that they are barely distinguishable. The maxim "there is a thin line between love and hate" is a truism. Often, we move from love to hate and back again. Within this principle we can uncover the art of polarization, a kind of mental alchemy that allows people to change their individual psyches, from hate to love, or from evil to good.

5. The Principle of Gender

"Gender is in everything; everything has its Masculine and Feminine Principles; Gender manifests on all planes."[13]

This axiom embodies the truth that gender is manifested in everything; the masculine and feminine principles are always at work. This is not only true of the physical plane but of the mental and spiritual planes as well. This principle has an affinity with the polarity axiom. On the physical plane, the principle manifests as sex, but on higher planes it takes other forms. No creation, whether physical, mental, or spiritual, is possible without this principle. Within our own individual spheres of existence we know that every male has elements of feminine energy, and every female carries the components of the masculine. When this law is employed, we see the creation of planets, solar systems, and animal life of all kinds.

6. The Principle of Rhythm

"Everything flows out and in; everything has its tides; all things rise and fall; the pendulum swing manifests in everything; the measure of the swing to the right is the measure of the swing to the left; rhythm compensates."[14]

The principle of rhythm explains the cycles of life, the truth that everything has a tide-like ebb and flow. Hermes stated that the ebb of the tide is equal to its flow and is set in motion and maintained by the rhythm of the universe. There can be no better example than that of the various races and their civilizations. Once there were opulent and great empires that were created, maintained, or influenced by the Black race. For thousands of

years, these civilizations flourished as a pinnacle of cultural influence, holding sway even over those nations that they did not
touch directly. But just as the great swing of the pendulum
brought about their ascension, so it brought about their demise.
Within every great experience, whether related to race, culture,
civilization, or individual magnanimity, the tide must eventually turn. This principle is eternally united with the concept of
the great, awe-inspiring cycles or ages of humankind, as well as
those of the Earth, which forever dictate periods of upheaval
and tranquility. There is always an action and a reaction, an advance and a retreat. This law manifests in the creation and destruction of worlds, the rise and fall of nations, and ultimately in
the mental states of humanity.

7. The Principle of Cause and Effect

*"Every cause has its Effect; every Effect has its cause; everything
happens according to Law; Chance is but a name for Law not
recognized; there are many planes of causation but nothing escapes
the Law."*[15]

This principle purports that everything happens according to
law — that nothing merely happens. Chance and coincidence do
not exist; these are terms human beings choose, or are forced to
use because of an ignorance of the principle at work. The masses
of the Earth are governed by a herd instinct: the many are lead
aimlessly by the few, destined to be carried along, obedient to
the wills and desires of others stronger than themselves. Because they are basically unconscious, they are forever subject to
the effect of environment, heredity, suggestion, and other outward forces moving them about like pawns on a chessboard.
Once this principle is understood and practiced, one becomes a
mover as opposed to being moved, a player in the game of life,
as opposed to being played by it.

PART II:

COMPREHENSIVE ANALYSIS OF THE SEVEN HERMETIC AXIOMS OF TEHUTI

1. This woman represents the Bonda, one of the oldest known cultures in India today. Called adavasi, meaning former inhabitants, the Bonda are only 800 in number. Speaking their own language, distinct from the Dravidian and other national tongues of India, the Bonda — with the exception of the Adamanese — are the closest descendants in physical feature to the ancient Harappans. The various tribes of South Asia constitute forty-five million of the present population.

CHAPTER 1

The Principle of Mentalism
and the Concept of God or the All

"That which is the Fundamental Truth — the Substantial
Reality — is beyond true naming, but the wise men call it The All."
— Kybalion

The idea of God in the functional and absolute sense has been elusive in Western civilization. The factors of this dilemma are worthy of examination in order to grasp fully the greater spiritual or religious dynamic that is being espoused by today's major religions. A comprehensive examination of the present state of Western religion must begin with the first Indo-European hordes, who stormed off the Ukrainian steppes circa 4000–2500 B.C.E., bringing new and different perspectives of culture, race, civilization, and religion. Traces of the polytheism, violence, and subjugation overwhelmingly inherent in their religious rites are still entrenched in the soul of India, where the Indo-Europeans made one of their earliest appearances. By the time the Indo-Europeans reached South Asia, they had given themselves the appellation *Aryan,* meaning "noble one." They traveled with a *host* (from Latin, meaning "enemy or hostile") of deities, the greatest or most supreme of which was Pater or Phater, the source of the term *father.* The Pater archetype was a crude and distorted model of what would later become the Aryan personification of God. It was crude in the sense that when one compares the Aryan religious beliefs with the cultures the Aryans would eventually conquer — Egypt, Sumeria, India, and Mesopotamia — Aryan beliefs seem to be based on the most rudimentary spiritual formulas and conceptual foundations. Pater had a chameleon quality: upon contact with other cultures, it would assume and subsume the position and identity of the local indigenous supreme deity. After the Aryan invasion of India, Pater became Brahma, usurping the religious beliefs (those that were comprehensible to them) of the indigenous population. The Aryans then enshrouded the entity of Brahma with their own pagan doctrine, creating a complex belief system that

2. European Crusaders pillaging Jerusalem.

retained elements of the higher spiritual axioms evident in the conquered culture.

Aboriginal inhabitants, called the *Harrapans*, formed and maintained the sociocultural complex of the Indus Valley civilization from 3500 to 1500 B.C.E. They had an extremely well integrated belief system that functioned on the universal principles of the cosmos. They did not believe that the universe was created, maintained, and destroyed by an array of anthropomorphic deities, but rather that these processes were the result of an established cosmic order of laws, which maintained the natural balance of life on its many levels. They were strictly monotheistic, believing in an all-encompassing divine force that permeated all forms of existence from the smallest particle to the most advanced life forms.

Upon contact with the Aryan warlords and their priests, the religious codex of India's inhabitants became warped and perverted. The introduction of Aryan polytheism into India created a model that in time would produce a theological paradigm that would not only influence India, but would eventually indoctrinate the world: Brahminism gave birth to the Hindu faith, complete with religiously sanctioned racism and sexism.

The Aryan mindset was never able to grasp, much less initiate, the more lofty philosophies of the spiritual aspirants whom they would inevitably trample underfoot. Later, this same socioreligious ignorance would allow such diabolical undertakings as the Crusades, in which military mercenaries set out across southern Europe killing, torturing, pillaging, and looting, all in the name of God. One crusading army, commanded by Godfrey de Bouillon, massacred the entire population of Jerusalem in 1098 C.E. According to one historical account, the Crusaders rode into the fallen holy city on horses wading "knee-deep in the blood of the disbelievers."[16] In 1204, Mephistophelian hordes descended upon Constantinople and ravaged what was once the very sanctum of Western Christendom. The siege ended at the Church of St. Sophia in a bloody, sacrilegious, and iniquitous orgy of monumental proportions: "The knights slaughtered a great multitude of people of every age, old men and women, maidens, children and mothers with infants, by way of a solemn sacrifice to Jesus."[17] Historians estimate that Europe was Christianized at a cost of eight to ten million lives. Unfortunately, this religious treachery did not expire with the

3. Knights do battle while the inhabitants flee the city with the women

Crusades. Until the advent of Hitler's Nazis in modern Germany, neither Europe nor the world knew of a system of organized terrorism that could rival the five-hundred-year reign of the Inquisition. Historian Henry Charles Lea, a leading expert on medieval Europe, called the Inquisition "a standing mockery of justice—perhaps the most iniquitous that the arbitrary cruelty of man has ever devised. . . . Fanatic zeal, arbitrary cruelty and insatiable cupidity [avarice] rivaled each other in building up a system unspeakably atrocious. It was a system which might well seem the invention of demons."[18] The Inquisition was created primarily to force various so-called pagan populations to accept a church and a god they did not want. Bulgarian writers recorded that the Roman Catholic priests were given to drunkenness and robbery, behavior that was not only condoned by the church, but encouraged. Peter von Pilichdorf wrote in the early fourteenth century, "the worst man, if he be a priest, is more worthy than the holiest layman."[19] In the twelfth century, several monasteries were converted into wine shops and gambling houses, while nunneries became private whorehouses for the Christian clergy. Nicholas de Clamanges, rector of the University of Paris, declared that the popes were ravishers not pastors of their flocks;[20] and the Fraticelli, a powerful order of Franciscan monks, lamented that the Pope and all of his successors were tainted with sin, then proceeded to label him an Antichrist. Immediately after that comment, Pope Martin V dissolved the order and destroyed its religious center, the town of Magnalata, which was razed to the ground. Every resident was slain.[21]

Economic greed also figured very prominently in the motives of the founding Christian fathers. Grim humor of the time speculated that the Church had not ten commandments, but only one: "Bring hither the money." Saint Bernard lamented the church's greed: "Whom can you show me among the prelates who does not seek rather to empty the pockets of his flock than to subdue their vices?"[22] In 1325, Pope John issued the *Cum inter nonnullos*, a religious decree that deemed heresy any statement to the effect that Jesus and his apostles owned no property. Inquisitors were ordered to prosecute those who believed Jesus was a poor man. The spiritual Franciscans scoffed the Pope's order, thereby forcing his hand: he had 114 of their members burned alive.[23]

This perverse pecuniary attitude within the Church became religiously consecrated with the advent of Calvinism. Calvinists believed in predestination—God would save a chosen few, regardless of their worldly behavior. But, they felt, individual economic success would be an indication, perhaps the only indication, of God's favor. Thus, the more money one accumulated, the more likely that one would be among the saved.[24]

During the Middle Ages, the European populace began to question Christian interpretations of the Bible. This skepticism was prompted by the influence of Gnostic philosophies from the East, which debunked certain myths of the Church such as the Garden of Eden, the fall from grace (the original sin), heaven and hell, the meaning of salvation, and the historicity of the personality known as Jesus Christ. Because of the growing number of religious discrepancies, the Catholic Church began to lose its stronghold in Europe; it was at this time that the papacy lost all of Bohemia to the formation of the Moravian Church.[25]

Two characteristics of Western religion are dramatized by these historical events: its corrupt and perverse foundations, and its lack of the spiritual sublimity (outstanding spiritual, intellectual, and moral worth) ideally intrinsic in any true religion. These ideals have not been represented in the biblical interpretation that has been so pervasive in the Western hemisphere, and thus morality has become more of a tenuous apparition with each passing moment. With a Bible in one hand and a gun in the other, missionaries still coerce the populations of so-called Third World countries to submit to their ideas of faith. Catholics wage war with Protestants in Northern Ireland and with Moslems in Bosnia, while Moslems and Jews have been massacring each other in the Middle East for millennia; Hindus are slaughtering Sikhs and Moslems in South Asia; and the rest of us seem to be sitting idly by, awaiting the second coming of whomever will end the moral deficit that is plaguing humankind. Thus, it seems that of the major world religions, the only God-inspired groups that are not killing or venting hostility on others or themselves, are the Yogis, Buddhists, and Taoists, who also happen to be the oldest and maybe the most illuminated of the many faces of religion. Furthermore, it should be stated that yoga and Taoism are not religions per se, but philosophies based on a scientific method for transformation.

One inescapable conclusion is apparent: Western culture and Western-influenced civilizations possess a fundamental misunderstanding of the constitution of God and religion. As the philosophies and religious practices of the indigenous Harrapans of ancient India became "Aryanized," the quintessence that had been passed from the ritual to the practitioner, and which allowed the true transformation of consciousness, was lost. In time, true religion was lost and then redefined in the West, along with the concept of God. Although religion is derived from the Latin *religare*, "to bind together," it is used to divide and conquer. Religion, in the perception of the ancient Harappans, was an intuitional realization of the existence of God, or the All, and their relationship to it. The West, consummate in its cerebral, positivist approach to life ("only that which is tangible is real"), was not capable of such a spectral experience, and replaced religion with theology—the human attempt to ascribe personality and character to God. Theology is the human theory regarding God's affairs, will, plans, desires, and projections for the human race. Inferences made about "Him" take on a purely anthropomorphic quality, which is no more than a religious aberration.

Sigmund Freud, whose controversial theories have been greatly contested, identified the warped perspective in the Western view of God:

> The ordinary man cannot imagine this Providence [divine guidance] in any other form but that of a greatly exalted father, for only such a one could understand the needs of his sons . . . or be softened by their prayers and placated by the signs of their remorse. The whole thing is patently infantile, so incongruous with reality . . . it is painful to think that the great majority of mortals will never be able to rise above this view of life.[26]

The obsession with infusing God with human qualities stems primarily from the Aryan attempt at comprehending what was, for them, incomprehensible. Aryan projections of God are obviously anthropomorphic in the earliest portrayals of Brahma, complete with head, arms, legs, feet, and in the initial biblical interpretation of "God made man in his own image," which was understood and applied literally.

As late as the seventeenth and eighteenth centuries, eminent European philosophers were still grappling with the concept of God. The work of German mathematician and philosopher

Gottfried Wilhelm von Leibniz (1646–1716) created a gauge by which this ever-growing concern in Europe's metaphysical and religious community could be measured. Though this work remained in a formative stage, his comments are worthy of reconsideration:

> God is an absolutely perfect being . . . there are many different kinds of perfection, all of which God possesses, consequently power and knowledge do admit of perfection and in so far as they pertain to God they have no limits. There are many who think that God might have made things better than he has. No more am I able to approve of the opinion of certain modern writers who boldly maintain that which God has made he might have done better. It seems to me that the consequences of such an opinion are wholly inconsistent with the glory of God. These modern thinkers insist upon certain hardly tenable subtleties, for they imagine that nothing is so perfect that there might not have been something more perfect. This is an error.[27]

Leibniz deplored his colleagues' superficial and materialistic approach to God. And though he himself struggled with the idea of the divine, he knew that there was a greater substantial reality to whatever it was that his five material senses could not reveal.

Another spiritual revolutionary of Western civilization was Mary Baker Eddy, who wrote at the turn of the century. Eddy was instrumental in introducing to Europe and America the concept of Christian Science. Born Mary Baker Glover, she was Pastor Emeritus of The First Church of Christ in Boston and president of the Massachusetts Metaphysical College. Her first domestic publication appeared in 1870, and before her death she had published seventeen highly acclaimed books on religion. Of her interest in the subject, she explained, "when quite young I was impressed that the Bible was not properly interpreted by the preachers, for I could not conceive of a God of wrath who was unjust enough to allow His little ones to suffer pain, misery, and death. I had hope, however, that some day the truth would be revealed. . . ."[28] Mary Baker Eddy dedicated her life to the acquisition of religious truth, committed to the veracity of the words of the Apostle John— "Ye shall know the truth, and the truth shall make you free" —and the words of William Shakespeare— "There is nothing either good or bad, but thinking makes it so." Her insights into an elusive component of religion that has managed to escape many, if not most of our current theologians, are notable for their qualitative correspondence to the ideas of the Hermetists of ancient Egypt. Eddy's ideas on the constitution of God represented both a departure from Western religious thought and a gateway to new and progressive concepts and practices in America:

> God is not corporeal, but incorporeal — that is, bodiless. As the words person and personal are ignorantly employed, they often lead, when applied to Deity, to confused and erroneous conceptions of divinity and its distinction from humanity. [God is an infinite Mind], and an infinite Mind in a finite form is an absolute impossibility.[29]

> God is Spirit; therefore the language of Spirit must be, and is spiritual. Christian Science attaches no physical nature and significance to the Supreme Being or His manifestation; mortals alone do this. Human theories are inadequate to interpret the divine. . . . Evidence drawn from the five physical senses relates solely to human reason.[30]

> Soul, or Spirit, is God, unchangeable and eternal; and man coexists with and reflects Soul, God, for man is God's image . . . . Mortals have a very imperfect sense of the spiritual man and of the infinite range of his thought. To God belongs eternal life. Never born and never dying. . . . The infinite has no beginning.[31]

Eddy's speculations on the constitution of God seem to, in retrospect, respond to the criticisms of the ancient Hermetists, who "regard[ed] all the theories, guesses and speculations of the theologians and metaphysicians regarding the nature of the All, as but the childish efforts of mortal minds to grasp the secret of the infinite. Such efforts have always failed and will always fail."[32] They referred to this entity as "the All," a concept which once constituted the very foundation of African religious thought, and can be identified in the cultures that would be born from the continent's soil.

It is this concept that we will now explore, beginning with a statement by Tehuti/Hermes which pertains to this entity: "*I cannot hope to name the maker of all majesty, the master of everything, with a single name, even a name composed of many names; it is nameless or rather it is all named since it is one and all, so that one must call all things by its name or by the names of everything, the only and the all, completely full of the fertility of both sexes and ever pregnant with its own will. Under, and back of, the universe of time, space and change, is ever to be found the substantial reality — the fundamental, the All.*"[33]

Substance here denotes that which underlies all perceptible or visible manifestations, as in the essence, or the essential reality. The term *substantial,* as used in this context, means actually existing, being the essential elements, and being real. *Reality* means that which is true, enduring, valid, or permanent. The Hermetic Principle of the All, therefore, represents the universal law that dictates that under and behind all outward appearances, there is a substantial reality.

The Hermetists of ancient Kmt (Egypt) stated that the All, that which we call God, is truly unknowable, for only the All itself can comprehend its own nature and being. The question then is, how does one identify the unidentifiable? The key to this question is humankind's unconditional acceptance of the unknowability of the All. Though the essential nature of the All is unknowable, there are certain truths arrived at through reason, with which humans must be content:

> 1. The All must be All that really is. There can be nothing existing outside of the All, else the All would not be the All.

> 2. The All must be infinite, for there is nothing else to define, confine, bound, limit, or restrict the All. It must be infinite in time, or eternal — it must have always continuously existed, for there is nothing else to have ever created it, and something can never evolve from nothing. It must exist forever, for there is nothing to destroy it, and it can never "not be," even for a moment.

> 3. The All must be immutable, or consistent, in its real nature to never change, for there is nothing to work changes upon it; nothing into which it could change, nor from which it could have changed. This the ancients held as the supreme truth, and that everything else is subject to changes, especially things on Earth.[34]

Hermes was quoted as saying, "*Truth alone is eternal and immutable; truth is the first of blessings; but truth is not and cannot be on Earth; everything has matter on it, clothed with a corporeal form subject to change, to alteration, to corruption, and to new combinations . . . the things of Earth are but appearances and imitations of truth; they are what the picture is to reality.*"[35] The axiom of Mentalism speaks to the All as being infinite, absolute, eternal, and above all unchangeable.

If the three truths stated previously acknowledge the various characteristics of the All, then perhaps reason can provide a guideline by which the All can be identified in its most transcendental form. Is the All purely matter? The answer would have to be no; for nothing rises higher than its own source, and it has just been established that matter is subject to constant change, reflecting rampant inconsistency and instability. Physical science testifies that matter is no more than an illusion—it is merely energy, power, or force combined at various vibrational frequencies.

But defining the All as pure power, force, or energy would not be totally accurate either. Energy or force as it relates to the All reflects only a residual component of its totality because energy and force are perpetually in a position of random flux in that they are always controlled by an outside influence, even when they appear to be moving of their own volition. Thus, there is no intrinsic intelligence in pure force or the power that guides or directs it. This is not the case with the All. What is perceived as energy and force in nature is but an outward manifestation, or projection, of the mind of the All. This is the feature that allows the definition of the All as Infinite Living Mind. Now, the term *spirit* is used as a means of general identification of the mind.

Most modern images of God are based on the line from the Book of Genesis, which reports that "God created man in his own image." Ironically, people have looked at themselves and projected their own image onto God, rather than allowing God's image to be primary. Instead of assuming that Genesis refers to God as a physically anthropomorphic being, we could instead assume that the human, or that which constitutes the essence of human, is a spiritual being: imperishable, infinite, and constant, like God. Thus, if spirit is living mind, then humans, like the All, have the ability to create and endure through the power of mind, only on a more minute plane of existence. This is the world's best-kept secret. This was the religious reality of antiquity, which today is unknown by most, forgotten by many, and practiced by few.

What exactly is spirit? As previously indicated, *spirit*, which means "real essence" in the Hermetic context, is simply a title that humans have given to the living mind. Because spirit

transcends our understanding, in our present state of consciousness, human beings must accept that it cannot be explained or
defined. One theory is that God or the All is the universe, but
this is pure conjecture and holds no basis in fact. The theory
probably arises from the fact that the universe is the largest tangible reality that humankind may mentally grasp and physically explore, but it is still matter that is subject to perpetual
transformation. The universe seems all-pervasive in its nature
or essence; it is connecting, binding, multidimensional with its
neutron stars, black holes and quasars, but it is not the All. The
mere fact that humans may understand and explore the physical universe disqualifies it as the character of the All, which cannot be perceived nor remotely grasped by humankind. The
conclusion is obvious: the universe is a creation of the All.

Spiritualists, metaphysicians, and philosophers theorize that
the All created the universe from its own substance, but this is
also inaccurate because according to the ancient Hermetists, the
All cannot be subtracted from nor divided. Furthermore, if it
were so, would not each particle in the universe be aware of its
being the All? Would not we, as spiritual entities, be born with
an innate awareness of our universal connectedness or oneness
with all life and with the All itself?

Some theologians and religious aspirants who acknowledge
the fact that spirit or living mind dwells within every human being, setting us apart from other animal life forms, proclaim that
"I am [or we are] God." But this, too, is an erroneous assump-
tion, comparable to a tiny human corpuscle claiming "I am the
body."

The process by which the All creates is very simple, and its
comprehension can be facilitated by the second Hermetic axiom, that of Correspondence—"as above, so below"—that is
based on the belief that there is a working correspondence existing among the many planes of the universe. According to the
Law of Correspondence, an examination of the human process
of creation will illuminate that of the All. Humans create in
many ways. We create by utilizing materials from outside of our
beings, such as metal, wood, clay, or combinations of materials.
This type of creation does not apply to the All, for "there is nothing outside of the All." Human beings also create from inside,
biologically, by the transformation of genetic substance into

new beings. Once again, this is not possible for the All, which can neither transfer nor subtract, reproduce nor multiply itself.

The manner of human creation that corresponds to that of the All is the human ability to create mentally, to imagine. As we create mentally, we use no outside materials, nor do we reproduce ourselves; yet the spirit of thought, or living mind, pervades our mental creations. Thus, according to the Law of Correspondence, we can assume that the All creates mentally. This is the key to the Hermetic riddle: "The All is Mind; The Universe is Mental."

Just as the reader may create a mental universe of her own, so the All creates universes in its mentality. The major difference between the two processes is that the human universe is the mental creation of a finite mind, whereas that of the All is the creation of an infinite mind. Therefore, that which is accepted to be the universe is just one mental creation of the All: "The All creates in its Infinite Mind countless Universes, which exist for eons of time—and yet, to the All, the creation, development, decline and death of a million Universes is as the time of the twinkling of an eye."[36] Creation does not take place within time; rather, time is an effect of creation.

This conception of time would, to Western culture, be considered a spatiotemporal impossibility. But the ancient Hermetists held that time is a mere illusion, subject to spatial manipulation by the wise who understood its inconstancy. But in order to grasp the dynamic mechanism within which the All creates, it is imperative to explore the concept of time and how it manifests itself in Western civilization. The misunderstanding of time as linear is directly related to the inability to understand the divine. Dr. Kamau Johnson, a Howard University psychologist who has done extensive research into human perceptions of time, points out,

> To the surprise of many, the sense of linear time presently experienced in the Euro-Americas has not always been the reigning orientation of time. According to Egyptian mythology, Thoth [Hermes] . . . was the divider and measurer of time . . . by observing successive patterns in nature, the Egyptians came to perceive time as cyclic. The sun, moon, and seasons returned with unfailing patterns and periodicity. As did their observations of the planets. So the concept of a cyclic worldview reflected the reliance on natural cycles . . . clever devices were designed to measure cyclic time. Sundials and

other such devices, reflected that a cyclic time was intrinsic to nature.[37]

Johnson identifies a pivotal shift in the perception of time analysis when, "[in] the mid-1600's, a Dutch scientist Christian Huygens, invented the pendulum clock, providing . . . its own recurring cycles independent of nature. This orientation was embraced by the western world . . . [and] became firmly ingrained in Euro-American culture. Reference to time became more rooted in concepts of hours, minutes, and seconds. . . . Today, it is assumed that time flows rigidly from past, present to future. Languages such as English are designed to describe a linear world . . . the tenses of English verbs indicate a rigid linear worldview. It is thus difficult to express non-linear . . . notions in our everyday language."[38]

Language, specifically descriptive or discursive language, is linear and consecutive. Descriptive or discursive languages cannot begin to capture or expound the simplest experience without depriving it of the essence that gives it life. Therefore, to try and use such a linear device to understand the All is nothing short of impossible.

Considerations of the Western perception of time as linear reinforce the inadequacy of Eurocentric thought and language to comprehend the cyclic nature of the divine. The cyclic nature of all natural elements on Earth corresponds to the nature of the All and constitutes the very hub of a universal dynamic, which connects the various planes of existence, whether seen or unseen. All things within the natural scheme of life move in cycles or continuous spirals. The double helix of DNA, the molecular basis of heredity in organic life, spirals up and out; blood spirals through living veins. Even the follicles of human hair, especially those of Blacks, spiral up and out of the head, creating the individual spiraling strands of helical, spring-like shafts so characteristic of that race. But the growth pattern of the hair in all human beings is cyclic in that it spirals from the lower top of the crania in a whorl pattern, no matter what the race. Seashells such as the nautilus are composed of a spiraling chain of chambers, the planets spin as they spiral in their orbits around the sun, and tornados and hurricanes also spiral as they move across the landscape. According to the Law of Correspondence, we may surmise that all of these natural phenomena are the mental creation of the All. In fact, the words *spiral* and *spiritual* originate from the Latin *spirare,* to coil.

According to ancient belief, the All—living mind or spirit—creates by projecting an incalculable number of mental images that seem very real to us as humans, but are as illusive as the mental images in our own minds. The birth and demise of stellar systems take place within a fraction of a millisecond in the mind of the All, but are eons in time to mortals.

The All creates these images through a process akin to our understanding of meditation. In the beginning of *Poimandres* (the Vision of Hermes), prior to his contact with the great Dragon, "Hermes, in search for divine truth, found himself seeking solitude. . . . He came to a place of rest and gave himself over to meditation." Meditation seems to induce the experience of an altered and higher state of consciousness, and through the study and use of it, human beings can create and achieve on a level much closer to that of the divine.

The Western meditative process differs greatly from the understanding and practice of meditation in the East, specifically South Asia or India. In the West, meditation means no more than to ponder or reflect, to contemplate or focus on a specific thought. Even transcendental meditation is simply an advanced technique of concentration in preparation for the meditative experience. In the East, meditation is regarded as a manner by which individuals encounter the nature of the divine within themselves, a procedure based on a scientific method to liberate the mind through serene reticence. After nearly a decade's worth of research on the biophysical advantages of meditation, UCLA physiologist R. Keith Wallace proved that, besides its nebulous spiritual implications, meditation has profound effects on the human body and mind. He showed that sitting in meditation induces the nervous system to enter a state of what he terms *restful alertness:* the mind remains lucid and awake, but the body goes into a state of deep relaxation. Dr. Deepak Chopra remarked that

> in a state of meditation, one undergoes definite shifts toward more efficient [biological] functioning such as lowered respiration, reduced oxygen consumption and decreased metabolic rate. The most fascinating aspect of this research . . . is that the biological process of aging itself does not have to be manipulated; the desired results can be achieved through awareness alone. In other words, meditation alters the frame of

4A. Spiral galaxy displaying the basic spiraling formula that permeates every aspect of the creative process, which is based on cyclic or circular movement.

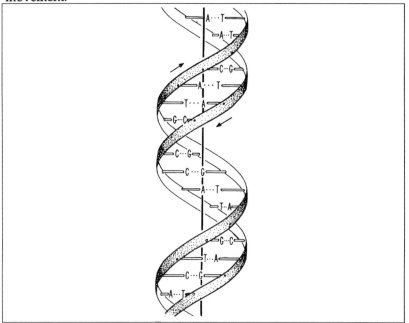

4B. *Double helix* of DNA showing spiral or coiling pattern. The word helix, from the Greek, means anything that coils or spirals.

reference that gives the person his experience of time . . . simply by taking the mind to a reality where time does not have such a powerful hold.[39]

Dr. Chopra's observations suggest the possibility of the cessation of biological decay, or premature aging. They also tantalize us with the prospect that we have happened upon one of the many secrets contained in The Book of Tehuti, which is reputed to have harbored the secret of regeneration. Dr. June D'Estelle, a psychologist who has done extensive research on meditation, concludes the following: "Through your thoughts, you create. With the gift of creative thinking, you are able to mold your life and to determine your destiny."[40] Scientific studies like these bring us closer to the realization that humankind most assuredly reflects the divine nature of the All.

Carl Jung aided Western civilization in its understanding of mentalism by his studies of the subconscious and supconscious parts of the human mind. The *subconscious mind* is the abode of the emotions, memories, habits, and instinct. Also called the *instinctive mind,* it establishes the order and assures that the incredible complexity of bodily processes will continue without conscious effort. The *superconscious mind* is that level of mind that few of us ever encounter. Here is where the divinity resides along with the soul, the spirit, the being of light that spiritual teachers regard as the true self, all-knowing and all-loving. Through this self, love is expressed and enlightenment is achieved.[41] Here, within the realm of the high self or divine mind, we may encounter, as Hermes did, Poimandres, the Great Dragon and emissary of the All. And it is here, through meditation, that human beings can receive the key to true biological, mental, and spiritual transformation.

The ancient Egyptians acknowledged the All's creative procedure as being manifested in two parts. This dual creative expression with respect to the All also helps one to identify the unidentifiable. The first part was the outward projection of infinite mind or spirit. The second, as a result of this projection, was the creation of the mental universe of which we are a part. The ancient Hermetists affirmed that at the base of this process lies a universal dynamic that serves as a common denominator with which all substance is brought into generation in the mental universe. This common denominator was form, and the form utilized was known to the Egyptians as *sacred geometry.* Geometry is

5. Young sadhu of India sitting in meditation. Many of India's spiritual aspirants become sadhus. Most wear their hair in *jata* — what are known in the West as "dreadlocks." They also cover themselves in a blue or white ash leaving only the feet and hands exposed. Regarded in India as some of the most dedicated aspirants, the sadhus wander freely throughout the subcontinent—enlightenment or the understanding of "the All" their only quest. Photo Credit: Dolph Hartsuiker.

6. Stone carving of Indian sadhu. Dated thirteenth century C.E.

one of the three principle branches of mathematics, the other two being algebra and analysis.

Historians of all ages (Pythagoras, Euclid, Descartes) have acknowledged and written profusely on what seemed to be an apparent geometric nonverbal language at the dawn of civilization. We find these forms in the guise of symbols deified and divinized in every human culture. The preponderance of these images, most of them identical from culture to culture, tell us of a mode of vocabulary entirely composed of geometric form. Rene Descartes (1596–1650), credited with the invention of analytic geometry, believed that all form was the object of various geometric patterns. He theorized that one may translate any geometric situation into an algebraic situation whereby the dominant system of algebra becomes accessible as a means of geometric investigation. Though Descartes wavered back and forth in his deliberations of the divine, some of his comments regarding his meditations on geometry and corporeal matter are worth noting. Descartes stated,

> It also occurs to me that whenever we ask whether the works of God are perfect, we should examine the whole universe together and not just one creature in isolation from the rest...And thus I plainly see that the certainty and truth of every science depends upon the knowledge of the true God...Therefore the very possibility of the existence of material things, in so far as they constitute the object of pure mathematics depends on the power of God...It remains for me to examine whether material things exist. Indeed, I now know that they can exist, at least insofar as they are the object of pure mathematics...For no doubt God is capable of bringing about everything that I am capable of perceiving. [42]

Scientists acknowledge that as infants we thought in images before we learned how to speak in words. This preverbal language is the most vital instrument we have for understanding the universe around us, remaining throughout our lives as the language of dreams and unconscious perception. Out of the several hundred images known, there are 125 common to all civilizations of the ancient world. Their meanings are analogous and they originate at such an early prehistoric epoch that their source is shrouded in mystery. Thus, the ancient Hermetists state that form, as expressed in geometric imagery, was the formula those of the ancient world used to comprehend the divine and its method of creating the material universe around us. Sacred geometry, therefore, is a creative learning experience as complex as the learning of language itself. In Egypt (Kmt), the concepts of sacred geometry are intimately connected with what is known as The Right Eye of Horus, which is a system of initiation based on left brain discipline. Hermetists inform us that the left hemisphere of the brain is male-dominated and functions on a must-know basis. It is the logical side and yearns to grasp how everything was created by spirit. The Hermetists of ancient Egypt professed the nature of sacred geometry to be absolutely flawless. Inextricably linked to the very genesis of the All's creative process, sacred geometry continued to unfold until the universe, in its entirety, was created. This was the grand design that the ancients so fully revered. Sacred geometry creates the web by which all things are bound in the material universe — every single part is entwined with everything else, creating the order to which the universe adheres.

Sacred geometry is the morphogenic structure behind all reality. The majority of physicists and mathematicians perceive numbers as being the prime language of reality, but the Hermetists declare that this is a misconception, that it is actually shape that generates all the laws of mathematics as well as physics, language, and biology, which includes the human species. It is imperative to understand that sacred geometry is not just lines on a page, but rather the sacred geometric motions of spirit in the void and in nature.

Stan Tenen, a California physicist, has after almost thirty years of research substantiated the presence of this divine maxim. Tenen, in his composition "Geometric Metaphors of Life," has been able to identify several key geometric patterns and formulas that seem prominent in the All's creative method. Out of these, he has distinguished one group of patterns whose position is preeminent in the formation of all others. The first figure identified by Tenen is what is known as a *tube torus*. This image is acquired by rotating a circular pattern until a small hole appears in the center. The faster the rotation, the smaller the hole becomes. The tube torus is the primal shape of the universe. It is unusual in that it moves in on itself; there is no other shape that can accomplish this. Tenen traced the spiral of a tube torus from the middle of its circular pattern then removed it out of the middle. He then placed it inside a three-dimensional tetrahedron. Tenen found that by shining a light through it so that its shadow appeared on a two-dimensional surface he could generate all

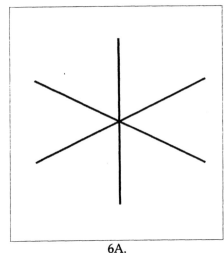

6A.

6A. This symbol denotes the Hermetic geometric concept of spirit being projected through the void in six directions, initiating what, in time, would become the foundation of the creative process. In many cultures, the number six symbolizes creation.

6B. The next procedure in the geometric order of creation, according to the Hermetists, was the rotation of spirit on an axis, creating a sphere. The circle creates the parameters by which spirit begins to operate and create within. The Hermetists believe that straight lines are masculine, and curved lines are feminine. But in order to create any and all things, curved lines must be brought into generation.

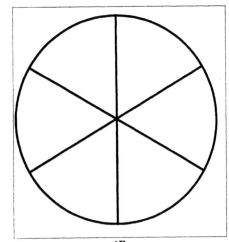

6B.

6C. With the circle or sphere now in place, inception of the seven laws, which will create the basis of universal order, takes place. This procedure is accomplished by connecting the various lines and angles, which creates a specific geometric pattern indicative of one of the seven Hermetic axioms. Each geometric symbol shown here equates to an axiom. Not shown is the projection of spirit in the six directions, the hub of this dynamic from which all others emerge.

6D. *Vesica Pisces.* The *vesica pisces* is the symbol for the creative feminine force that brought the material universe into being. It represents the fundamental energy which lies at the basis of all creation, and without it nothing could be. To remove its energy from all form and matter would bring about immediate disintegration of the universe.

6C.

6E. This symbol, known in sacred geometry as the "flower of life," is held by Hermetists as the penultimate of all geometric symbolism. This symbol is comprised of numerous *vesica pisces*, overlapping one another at their respective centers. The ancient Hermetists state that everything in existence—whether past, present, or future— is contained within this structure. It contains all of our laws of biology and physics, as well as all languages current and obsolete. Enclosed within the geometric expression of the "flower of life" is all of creation.

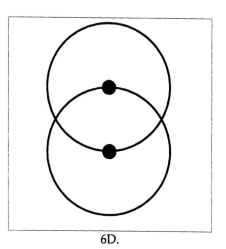

6D.

6F. The following diagrams show the role geometry plays in the genesis of human life. Science acknowledges that prior to conception the ovum is a sphere—a sphere that also contains the female pronucleus, which contains half of the chromosomes for creating a human being, twenty-two plus one. When the male sperm reaches and penetrates the ovum, conception commences. The events which lead up to this event are extremely noteworthy in dramatizing this concept. When that one chosen sperm penetrates the ovum, its tail breaks off, and its head forms a sphere the same size as the female pronucleus. These two merge, forming a perfect *vesica pisces*, which contains the blueprint for all universal knowledge. The sperm and ovum pass through one another creating the first cell identified as the human zygote, containing forty-four plus two chromosomes. Next in the process is mitosis where opposite or polar bodies are created that travel to opposite ends of the cell nodes, forming northern and southern polarities. The next phase is the formation of a tube splitting the sphere and the chromosomes—half going right and half going left.

6E.

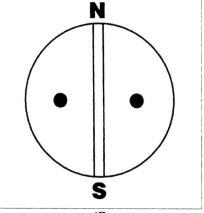

6F.

6G. The zygote splits into four cells and forms a tetrahedron inside a sphere, an expression of sacred geometry in one of its most universally primordial dramatizations.

6G.

6H. The next division creates eight cells and a star tetrahedron, with the eighth cell lying directly under the center cell and star tetrahedron. This affirms conclusively that creation, from the formation of star systems to the development of human beings, is a geometric process. The location of these eight cells are at the base of the spine or perineum, where the powerful "kundalini" force, spoken of in the yoga traditions of India, resides. Hermetists hold that the energy fields which emanate from the human body originate here at the perineum. These cells divide into eight more cells forming a cube within a cube. At this point, development begins to become asymmetrical. The embryo hollows, returning to the form of the sphere. The north pole enters the hollow ball, descends, and connects with the south pole, forming a hollow tube in the middle. One end becomes the mouth and the other the anus. Such is the miracle of life.

6H.

6I. The five perfect or Platonic solids.

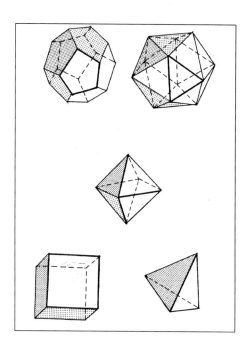

6I.

6J. The mystical "tree of life" represented geometrically.

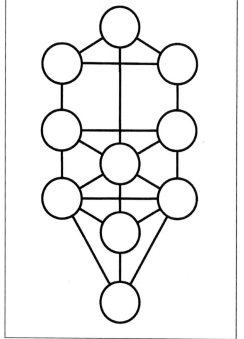

Illustrations
6A.– 6J. David Kennedy.

6J.

the letters of the Hebrew alphabet, exactly in the shape and order that they are written. Tenen also found that by changing the shape inside the tetrahedron to different positions, he could project all the Greek and Arabic letters as well. From this example, we may see the influence geometry has on language. Stan Tenen went on to equate geometric form to the first seven days of creation as espoused in the Biblical tradition with astounding revelations, all supported by science.[43] Another major image in sacred geometry and central to the theme of generation is the *vesica pisces*. The *vesica pisces* is simply a circle next to another circle exactly the same size so that the edge of one circle passes through the center of the other. The common area created by this intersection is the *vesica pisces,* which means "vessel of the fish." In ancient symbolism it stood for the feminine creative force or mother-spirit that gave birth to worlds and to the gods that maintained them. The vesica pisces in prepatriarchal history is found in India, where it is referred to as the *Jagad Yoni* meaning "womb of the world." Two pyrmordial equilateral triangles fit inside this image.

The five- and six-pointed stars, the golden mean rectangle, as well as the spiral, are basic geometric shapes that aid in the generation of all others. The ancient Hermetists include five other configurations that are also paramount to stellar generation. These are the hexahedron or cube, composed of six square faces, eight corners, and twelve edges; the tetrahedron, made up of four triangular faces, four corners, and six edges; the octahedron, which has six triangular faces, six corners, and twelve edges; the dodecahedron, formed of twelve pentagonal faces, twenty corners, and thirty edges; and last, is the icosahedron, which has twenty triangular faces, twelve corners, and thirty edges. Though these forms were an integral part of Egyptian mathematics and Hermetic alchemy, they have come to be known as the *Platonic solids;* though they were named after Plato, we know they were introduced to the West at least two hundred years earlier by Pythagoras, who called them the perfect solids because all their edges were equal, they had only one surface and one angle, and their points all fit on the surface of a sphere. These are the only five shapes known that fit these criteria.

The cube, whose two-dimensional form is the square or quadrangle, was emblematic of a solid foundation and the four corners of the Earth. Three Russian scientists have gained important insights with respect to the perfect solids; Nikolai Goncharov, Vyacheslav Morozov, and Valery Makarov discovered that the Earth projects from within itself to its surface a dual geometrically regularized grid. The first part of this grid formed twelve pentagonal slabs, which the scientists said indicated the original shape of our planet—a dodecahedron. The second or remaining portion of the grid formed a geometrically perfect icosahedron. Their research and revelations are explored in-depth in the ensuing chapter on Rhythm. It becomes obvious that what the Egyptians identified as sacred geometry comprises an overwhelmingly integral part of the All's creative process, extending to the very formation of our globe. This alludes to a greater substantial reality—that sacred geometry is the universal template that generates all form in the material universe. (See chapter 6 for further discussion.)

Through examination of the previous concept, that form is geometric and is intimately related to function, human beings may arrive at a deeper understanding of this universal dynamic. The idea of sacred geometry as an all-pervading axiom is worthy of much consideration. Are we to assume that it is merely by chance that the ancient Egyptians chose the upper half of a perfect octahedron in which to fashion their pyramids? The octahedron or double pyramid is the most dense geometric form. It occupies the smallest percentage of the volume that encloses it, and the sphere or circle occupies the greatest. The ancient Egyptians held the octahedron to be the imprisoned fire of the seed, the materialized aspect of the sphere, which is the symbol for spirit—having no beginning and no end. We in the West like to identify ourselves as visionaries, but the truth is that our vision does not exceed beyond the globe in which we exist.

The Hermetic philosophers of old remarked that human beings should never make the mistake of supposing that the world around us—the Earth, a mere grain of dust in the universe—is the universe itself. There are countless millions of such worlds, stellar systems, and universes that exist within the infinite mind of the All. The Hermetists assert that, even within our own little solar system, there are regions that harbor forms of life far higher than ours and illuminated beings who view us as we view the one-celled life-forms that dwell on the ocean's floor: "There are beings with powers and attributes higher than Man has ever dreamed of the gods possessing. And yet these beings were once as you, and still lower and you will be even as they, and still higher. . . ."[44]

To embrace such an ideal as reality gives a radical perspective on life. Much of the senseless futility of daily life takes on a new and divergent quality. Events and situations that seem hopeless and finite are but lessons to be encountered on an infinite journey. Death is not real, even in the relative sense; it is but birth to a new life:

> *The Universe is your home, and you shall explore its farthest recesses before the end of time and space. And at the end of the Grand Cycle of Eons, when the All shall draw back into itself all of its creations, you will go gladly, for you will then be able to know the whole truth of being at one with the All. Such is the report of the illumined, those who have advanced well along the path.*[45]

CHAPTER 2

The Principle of Correspondence

"As above, so below; as below, so above." — Kybalion

The second Hermetic axiom is based on the belief that there is a working unison, consistency, or correspondence between the many planes or levels of the universe. Stated plainly, "as above, so below" addresses the reflecting or mirroring relationship between the macrocosmic and the microcosmic reality. The ancient Hermetists based this law on the truth that all within the universe emanates from the same source, and this source — the All — instills its formula in each and every aspect of creation. In acknowledging the presence of this formula or maxim in the natural scheme of universal procedure, one may understand the higher planes of life by studying the lower, and know the lower planes through examination of the higher.

Many people, if not most, have seen the symbol that represents this axiom; it is now referred to as the Star of David or Solomon's Seal, the hexagram of Judaism. Its origin and meaning are far more auspicious than that of an emblem used to categorize a particular creed or group of human beings. What is ironic is that this symbol has been regarded as officially Jewish only for about a century. The hexagram reached Judaism via the eastern Tantric influences on medieval Jewish cabalists, who chose to elaborate on the union of God and his female counterpart, *Shekina*.[46] Historically, at the time the biblical stories were being spun about David and Solomon, this star had nothing to do with the Jewish people, but had been previously employed in cultures such as India and Egypt for more than 2,000 years.

In India, its earliest appearance was discovered in the Indus Valley civilization (3000 B.C.E.), and soon after was regarded as a Jain philosophical symbol. It would later be utilized by the Buddhists and Tantrikas of India to symbolize divine sexual energy and the union of the male and female elements in creation. The linguistic origins of the word *sex* is rooted in mathematics, as in the biblical reference to "six days of creation." *Sex* in Sanskrit means six. Currently, in India the six-pointed star is called the Star of Vishnu, reflecting the cosmic union between Kali and Shiva, the male and female forces in the universe.

These references attributed to the hexagram are incomplete. It is in ancient Egypt where the six-pointed star resided in full splendor. Heralded as the *Star of Creation* by the Egyptians, it represented the union of male and female energy in nature and on all planes of existence; but it was also held to be the symbol that reflected the Hermetic law of Correspondence. The upward pointing triangle represented the macrocosm and the downward triangle represented the microcosm; two identical forms interlocked yet independent, each one a part reflecting the whole.

There are many examples of Correspondence, such as the previously discussed models of the atom and solar systems of the universe. Upon examining existence at the atomic level and its relationship to solar symmetry, it becomes quite clear that there is a radical, pervasive unity bonding the ultimate essence of each part of nature. From galaxy to star, and from star to atom, everything in the universe follows analogously.

In an atom there is the nucleus, which is its hub or core, and there are the various particles that spin and orbit around this nucleus—neutrons, protons, and electrons—each charged positively, negatively, or neutrally. When astronomers observe our stellar system, they see a model much like that of the atom, with the Sun at its center, and the many planets that, like protons and electrons, spin on their axes as they orbit the Sun.

Another example of this correlation is our own bodies. The human organism contains all of the agents, elements, and compounds that we identify in the world around us. In fact, our physical bodies are but a composite of the multitudinous components found on, in, and around the Earth. If we examine the periodic table of the elements, we will discover that most if not all of these elements are found within the human body—from carbon and arsenic to hydrogen and boron, from solid to fluidic to gaseous matter. Thus, the biblical statement, "then the Lord God formed man of dust from the ground, and breathed into his nostrils the breath of life," finds basis in fact. When we stand in awe of the streams of electrical current that bolt through the heavens during an electrical storm, we should know that these same electrical currents run through our own bodies, creating what the ancient metaphysicians called the electrical body.

7. Egyptian Star of Creation now known as the "Star of David."

For the purpose of instruction and convenience, the ancient Hermetists taught that the universe could be divided into three strata called the Great Planes of Correspondence. Though these planes, or divisions, are more or less artificial and arbitrary, they serve as an invaluable device for comprehending the Correspondence axiom. The planes are the Great Physical Plane, the Great Mental Plane, and the Great Spiritual Plane.[47] The planes in this order symbolize humankind's ascension from matter to spirit. Each plane has seven subplanes, which shade into one another in a gradual process of development. Thus, no distinct line of demarcation exists between the higher phenomena of the Physical Plane and the lower of the Mental Plane.

This pattern saturates every aspect of the creative method, leaving no vacuums. Thoth/Hermes once stated,

> There is no such thing as a void, nor can there have been, nor will there ever be. For all members of the world are completely full so that the world itself is complete and filled with bodies diverse . . . some are larger, some smaller, and they differ in density and rarity. The rarer are very difficult or altogether impossible to see. . . . Hence, many believe that these are not bodies and that they are empty places – which is impossible.[48]

By reversing the order in which humankind scales the various planes of life, we can establish the procedure of divine providence by which the All manifests creation, from the Great Spiritual Plane to the Great Mental Plane to the Great Physical Plane. Poimandres, in his discourse on universal genesis, thus instructed Hermes,

> Hear how it is with God and the universe . . . God, eternity, cosmos, time, becoming. God makes eternity; eternity makes the cosmos; the cosmos makes time; time makes becoming . . . the energy of God is mind and soul; the energy of eternity is permanence and immortality; of the cosmos, recurrence and counter-recurrence; of time, increase and decrease; of becoming, quality and quantity. The source of all things is God; eternity is their essence; the cosmos is their matter.[49]

By employing the Principle of Correspondence, we can understand fully the Great Planes of Correspondence. It is important to remember when dealing with an atom, with force and power, or with the human mind, that these are but varying degrees on one scale, and therefore are fundamentally the same in their essence. They may shade into or occupy higher aspects of a mutual plane, or one may exist totally within a different strata or frequency, but they all are manifestations of the All.

Before proceeding further, an explanation of the term *plane* is in order, for its definition by the Hermetists differs somewhat from that held by Western science. In the West, the term plane relates to consciousness, a level of existence or intellectual development, a condition or a state. It also denotes a place having dimensions. Hermetists believe that a plane encompasses all of these characteristics and more. It is considered a state or condition, and yet this state or condition is in itself a degree of dimension on a scale subject to calculation and measurement. The mechanism used to gauge the various planes of existence is vibration. The higher the rate of vibration, the higher the plane; the higher the plane, the higher the manifestation of life that occupies that plane.[50]

As previously stated, there are seven subplanes within the three Great Planes of the universe. Each subplane not only vibrates at an ever-increasing frequency within its own category (ascending degrees of matter on the physical plane from, for instance, gross rock to rarefied matter such as fire or electricity), but continuously enhances its rate of vibration as it merges into higher planes, from the physical to the mental.

The Great Physical Plane and its seven minor planes comprise the physical universe, and all that relates to physics — force, power, and things that tangibly manifest on the physical plane, seen or unseen. It includes all of what we call *matter* and *energy* — from solids, liquids, and gases to heat, light, electricity, gravitation, cohesion, and chemical affinity. The Hermetists maintain that there are planes within this category that produce higher forms of energy not yet discovered by science. These planes create the higher vibratory frequencies that connect the Great Physical Plane to the Great Mental Plane.

The Great Mental Plane and its seven subdivisions contain various living forms. Many of these are known to science, but there are forms, according to the Hermetists, of which we are not aware because of our limited and underdeveloped perceptive abilities. The subdivisions of this plane span from what is called *mineral mind* to *human mind*. The Hermetists profess that minerals too are endowed with intelligence or mind, not in the way we perceive it perhaps, but mind nonetheless.

This concept was substantiated in 1977 by Johann Gradsky, a physicist at Berkeley and later at Cleveland State University. During the 1970s, Gradsky was one of the world's few theoretical physicists, part of a movement exploring new, unproven, and controversial concepts in the field of physics. Gradsky pioneered a radical branch of this field, establishing the unknown as known and the uncommon as common. Using an electron gun, he demonstrated to the global scientific community that mind is inherent on the atomic level. In an atomically impenetrable wall within a fission chamber, Gradsky made two incisions, a right and left, and fired an electron from the gun at the left incision. It went through. Gradsky then replaced the wall with one that had only one incision in it, on the right. He refired the same electron in the direction where the left incision had been, and a remarkable event occurred: When the electron reached the wall and found that the hole was gone, it stopped, hesitated, and went to and through the incision on the right. This led Gradsky to believe that not only do atomic particles have a degree of intelligence (recognition that the hole was no longer there), but they have the ability to make decisions (entering the alternate incision).

What are the implications of this discovery? All matter, including minerals, rocks, and other solid compounds, is composed of atomic and subatomic particles. Therefore, to establish mind on an atomic level is to acknowledge mind in these many aspects of matter.

Another subplane of the Great Mental Plane is that of plant mind. The provocative and popular book *The Secret Life of Plants* by Peter Tomkins is the culmination of years of research that prove, conclusively, not only that plants have mind, but that in many respects their extrasensory mechanisms are much more developed, functional, and detectable than those of humans! To stand under or beside a giant sequoia or redwood in the woods of California is to be overcome by an eerie feeling of actually hearing the stories of these ancient wonders. [51]

The remaining subplanes in the Great Mental Plane are *animal mind, elemental mind,* and *human mind,* which is composed of the many stages of human development in both its splendor and its decadence.[52]

When observing the animal mind, many factors abound. Contained within this category are our ever-present and ongoing relationships with domestic animals that have become our guardians, emotional cushions, and companions. From birds such as parrots, which have speaking capabilities, to dogs and cats, from the exotic to the ordinary, one experience that animal owners often share is the ability to communicate with their pets. Few, if any, can deny the profound levels of comprehension consistently seen in animals, wild or domestic, that allows animals to understand our tones, words, needs, and desires. As humans we deem ourselves the superior species, but upon closer examination, this may not be the case. Animals seem extremely capable of understanding us and being instructed or taught by us. Though humans may feign a position of superiority, many animals seem to reflect a more responsive and evolved degree of sensory perception.

Many cultures in South America, India, and Africa, profess with respect to evolutionary status, that humankind is only fourth in an evolutionary line preceded by whales, dolphins, and elephants. They regard these animals as totally conscious beings, utilizing their brain capacity far in excess of human beings. These cultures maintain that these animals are the guardians of our planet and the merciless slaughtering of them is one of humankind's greatest atrocities.

The Dogon of Africa, who live near Timbuktu, retain in their ancient mythological traditions the belief that they were imparted the knowledge that constellations Sirius A and B exist by dolphin-like beings more than 700 years ago. The Dogon and their astronomical comprehension of Sirius is one of the greatest mysteries of modern science. In studying the dolphin, scientists have found that their species is approximately 35 million years old. They also believe that dolphins were once land dwellers, but eventually returned to the sea. Close examination of their frontal fins reveals human-like hands inside of them. But the most astounding find concerning dolphin research is their brain capacity. Both hemispheres of a dolphin's brain function at 100 percent, indicating a fully conscious entity. When dolphins are at rest, they suspend usage of one hemisphere in the brain, thereby conserving power. Human beings have only half of their brain working at any time leaving the other half non-functional and dormant. Of that half of the human brain that is operational, we use on an average only 5 to 10 percent. So from a dolphin's vantage point, we are not only consciously dormant, we are also mentally unconscious beings. This verity is evidenced daily in our struggle to survive.

The last of the Great Planes of Correspondence is the Great Spiritual Plane. Hermetists deem this plane's entities to be incomprehensible to humans at our present level of understanding; thus, the task of explaining them is an impossibility. How can color and light be described to a man born blind? How can the taste of honey be explained to a woman who does not know sweet, or harmony to one born deaf? These are questions the Hermetists would ask rhetorically in their attempt to describe the unfathomable. We can, though, using the principle of correspondence, see the unfathomable in tangible examples.

On the lowest strata of the spiritual plane dwell the *adepts, arahants, sages,* and *masters.* These are "divine angels" who walk the Earth with humankind constantly assisting in the evolution of the human race. The term *adept* implies one who has mastered organic alchemy, that is, one who has mastered all seven bodily senses and, like the caterpillar that has transformed into a butterfly, has become that which can truly be considered a human being. An *arahant* is one who has totally extinguished all worldly desires, thereby putting an end to her lifetimes or reincarnations. *Sages* carry qualities of both the adept and arahant, in that they have mastered the body through various spiritual austerities, but have chosen to remain in contact with the human race, to aid and assist it. Sages are known as *tirthankaras* in South Asia, and are said to have been given the responsibility of preserving the divine word or ultimate truth, which guides and directs those human beings who have chosen the path to spiritual realization.

Bearing the titles *adept* and *arahant* are individuals such as Tehuti/Hermes, the Buddha, Krishna, Osiris, Isis, Jehoshua or Jesus Christ, and the Jain saviors Mahavira and Parsava. There have been many sages who have walked the Earth, and they too are recognizable: Imhotep, the multitalented master of Kmt's Old Kingdom; Sui Nu, "the Dark Girl," who imparted the knowledge of all things to Hwuang-Ti; China's greatest emperor, Lao-tzu; Quetzalcoatl of Meso-America; Moses; Mohammed; and Abu Bakari, among many. These are the great souls so often referred to as *avatars, adepts,* or *masters.* They appear upon Earth in its darkest periods to illuminate humankind and to renew hope. They are the sentries of what the Bible calls

Heaven—the gateway to the Great Spiritual Plane of Correspondence.

"As above, so below" is a principle that manifests on all planes and is an integral component of the axioms to follow. Further analysis of the laws will actually illustrate how these dynamic principles are at work in our daily lives, as well as their impact on times past.

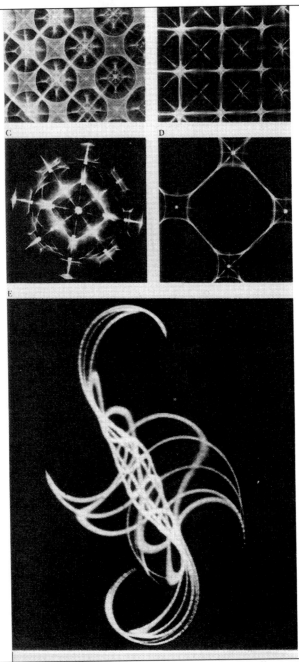

8. The study of wave patterns is known as "cymatics." It illustrates the relationship between frequency and form. What this implies is that specific materials subjected to specific vibrations assume specific geometric forms;

CHAPTER 3

The Principle of Vibration

"Nothing rests; everything moves; everything vibrates." – Kybalion

This principle embodies the fact that motion is manifest in everything in the universe. Whether we acknowledge or perceive the motion, nothing is at rest; everything is moving, constantly vibrating. As human beings, we use vibratory metaphor constantly, for example, "being in tune with the times" or "out of tune with one another." How often have we all heard the expression, "being on the same wavelength?" The Gospel of St. John begins, "In the beginning was the Word, and the Word was with God, and the Word was God." In the Egyptian *Book of Coming Forth by Day*, now referred to as *The Book of the Dead*, the oldest written text in the world parallels the biblical passage with, "I am the Eternal, I am Ra . . . I am that which created The Word . . . I am the Word." The Word, or any word for that matter, is scientifically a vibrational complex of sound. These expressions speak to an unconscious and metaphoric understanding of vibratory influence. Even colors are vibrations that resonate at specific frequencies. Sodium lights are yellow because sodium atoms vibrate with those frequencies that your brain perceives as yellow. Mercury atoms vibrate with a bluish light, and neon atoms send out vibrations that reach the brain as red.

The most profound minds of ancient Greece—Thales of Miletus, Xenophanes of Colophon, Socrates, Plato of Athens, Pythagoras of Samo, among many others—were aware of and taught this principle. Besides being Greek, they share one other common experience: they all studied in Egypt and were intimately acquainted with the Hermetic teachings.

With the inevitable demise of Greek civilization, and later (1492 C.E.) the brutal destruction of the Moors and Moorish influence in Europe, the principle of vibration and others were lost to the West. In the nineteenth century, it was rediscovered by Western pioneers in physical science, and since that period tremendous progress has verified the presence of vibration in the overall fabric of universal substance.

Scientists agree that what appears to be stable matter in our universe is fashioned from indivisible particles of vibrating energy known as *quanta*, which in themselves are elusive because quanta will melt when they are probed in attempts to see how they are made, as surely as snowflakes in the palm of your hand. But matter has wave properties, and therefore frequencies. Each particle wave, for that matter, has a specific frequency, and that frequency corresponds to a specific energy. Energy equals mass according to Einstein's theorem, $E = mc^2$. So in a fundamental sense, the way matter vibrates determines its form. Since modern science has proven that all matter and energy are no more than modes of vibratory motion, the focus here will be the different perspectives on vibration held by conventional Western science and by traditional Hermetists.

What is essential in Hermetic thought is not the obvious fact that everything vibrates or is in constant motion (the focus of popular Western science), but that there are different rates or frequencies of vibration, and the higher the vibration the more advanced the life form. The ancient Hermetists maintained that the All retains a constant vibration of such an infinite degree of intensity and rapidity that it may be considered at rest. The teachings of Tehuti describe the scope of vibration as having spirit at one pole and gross matter at the other. Between are countless varying rates of vibratory modes, each representing a specific station in the spectrum of cosmic order.

Note the differences in consideration of these principles by modern science and by Hermetic science. Modern science recognizes three characteristics of matter: *cohesion* (now defined as a principle of molecular attraction), *chemical affinity* (the principle of atomic attraction), and *gravitation* (the principle of attraction, by which every particle or mass of matter is bound to every other particle or mass). Hermetists believe these principles to be manifestations of some form of vibratory energy.

Universal ether is regarded by conventional scientists to be a rarefied element that fills and permeates all space, and transmits transverse waves to which light and radio waves adhere. The Hermetists call this ether *the ethereal substance*. They view it as a web of extreme tenuity and elasticity pervading the cosmos, serving as a conduit or medium for several forms of vibratory energy waves: heat, light, electricity, and magnetism. This ether, according to the Hermetists, manifests a degree of vibration entirely its own in rate and mode.[53]

One of the most intriguing aspects of vibration taught by the Hermetists is its relationship to thought patterns. Hermetists teach that all aspects of thought—emotion, reason, will, and desire—are accompanied by vibrations, a portion of which are projected and then received by individuals in close proximity: "The teachings of all lands and ages, as also those of modern Mental Science, are to the effect that the Mind, in its manifestation of Thought in the brain, generates a form of energy of intensely high Vibration, which energy may be, and is projected in vibratory waves from the brain of the thinker, and which affects the brains of other persons within its field of influence."[54] The Hermetists teach that by understanding the principle of vibration, when applied to mental phenomena, individuals may polarize the mind at any degree, thus gaining absolute control over their various mental states. This process of mental transmission is called *induction,* or "mind over mind." Many of us are aware of our mental/emotional influences on others, subtle though they may be. Adolf Hitler was reputed to have had exceptional inductive abilities that were akin to mesmerism, and he used this faculty of mind to control multitudes in early twentieth-century Germany.

Within the last sixty years, another form of mind influence, mental telepathy, has been under close scrutiny in and around scientific laboratories: "Experiments have shown that the temperature of the brain is increased in accordance with the intensity of feeling and thought, and that there is undoubtedly a generation of energy which bears a very close resemblance to the process of the generation of electrical energy."[55] As early as the 1920s, Western science was exploring the possibility of thought induction. The eminent French scientist Camille Flammarion, who was doing extensive research on the subject during this period, concluded, "one mind can act at a distance upon another, without the habitual medium of words, or any other visible means of communication. It appears to us altogether unreasonable to reject this conclusion if we accept the facts. The action of one human mind upon another, from a distance, is a scientific fact."[56] Because of this phenomenon and others like it, the 1970s would see the birth of a new branch of psychology, known as *parapsychology*. In this field, research in the area of mental influence, namely telepathy, is ongoing.

India, one of the oldest cultures in the world, has a tradition of telepathy that extends into very remote antiquity. The science of induction is practiced extensively by South Asia's Yogic community, and for centuries has been a point of fascination for the West. Ironically, this ability is one of the more rudimentary qualities that Yogis possess as they aspire to achieve greater states of mental clarity or consciousness. This is substantiated by the many anthropologists, philosophers, and psychologists who have journeyed to the area to research this culture:

> Simplest of the Yogis' psychic abilities is that known as telepathy. This phenomenon consists of the conscious projection and reception of the vibratory thought waves emanating from the minds of persons performing the processes of thought. The Yogis hold that there is always more or less unconscious telepathy in operation among people. Everyone is constantly emanating thought waves, and everyone is constantly receiving such; but the performance is chiefly along unconscious lines. The conscious projection and the conscious reception of these thought vibrations constitutes the psychic phenomena of telepathy. The Yogis hold mastery of the skill as elemental.[57]

Physician Rudolph Ballentine and psychiatrist Allan Weinstock performed extensive clinical research into this phenomenon to gather evidence that would explain to the Western world the functional mechanics of induction or telepathy and how it is applied:

> Telepathy . . . is inexplicable in terms of the ego's notion of "reality." The boundaries of I-ness are temporarily interrupted to allow contact with something outside the I which cannot be encompassed by it. When the ordinary waking consciousness is stopped, the usual filtering of sensory data ceases. When input is no longer "censored" to maintain a predetermined "reality," mind is open to a much greater range of information. At this level there is access to information beyond the field of the ego's consciousness. This is the merging of differentiated consciousness . . . that allows "extrasensory perception."[58]

We learn from this principle that there are experiences that surround and involve us, of which we can be totally unaware. The principle of vibration gives us insight into unconventional, yet scientifically proven, ideas about the material world around us and the inner universe of our own minds.

CHAPTER 4

The Principle of Polarity

"Everything is dual; everything has poles; everything has its pair of opposites; like and unlike are the same; opposites are identical in nature, but different in degree; extremes meet; all truths are but half-truths; all paradoxes may be reconciled." – Kybalion

According to *Foundations of African Thought*, "The ancient Africans . . . believed the world to be founded upon contradictions . . . and this belief was expressed in the form of the Principle or Doctrine of Opposites."[59] This principle—probably the most visible, most employed, and most widely known of the seven—continues as the basis of many African societies, including the Dogon of Mali, the Fon of Dahomey, the Bambara of eastern Guinea, and the ancient Ife of West Africa. The Ife employ this law today in the form of an oracle known as *Ifa*. They profess the genesis of the Ifa system of divination to be 20,000 B.C.E. and speak to its pervasive influence in the dissemination of the concept of polarity in various cultures and lands outside of Africa (see notes 60 and 61).

Ancient and contemporary African cultures hold polarity paramount in the formation and maintenance of creation and universal order. Nigerian-born Dr. C. Kamalu defined life itself as "with the duality of being and becoming . . . the product of being and becoming is the Life Force, that which gives rise to change and motion. . . . The Life Force is also the organizing power bringing order to the primeval chaos. This organizing power, this force of life and motion, is sometimes described as the first created [thing]."[60]

Here in the West, the notion of an ever-present cosmological duality is slowly being accepted. Influenced by the metaphysical iconography of the Far East, the Western hemisphere has been inundated with the two primary symbols on which Chinese philosophical tradition was conceived: yin/yang and the oracle of the I-Ching. The concept of yin/yang essentially translates into the positive and negative duality that permeates the material universe; it is the absolute or ultimate reality of all existence, which existed from the beginning. Introduced into

Ogbe	Oyeku	Iwori	Edi	Obara	Okanran	Irosun	Owonrin
I	II	II	I	I	II	I	II
I	II	I	II	II	II	I	II
I	II	I	II	II	II	II	I
I	II	II	I	II	I	II	I

Ogunda	Osa	Irete	Otura	Oturupon	Ika	Oṣe	Ofun
I	II	I	I	II	II	I	II
I	I	I	II	II	I	II	I
I	I	II	I	I	II	I	II
II	I	I	I	II	II	II	I

9. Ifa oracle, which like the I-Ching is based on the binary principle. Each column is headed by an Odu, which corresponds to a specific Orisha or deity.

10. The symbol of yin and yang encased within the oracle of the I-Ching.

11. Tieguai, one of the nine immortals of Taoism who lived during China's "Golden Age." It was Tieguai who aided in disseminating the I-Ching and the Tao throughout China. An accomplished martial artist, Tieguai was known as the "Iron-Staff Immortal," whose staff when let loose into the air turned into a waterfall. Hand painted on silk, early Yuan Dynasty thirteenth century C.E.

China during the Xia dynasty by the cultural hero Hwang-Ti (2697–2597 B.C.E.), it soon became the hereditary symbol of Taoist philosophy. The I-Ching or *Yih King* entered China at an earlier period (2852–2738 B.C.E.) and is reported to have been the invention of a man the Chinese called Fu-Hi. Based on an arrangement of eight trigram figures, the I-Ching oracle was reputed to hold the key to creation. Though these two systems of divination are considered synonymous with Chinese thought, ironically, their origins may not be Chinese.

In his book *Chinese Thought*, Paul Carus discussed a Babylonian tablet found in the Library of Ashurbanipal (700 B.C.E.) called the Tablet of Destiny, said to "contain the Mystery of Heaven and Earth." Carus speculates that not only are the I-Ching and the Tablet of Destiny one and the same; but since the tablet predates the I-Ching by several centuries, the latter may have evolved from the former. A translation of a fragmented text from the Library of Ashurbanipal, identified as the *Text of Enmeduranki*, stated: "Enmeduranki, king of Sippar, is the seventh of the *aboriginal* kings, and he declares that he received the divine tablet from Anu."[61] Sippar is located in the region of Mesopotamia known now as Iraq and is one of the most ancient cities in that area, which prior to the Indo-European incursions, was controlled and culturally dominated by some of the oldest populations of West Asia. Carus went on to say, "Chinese sages have their own interpretation of the phrase 'the mystery of heaven and earth.' They would at once associate the words 'heaven' and 'earth' with the two opposing principles yang and yin. . . . It seems not to be impossible that the Chinese tablet in the hands of Fuh-Hi is the same as the 'Tablet of Destiny' of the [Mesopotamians]."[62]

One of the most outstanding contributors to the history and origins of the Chinese people and their philosophies was Professor Albert Etienne Terrien de Lacouperie. Lacouperie's work in this area of investigative study has never been rivaled, let alone surpassed. Lacouperie held appointments as professor of Indo-Chinese philology at the University of London, president of Council of the Royal Asiatic Society and Philological Society, and board member of the Peking Oriental Society. He authored twenty-five books, among them the provocatively titled *The Languages of China Before the Chinese, West Asian Origins of Chinese Civilization, The Black-Heads of Babylonia and Ancient China,* and

12. West Asian population known as the Elamites whom Lacouperie identifies as the Bak. Limestone relief ca. 900B.C.E.

13. Akkadian ruler, thought to be the great Naram-Sin, grandson of Sargon. Naram-Sin ruled virtually all of West Asia for thirty-seven years (2270–2233 B.C.E.). Sin is depicted here with the false beard and crown of West Asian kingship.

The YH-King and Its Authors. It is this last volume that documents those who introduced to the Chinese people the concept
of duality (yin/yang) and the oracle of the I-Ching.

An accomplished philologist, Lacouperie used language and
various historical documents to launch what seems to be an impenetrable defense for a West Asian origin of China's I-Ching.
Lacouperie began by identifying a group of families known as
the *Bak,* who immigrated into China carrying with them the be-
ginnings of civilization: a well-defined sociopolitical structure,
writing, philosophy, and economic fortification. Culturally, this
group was intimately related to the Meso-Sumerians of West
Asia. Racially and ethnically, the Bak were descended from the
Akkadians and Elamites of Mesopotamia:

> The language of the Bak families, which under the leadership
> of Yu Nai Hwang-ti (HuNak-Kunte) arrived about 2282 B.C. on
> the banks of the Loh River in Shensi, [and] was deeply connected
> with that of the Akkado-Sumerians of Elam-Babylonia. This
> alone might be sufficient to show that previously [*sic*] to their
> migration to the East and the Flowery Land [China] they were
> settled in the vicinity of these populations and, therefore, in
> proximity of Chaldean civilization, with which we have shown
> them to have been well-acquainted. The relationship of their
> language with that of the Akkado-Sumerians was pointed out
> and exemplified by me in 1880 . . . an extensive comparison has
> shown me that the Akkado-Sumerian words in Chinese belong
> [to] the Bak families from the Elamo-Babylonian civilization in
> which they were current terms.[63]

These statements by Lacouperie are extremely significant for
three reasons. First, the identification of Yu Nai Hwang-ti as a
family of languages removes the shroud of ambiguity from
China's first Emperor Hwang-ti. We know that the name does
not refer to an individual but to a group or entire population.
Second, the transliteration of *Yu Nai Hwang-ti* into *Hu Nak-Kunte*
is very revealing. The fact that Kunte is a common clan name
among West African Mande speakers and that their linguistic
presence in 2282 B.C.E. was prominent in East Africa could suggest a link between the linguistic patterns of the two geographi-
cally distinct regions. Finally, the mention made by Lacouperie
to the Akkado-Sumerians indicates that the Akkadians play a
very significant role in the transmission of culture from West
Asia to the Far East. Their influence is acknowledged more than
once by Lacouperie. Shedding more light on the Bak culture, he
remarked, "The language of the...invading Bak tribes was

entirely distinct from that of the Aborigines of China.... The result of this advance was for a time an intermingling of the language of the conquerors with that of the previous inhabitants."[64] What is evident among the Bak tribes is that though they spoke a language derived from a common source, there were various dialectical branches that included syntaxes, syllabaries, and polyphonics of a different origin.

Lacouperie documents that the Yh-King appears in early texts of the Xia dynasty (2000 B.C.E.), whose writing and language "correspond to linguistic features peculiar to the Mon and *Tagalo-Malayan* languages, and cannot be mistaken."[65] This language group was and to some extent is still found on various islands throughout Melanesia and Southeast Asia, which are presently inhabited by the ethnic groups who originally spoke the languages. Currently these dialects fall within the category of the Austronesian family of languages.

Focusing more specifically on the origin of the I-Ching, Lacouperie wrote, "before their emigration to the Far East, the Bak families had borrowed the pre-cuneiform writing . . . from South-Western Asia. A most interesting feature of the literature embodied in the cuneiform characters is the numerous vocabularies of several kinds giving the different meanings, [and] various sounds, . . . [they are] Sumerian, Akkadian, and the Akkadian descriptive names of the characters, single and compound."[66] Lacouperie went on to say, "the Yh-King is the oldest of the Chinese books . . . some of the Yh-King's chapters, would suggest that some of the Yh-King's vocabularies are imitated from old pre-Cuneiform ones . . . what is pretty sure is that the Chinese vocabularies have been framed in obedience to the same principles, with the same materials, and undoubtedly according to the [same] tradition of the old syllabaries of South-Western Asia."[67]

Through writing and language, Lacouperie skillfully unraveled the important roots of a system whose originators are not only forgotten, but have become strangers in their own land. Lacouperie's evidence both supports and is corroborated by the words of world-renowned historian and theosophist Helena Petrova Blavatsky:

> One of the oldest known Chinese books is the Yih King, or Book of Changes. It is reported to have been written 2850 B.C., in the dialect of the Accadian black races of Mesopotamia. It is a most

> abstruse system of Mental and Moral Philosophy, with a
> scheme of universal relation and divination. Thus a circle
> represents YIH, the Great Supreme; a line is referred to YANG,
> the Masculine Active Potency; two half lines are YIN, the
> Feminine Passive Potency. . . .[68]

Though he meticulously dissected the I-Ching, daringly blazing his linguistic trail, Lacouperie was never able to perceive the I-Ching as anything more than a codex that recorded historical events. Lacouperie believed that its functions as an oracle were unfounded, and therefore dismissed them. This is unfortunate. To the Akkado/Elamite families of West Asia, the I-Ching was a scepter of power that contained the secrets of the solar cosmology as well as the biopsychic unfolding of the human race, all of which was contained within its principle of duality — its yin and yang.[69] The I-Ching, like Ifa, reflects the fundamental reality in the material universe based on the primordial binary elements of positive and negative, dark and light, yin and yang. The term *binary* simply indicates something that consists of two parts. In respect to numerics, binary signifies any mathematical system that has two at its base, and so it is with the I-Ching or Book of Changes. Yes/no, on/off, positive/negative are all encounters of a binary nature. Several examples will dramatize the power of polarity as it is represented in the I-Ching. At the base of the individual lines of the eight binary triplet figures are the units of duality expressed as − and − −, or yang and yin respectively (See Photo 16). These two lines are then arranged in three-line structures, enclosed in a circle, and read from the bottom up. The binary trigram configurations in the upper hemisphere of the circle correspond to the energy that emanates from the Earth's electromagnetic field, while those at the bottom of the circle pertain to the Earth or the gravitational field rotating in time. When the two are combined, they produce the sixty-four permutations, or hexagrams. These sixty-four six-line structures comprise the changes and correspond to the *biopsychic field* — energy which surrounds every human being.

In 1675, German mathematician and philosopher Gottfried Von Leibniz was given credit for the discovery of differential and integral calculus. According to research reported by Dr. Jose Arguelles in *Earth Ascending: The Law Governing Whole Systems*, Leibniz had begun work on a theory involving the concept of binary mathematics, but encountered great difficulty finding evidence to prove his theory. Through a Jesuit priest who had

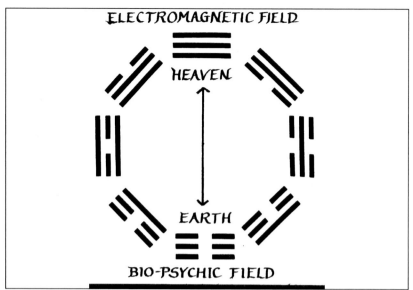

14. The eight linear binary hexagrams which comprise the I-Ching, the oracle said to unravel the mystery of Heaven and Earth. The upper portion of this oracle corresponds to Heaven and the electromagnetic field, while the lower relates to Earth and the biopsychic field which envelops each individual human being. The blending of the various hexagrams can result in sixty-four combinations and no more. This correlates to the sixty-four combinations found within the genetic code.

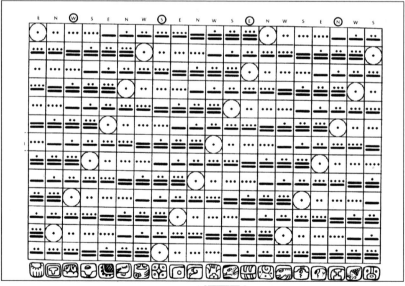

15. This Mayan grid (the Tzolkin), the sacred calendar of ancient Mesoamerica, demonstrates (like the I-Ching and DNA) that there are fundamental patterns represented in nature, perceived but not created by humans.

traveled extensively throughout the Far East, Leibniz was introduced to the I-Ching. After close study of this oracle, he was able
to confirm his system of binary mathematics, which has become
the basis of present-day computer science.

Less than two hundred years ago, another German philosopher and historian, George Hegel, acquainted himself with the
binary system of Leibniz. Hegel would go on to construct the
dialectical theory of history, which equates the rational with the
real and uses dialectic to comprehend an absolute idea. This theory of dialectical history had a profound impact on the great social philosopher Karl Marx, who used this binary concept as the
foundation for his theory of dialectical materialism.[70] Thus, in
the course of several centuries, three men who would radically
effect the philosophical direction of Western civilization inher-
ited from their predecessors and accepted as fact the fundamental reality of binary law as postulated and espoused by the
I-Ching.

Carl Jung was attracted to the I-Ching for what he perceived as
its psychological applications. Jung believed that it confirmed
many suspicions concerning the archetypes of human consciousness as well as the notion of synchronicity, the idea that
events gain significance from their simultaneous occurrence. So
impressed was Jung with the I-Ching that he would eventually
write the forward to the most authentic translation of the book
in the Western hemisphere, the 1949 Wilhelm/Baynes edition.

Though the validity of the I-Ching had been confirmed and
embraced by four of the most influential minds of this era, the
most stunning revelation was yet to come. In 1953, two scientists, James Watson and Francis Crick, announced to the world
their discovery of the genetic code, consisting of sixty-four binary triplet figures called *DNA codons*, which correspond directly to the sixty-four binary triplet hexagrams of the I-Ching
oracle. The genetic code is written with four nucleic acid letters,
each one represented by the two basic linear units of binary language $(- -, -)$, yin and yang. Like the hexagram of I-Ching,
there are sixty-four codons, and only sixty-four such structures
possible. From these codons, the twenty amino acids are derived, which make possible every biochemical and physiological action in the human organism. Thus, we are able to say that
the I-Ching contains the key to unlocking the very mystery of
life itself. Whether identified as *The Book of Changes, The Tablet of*

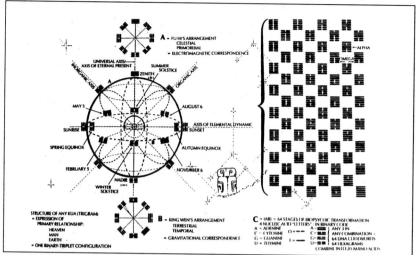

16. Map showing the relevance of the I-Ching to terrestrial and stellar phenomena. It also demonstrates the two different arrangements of the oracle. Fu-H's, the original arrangement utilized by the Xia and Shang dynasties, pertains to Heaven while King Wen's of the Zhou, relates to Earth. In the far right, we find the chart (Letter C) that corresponds to the code of genetic dialect.

17. A bronze mask depicting the visage of the inhabitants of the Chinese Shang Dynasty (1766–1000 B.C.E.). The Shang were the successors of the great Xia dynasty and carried on their traditions until they were overthrown by the Zhou. Historians agree that it was during the Shang dynasty that writing was developed as well as the cultivation of the silkworm, the silk industry, sophisticated bronze work, and sculpture in jade. These contributions, along with the philosophical concepts imparted via the Xia, literally laid the foundation for Chinese culture and civilization.

Destiny, or the *I-Ching*, one thing is certain: the power of this oracle has been used consciously at times to mold or influence specific periods of human history. That the I-Ching derives its
power from the principle of duality or polarity is the radical but
undeniable lesson here. Ironically, what the West has gained
from this axiom is far less than what it has to offer. Though
many have acknowledged the reality of opposites, there is a tendency to overlook or neglect the countless levels between the
two extremes.

The Hermetists of ancient Egypt had a thorough understanding of the functional dynamics of the Law of Polarity. This,
the fourth great axiom from the Hermetic perspective, embodies
the truth that all things manifested in the mental universe have
two sides, two aspects, two poles, and a pair of opposites with
multiphasic degrees between them. Thus, everything has inherent duality or poles, which manifest the multitudes of opposites
that we encounter on a daily basis. Batteries have an anode and
a cathode, or positive and negative aspects that, when properly
connected, will generate power or electrical force. Electrical current is a flow of actually two currents, AC (alternating current)
in which the poles reverse and DC (direct current) where the
poles are constant. The expression *AC–DC* is also English slang
to describe someone who is bisexual, or who alternates between
their sexual poles. Manic depressives, who exhibit wide mood
swings from the depressive pole to the manic pole, are called *bi-
polar*. Love and hate, hot and cold, good and bad, not to mention
male and female, are all manifestations of universal opposites
that consistently prove to us, regardless of our acknowledgment, that everything in creation has its opposite.

All of these opposites may at any time be transmuted, provided the practitioner understands the law. Things belonging to
different classes cannot be transmuted into one another, but elements of the same class may have their positions reversed. For
example, love can never become east or west, but it may become
hate; hard things may be rendered soft, hot things may become
cold, and sharp things may become dull. The principle of polarity states that like and unlike are the same, that opposites are
identical in their nature and different only in their degree. This
can be easily substantiated. Hermetists proclaim that spirit and
matter are but two poles of the same element, the intermediate
planes are various degrees of vibration. Infinite mind and finite

mind are the same in their nature (that nature being mind), and are different only in that the two are among the many planes of correspondence comprising multiple vibratory frequencies. Heat and cold are identical in nature and are different only in degree. A thermometer registers many degrees of temperature, the lowest point or pole being cold, and the highest hot. Between these two points are many variances of the two and in the absolute sense there is no place on the thermometer where heat ceases and cold begins. The same is true of short and tall or high, and low (height); large and small (size); wide and narrow (breadth); and day and night, which in a twenty-four-hour period exhibit many degrees that gradually shade into one another.

What is imperative to understand is the relativity of all of these varying degrees. We are compelled to use these terms in a descriptive context so that others may understand us, but they are relative from person to person, let alone in the absolute sense. If you travel around the world in an eastward direction, you will eventually arrive in the west. If you go far enough south you will find yourself in the north. That which we deem good and bad are not absolutely so. The expression "the lesser of two evils" refers to something that is less good than the next higher in the scale; but what is less good in turn is better or "more good" than what is below.

Love and hate are emotions humans categorize as diametrically opposed, or irreconcilable. But according to the principal of polarity, there is no such thing as absolute love or absolute hate. Envision a polar scale that measures these two emotional extremes. At any point on the scale, there will be more love and less hate, or vice versa. As we ascend the scale we encounter less hate and more love, but if we descend the scale we find just the opposite. These intermediate areas are the jurisdiction of like, dislike, disdain, fondness, amiability. Therefore, there are no absolutes that introduce the next subcategory.

The proclamation of the axiom, "all truths are but half truths" (and all paradoxes may be reconciled), echoes many ancient philosophical aphorisms: everything is and is not at the same time, and there are two sides to everything. The reality is that all truths are but half truths, simply because there are no definitive absolutes, although humans are forever trying to create them.

Though much of the principle of polarity has been discussed, the best way to understand what remains of this principle is through personal experience. In the human promenade through life, there is a continuous parade of new lessons that inevitably create perspectives, convictions, and directions in and about life. These personal realities become our truths, and we live and relive them daily. As we grow and mature, many, if not most, of our notions about our realities change, and what we once held to be hallowed is modified, sometimes radically, demonstrating that our truths and realities are in a constant state of flux. Those who are too rigid to see change on their paths eventually succumb to a fixed view of the world, making themselves and those around them miserable.

All experiences, events, items, and emotions can be classified as positive or negative. For example, love is positive, and hate is negative. The positive pole is considered a higher degree of vibration than the negative pole and is therefore dominant. The ancient Hermetists stated that the tendency of nature is to move in the direction of the positive pole, which is forever increasing its vibration. Here we see that the Laws of Vibration and Correspondence work intimately with the Law of Polarity. By understanding this relationship, the transmutative abilities of polarity become clear. When properly applied, the Law of Polarity leads to a greater sense of self-awareness and clarity.

CHAPTER 5

The Principle of Gender

"Gender is in everything; everything has its Masculine and Feminine Principles; Gender manifests on all planes." – Kybalion

It has been said that "The union of man and woman is like the mating of Heaven and Earth. It is because of their correct mating that Heaven and Earth last forever. Humans have lost this secret and have, therefore, become mortal. By knowing it, the Path to Immortality is opened."[71]

This axiom embodies the truth that within all things is ever-present the reality of the masculine and feminine principles, which are constantly exerting their influence on each plane of life. I feel it is important to clarify my usage of terms in explicating this law. My use of the terms *masculine* and *feminine* do not correspond one-to-one with the terms man and woman since, by the Law of Polarity, masculine and feminine are not necessarily opposites, but are simply the two shades of gender. And, since by the Law of Gender all things are masculine and feminine, it follows that all people embody all shades of gender. If gender is conceptualized as a scale, the poles of which are pure maleness and pure femaleness, then we can see how we have come to label people male or female. Those who are psychologically and physically closer to the male pole are called *men*, while those who are closer to the female pole are called *women*. Though many of us choose to view this scale as fixed or steadfast, our present social, cultural, as well as psychological, circumstances dictate a broader reality, informing us of the potentiality of more than two types of sexes. It is gender, operating within the parameters of polarity, that makes this a possibility.

Currently in American discourse, gender is associated with sex, which we inadequately explain by equating the terms *male* and *female* with the words *man* and *woman*. The word *gender* is derived from the Latin root *genre* or *gener*, meaning to beget, to procreate, or to generate. The sexual union of male and female is merely one manifestation of gender on the Physical Plane of

18. The symbol of yin and yang, which characterizes gender in all its many aspects of creation. Each part contains an aspect of the other, the phenomena which lends itself to perpetual generation.

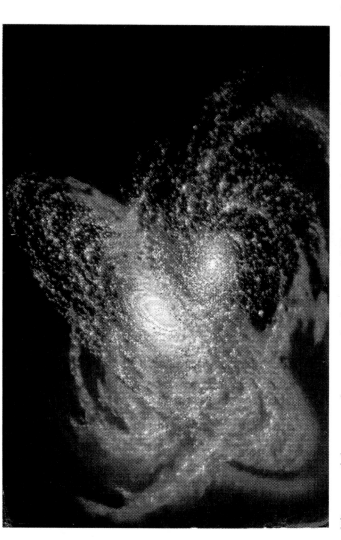

19. This photo exemplifies one of the great phenomena in the material Universe. Science recognizes that most galaxies belong to groups bound together gravitationally resisting the over-all tendency to fly apart. But there are periods when two galaxies will merge without sustaining damage to one another – creating a new galaxy. The Hermetic Philosophy would dictate that these galaxies are charged with either positive or negative forces or yin and yang energy. Therefore, we see in this example, creation through gender, in one of its most abstract, yet dynamic, manifestations.

Correspondence. Gender, apart from its modern association with sex, is the process of begetting, generating, creating, and producing on all planes of creation. In the parameters of the human experience, this phenomena is symbolically expressed in the spherical icon of yin and yang, expressed in the colors black and white. Within each aspect of the divided circle is a portion of the other. Thus, in the black half denoting yin is the white dot of yang and within the white yang is found the black dot of yin. Within each man is a portion of woman, and within every woman is an aspect of man. This symbol, when applied universally, encompasses the generative principle in all of its fundamental features from the creation of atoms to the birth of solar systems and galaxies. Positive and negative as applied to gender are never antagonistic to one another but work mutually in continuous harmony. One is dependent upon the other in the process of being and becoming; they are compliments, not opposites.

In a dialogue with Thoth/Hermes, Asclepius (Imhotep) asked Hermes, "Do you say that God is of both sexes, Trismegistus?" Taking but a second to ponder, Hermes replied, *"Not only God, Asclepius, but all things ensouled and soulless, for it is impossible for any of the things that are to be infertile. Take away fertility from all things that now exist, and it will be impossible for them to be forever . . . . "*[72]

This postulate is dramatized in the East Indian creation myth. The universe is created by the Supreme Yogi Shiva, the exalted male principle, and his consort Shakti, the active creative energy of femininity, who is called *Parvati* in her benign aspect and Kali in her awesome aspect: "The whole universe is created out of the union of Shiva and Shakti. Shiva and Shakti's love play transforms the universe. The sexual activity of Shiva and Shakti makes the moon wax and wane."[73] Examples such as these that allegorically reflect the Law of Gender are globally evident in the doctrines of the ancient world as well as present-day societies. In ancient Kmt, there were Nu and Nut, male and female counterparts of the primeval spirit. The Bambara of eastern Guinea see this as Pemba and Faro, or Heaven and Earth, whose interaction brings about conservation and change. The Dogon identify Amma and Nummo while the Fon of Dahomey identify their principle of duality as mawu-lisa.[74]

Interestingly, this principle of duality is absent in Western culture, most probably due to the entrenched patriarchal customs and mores of a male-dominated culture and society. The Judeo-Christian tradition attributes the genesis of all creation to a lone male deity, God. In the Christian tradition there is the Trinity of God — three persons in one God — the Father, the Son, and the Holy Spirit (or Ghost), all of whom are masculine. The absurdity of the Western notion of creation as an exclusively male activity can be traced in part to events that took place almost 5000 years ago: "the Indo-European-ruled nations of the historic periods, explain the creation of the universe by the male deity or the institution of kingship, when none had existed previously. . . ."[75]

This forced exclusion of the feminine aspect of creation has wreaked havoc on virtually every individual psyche in all Western and Western-influenced cultures and civilizations. Jungian psychologist Marion Woodman has asserted that because of the dominant influence of patriarchy, our present culture has substituted *mater*, the word from which we derive the term *mother*, for *matter*, the menial expression of our current sociocultural condition, which has created our blind and destructive indulgence into overt materialism. Thus, with respect to mental gender, the feminine or mother aspect has been replaced by a masculine expression indicative of a left-brain, mundane material existence. It is noteworthy that the word *matter*, though a corruption, is also derived from the term *mater*. As human beings engage one another with this unhealthy and sometimes perverse perspective of social and mental gender, a myriad of problems are created.

What are social and mental gender? *Social gender* is simply the way men and women are conditioned and expected to act in the social environment. Social gender is built into the very norms and mores of the culture; and because of the severity of early indoctrination, it is impossible to eradicate these behavioral patterns completely. *Mental gender* is the state or condition of mind that allows social gender to be a reality. The conventional wisdom, "as a man thinketh, so is that man," is surely applicable in this instance. Men are so fervent in their quest to epitomize the "macho" mentality that currently pervades many societies. This behavior is self-destructive according to the Law of Gender,

20. Shiva and Shakti, the two eternal manifestations of gender. Shiva is the oldest of the great gods of India, pre-dating the gods of the Hindu or Aryan pantheon by millennia. Traces of Shiva extend as far back as 3000 B.C.E., placing him firmly in the Indus Valley civilization. The original inhabitants of ancient India held Shiva as the Supreme god, for he was forever in a state of actualization due, in part, to his constant awareness of his feminine active principle, the goddess. The ancients of India held that Brahma and Vishnu, the Vedic gods of the Aryans, were "puny insignificant upstarts when compared to Shiva." Here Shiva is joined with Shakti to produce the *Bindu* or *Seed of the Universe.*

which describes a reality of mind based on both masculine and feminine components.

Many writers have theorized on various divisions of the mind, such as conscious and subconscious, voluntary and involuntary, passive and active. All of these divisions announce the presence of mental duality. The Hermetists equate the masculine principle of mind to what is now considered the objective or active mind. Taoists would denote this aspect as yang. The feminine principle of mind corresponds to the subconscious, passive, or involuntary state of mind. For Taoists, this aspect is yin. Hermetic Philosophy labels these two states of mind the *I* and the *me*. The I represents the masculine principle of mental gender, while the me is indicative of the feminine; I reflects a state of being, while the me component represents the aspect of becoming. The I or masculine mind equates to the intellect and is that level of our mentality that concerns itself with the work of the will. The feminine principle of mind is much more expansive and far-reaching in its field of operation. It concerns itself with the task of generating new and innovative thoughts, concepts, and imaginative formulas. Furthermore, "The tendency of the Feminine Principle is always in the direction of receiving impressions, while the tendency of the Masculine Principle is always in the direction of giving out, or expressing."[76]

Psychiatrist Rudolph M. Ballentine, in speaking about the I or masculine mind, which he refers to as *I-ness,* says, "When sensory impressions come in via the lower, sensory-motor mind, this I-ness serves to transform them into a personal experience by relating them to individual identity. It provides a sense of separateness from the rest of the world, a feeling of distinctness and uniqueness. . . . It is the property of subjectivity. . . . I-ness does not instinctively flow with nature. It makes possible the question: 'What's in it for me?' and lends the ability to say, 'These are mine.'"[77] Though he concurs with his colleagues about the complexity of the term *ego* — it is much more than egotistical behavior — Ballentine draws correlations between I-ness and the ego: "I-ness is often translated ego. It thinks logically and sequentially. Ego means 'I' in the everyday, ordinary sense: it is the adaptive, competent, common sense self that operates in the world of competition and achievement."[78]

Though the two aspects of masculine and feminine mind are similar in kind, they are vastly different in degree. The masculine

MICROCOSMIC ORBIT

THE FRONT OR FEMININE CHANNEL   **THE BACK OR MASCULINE CHANNEL**

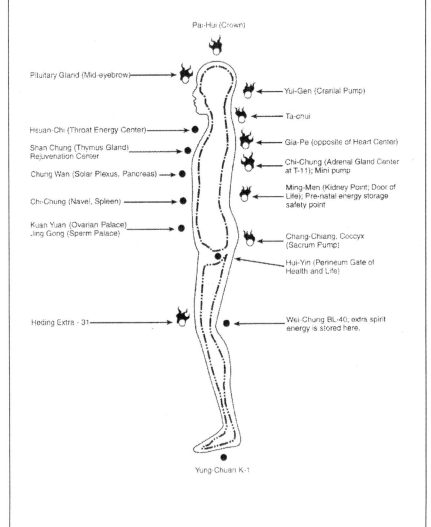

Pai-Hui (Crown)

Pituitary Gland (Mid-eyebrow)

Yui-Gen (Cranial Pump)

Ta-chui

Hsuan-Chi (Throat Energy Center)

Gia-Pe (opposite of Heart Center)

Shan Chung (Thymus Gland)
Rejuvenation Center

Chi-Chung (Adrenal Gland Center
at T-11); Mini pump

Chung Wan (Solar Plexus, Pancreas)

Ming-Men (Kidney Point; Door of
Life); Pre-natal energy storage
safety point

Chi-Chung (Navel, Spleen)

Kuan Yuan (Ovarian Palace)
Jing Gong (Sperm Palace)

Chang-Chiang, Coccyx
(Sacrum Pump)

Hui-Yin (Perineum Gate of
Health and Life)

Heding Extra - 31

Wei-Chung BL-40; extra spirit
energy is stored here.

Yung-Chuan K-1

21. The Path of the Microcosmic Orbit. Dr. Michael Frost.

mind is confined strictly to mundane cerebral impulses, while the feminine mind relates to the more lofty experiences of a greater refined consciousness serving nature, oneness, and humanity.

The ancient masters also acknowledged that gender was not limited to the mind — mental perspectives and processes — but that the entire human body (organs, glands, etc.) was divided into specific areas of gender, which the ancient Chinese categorized as yin and yang. The ancient Egyptians, Indians, and Chinese believed that by practicing particular exercises they could harmonize these elements of yin and yang to create a more balanced masculine and feminine perspective within the mind, which would allow the consciousness to expand beyond the physical body prior to its demise. They referred to this process *as developing the energy body.* Developing this energy body awakens a part of the individual that moves instinctively, free from environmental, educational, and karmic conditioning.

Organic or internal alchemy is the outcome of these practices. The elements of water and fire and sex and love (called *kan* and *lin* by the Chinese) reunite the male and female within each of us. The reuniting of male and female involves the practice of self-intercourse, which through the fusion of the internal sexual energies enables one to give birth to more profound states of awareness. This process also aids in the development of the soul body, which inevitably leads us to the body of immortality. We must remember that although the terms *sexual* and *sex* are being used, they are — with respect to the process of creation — inadequate. Inexhaustible in its essence, sexual energy is no more than the primordial creative energy locked within all that is.

By using tonal or sound vibrations, manipulation of the pubococcygeal muscle, and breathing exercises, our ancestors eventually discovered within the body what has come to be known as the *microcosmic orbit.* The microcosmic orbit is a pathway within our bodies that channels energy or *chi* up the back from the perineum through the spine, over the head, ending in the palate of the mouth. This is the yang or masculine channel, and all other yang channels connect to this major pathway and are nourished by it. The yin or feminine channel ascends from the perineum, up the front of the body, ending at the tip of the tongue. The six yin channels connect to this main channel and are nourished by it. Touching the tip of the tongue to the palate connects the two yin and yang channels, which allows the chi to circulate continuously in our bodies. *Chi, ki,* and *prana* are words used to identify a form of vital energy that flows through our bodies. It cannot be created or destroyed, but merely transformed. *Chi* is the source of all activity in the universe. In humans, primordial or original *chi* is stored in the kidneys, just below the navel, and the sexual center. The ancient masters perceived that this circuit, or microcosmic orbit—a conduit for *chi*—connects our physical, electro/energetic, and spirtual bodies.

Thus the ancients, by their understanding of gender, were able to vary the universal force into two qualities of primordial energy—positive and negative, masculine and feminine, or yin and yang. They believed that yin and yang were inseparable tendencies of all energy, and it is impossible for one to exist without the other. With respect to gender, the merging of yin and yang is at the source of all universal action, making it a factor intrinsic to the creative process and therefore innate in all manifestations of the human experience.

The irony before us is that men constantly deny that which is feminine within us while women, forced to live in a patriarchal culture, are constantly fighting for greater expression of equality, which forces them to consistently engage the more aggressive male-oriented patterns of survival on both a mental and physical level.

Because of improper perceptions of men as being strong and women as being weak, qualities associated with women that are characteristic of the feminine component of the mind are suppressed in men. Therefore, a sensitive man is perceived as weak, for men are supposed to be macho; for a man to cry is weak, for only women do such things. The vision of why we are on Earth, which is contained in the feminine mind, is muddled with the aggression, arrogance, and insensitivity of the masculine ego. Joan Armatrading, a modern-day poet/musician, allowing the words man and woman to represent the masculine and feminine aspects of the mind, has written, "Man likes to own/a woman shares/man has his needs/a woman cares."[79]

Until men allow the part of their minds that is feminine to be fully engaged with their masculine aspect, they will never understand their true nature and connection with the divine, since they are only half-functional and incomplete. Though gender manifests itself in all things and on all planes, humans play a primary role in the evolution of those things through the evolution of our own consciousness. The feminine aspect of mind is the doorway through which all men must sooner or later pass. What men perceive as strength is one dimensional and finite. The Indian goddess Tara embodies the true power of the feminine aspect of mental gender:

I guide man to the path of the Divine
And guard him from the red Wolf and the Snake.
I set in his mortal hand my heavenly sword
And put on him the breast-plate of the Gods.
I break the ignorant pride of human mind
And lead the thought to the wideness of the Truth;
I rend man's narrow and successful life
And force his sorrowful eyes to gaze at the sun
that he may die to earth and live in his soul.
I know the goal, I know the secret route,
I have studied the map of the invisible worlds
I am the battle's head, the journey's star. [80]

CHAPTER 6

The Principle of Rhythm

*"Everything flows out and in; everything has its tides; all things
rise and fall; the pendulum swing manifests in everything; the
measure of the swing to the right, is the measure of the swing to the
left; rhythm compensates." – Kybalion*

The Law of Rhythm is closely connected to that of polarity. In
fact, rhythm actually functions within the polar parameters created by the polarity axiom. The Hermetists hold that all actions
are followed by a reaction — an ebb and flow, a rising and sink-
ing that manifests in all aspects of universal order. Solar systems, suns, planets, races of humanity, and civilizations are all
subject to the Law of Rhythm. It applies to religions, creeds, philosophies, governments, and social and national movements.
The Principle of Rhythm makes itself evident in the creation and
destruction of worlds, as well as in the rise and fall of nations.
The Brahmans of India dramatize this process as the *outbreathing*
and *inbreathing* of the god Mahavishnu. As Mahavishnu ex-
hales, universes are created, spiraled to a summit of efficiency,
and maintained. As Mahavishnu inhales, so begins the decline
of these star systems until they reach their lowest point of decadence, only to once again begin their ascent. This procedure
manifests on every level of existence. The ancient Hermetists
saw this pattern in all things: people are born, grow, meet their
demise, and like the phoenix are reborn. We can see rhythm
manifested plainly in the seasons. Spring is the birth or beginning, summer is the period of maturation and constancy, and
fall is the encroaching ebb or decline, which ushers in winter, the
season of death; with the passing of winter, there is rebirth in the
spring.

One lesson of this law is that there is no absolute rest, no cessation from rhythm's cycle. That all movement is contiguous with
this principle is evident in all natural phenomena — the seasons,
the recurring orbits of planets, the rise and ebb of ocean tides,
and the repeated occurrence of comets traversing our solar system. This rhythmic process is also found in human sociopolitical
and economic patterns. Events in American history have followed

22. Two faces carved in stone from South Asia (India) dated the fourth or fifth century B.C.E. The images depicted here are most assuredly representative of the Harappans who occupied the Indus Valley complex.

23. Sai Baba, a Dravidian spiritual master from India whose philosophy incorporates the science of the Manvantara.

this pattern. These events are believed by some to have been engineered by humans, but these humans were unknowingly acting in accord and by the dictates of this axiom. Beginning arbitrarily with the nineteenth century, we can see that each phase of acceleration was followed by a phase of deceleration. Expansion gives way to downturn. The economic upturn of the industrial revolution was followed by a period of depression between 1826 and 1847, which involved the shrinking of markets for industrial products. The period of machines and massive railroad building, which allowed the rapid production of iron, steel, and coal between 1848 and 1873, gave way to the depression of 1873 to 1894. This downturn was marked by a growing export of capital and by efforts to reduce the costs of raw materials. The brief boom of 1894 to 1913 was due to reaping the harvest of the previous period's capital exports and to the introduction of new technology.

World War I ended this boom, and a period of economic and political gyrations followed from 1914 to 1929. Berlin experienced a revolution as the United States headed into the era of prohibition and racketeering of the roaring twenties. The gross spending and illegal financial pursuits of the 1920s created an economic tailspin, ending in the 1929 stock market crash and the beginning of yet another depression, popularly referred to as the Great Depression. The economic, moral, and physical despair of the 1930s ended only with the entry of the United States into another world war in 1942.

Although America fought and defeated two enemies, World War II did not last long enough for the country to recuperate financially. It did, however, remove all vestiges of the depression that had engulfed the nation. As the United States entered the 1950s, it was still recovering from its past political and monetary entanglements. This was the time of the Korean War, crop failure, a recession, and the 1954 Supreme Court ruling on the unconstitutionality of segregation and the beginning of the American Civil Rights Movement. The tumultuous, yet economically prosperous, 1960s gave birth to another recession and the fabricated energy crisis of the 1970s. The lavish, self-indulgent 1980s were followed by economic hardship in the 1990s.

We could cite example after example, but the point here is to dramatize the obvious: there are cyclical patterns, rhythms that are in operation on several levels of existence. To sociopolitical

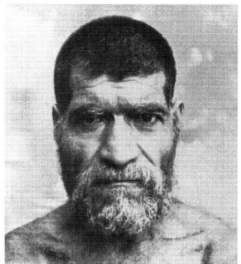

24 A and B. Current direct descendants of the Indo-Europeans who overran Europe, Northeast Africa, and West and South Asia. These men, the last group of their genre, are known as the Kalash and only number 1200. Labeled as *kaffirs* or barbarians, they are despised by the people of Pakistan. In the nineteenth century, the Emir of Kabul ordered their annihilation and sent thousands of troops onto the steppes and into the mountains. His soldiers slaughtered multitudes of these people, leaving the Kalash as the only survivors.

analysts, these events may seem the cause of basic detectable patterns that reflect the human machine and how it functions within its environment, but such an observation would be superficial at best. Beneath the mundane realities of daily life lies the Principle of Rhythm, shaping the destiny of the human race.

Of the varied cyclic manifestations of this principle, the most intriguing are the recurrent periods of human activity upon the Earth, even those periods that occurred in epochs now forgotten or intentionally dismissed. The ancients believed that by understanding the nature of these cyclic periods one could not only foresee the future of humankind, but could also glimpse the past.

The oldest and most accurate of these systems known at this time originated with the indigenous population of ancient India, the Harrapan or Indus Valley civilization, which is presently yielding carbon dates from 7000 B.C.E.[81] The Harrapans believed that the universe was organic and imperishable and that its existence was divided into an ongoing and recurring infinite number of cycles, each consisting of a period of improvement and a period of decline. In his book *The Divine Science*, P.K. Manikkalingam reported that in a period of improvement, people are of enormous size and live to a very advanced age. They have no need for laws or ownership of property. Human beings are spiritually in touch with themselves and the divine. There are no wars or malice of any kind.

In an age of decline, humans live a primitive life, contemplating whether they are a product of civilization or barbarism. All true religion is lost or falsified, and people become dwarf-like in stature, with an average life span of only sixty to seventy years, the last thirty-five of which are immersed in physical pain and suffering. Wars and disease are rampant, and the moral and spiritual fiber of the human race is at its lowest point. Then the pendulum begins to swing in the opposite direction, at times following cataclysmic destruction, and improvement begins.

This system is still alive in India today and is known as the *Manvantara*, the "race cycles," as they apply to the evolution and deterioration of the human species under the Law of Rhythm. Tehuti expressed this phenomenon in terms of the necessity of corruption to beget aspiration: *"And corruption hath laid hold upon all things on Earth, and the Providence of the True encompasseth, and will encompass them. For without corruption, there can be no*

Generation consist. For corruption followeth every Generation, that it may again be generated. For those things that are generated, must of necessity be generated of those things that are corrupted, and the things generated must be corrupted, that the Generation of things being, may not stand still or cease."[82] The Manvantara speaks to this very cyclic process. The Manvantara is divided into four *yugas* or ages. These ages succeed one another and repeat themselves *ad infinitum*. Each age is preceded by a period of transition called *Sandhya* or twilight, the time of pruning or purification in preparation for the age that is to follow. The ages or yugas are as follows:

1. *Krita* or *Satya Yuga*, which lasts 1,728,000 years, is considered the golden age, or the age of truth and purity.

2. *Treta Yuga*, which lasts 1,296,000 years, is also an age of purity, but of less perfection than the first.

3. *Dwapara Yuga*, which lasts 864,000 years, is characterized by the emergence of conflicting forces and, though the cycle within this age begins in harmonious accord, it eventually exhibits the struggle between the high and low, good and evil.

4. *Kali Yuga*, which lasts 432,000 years, is considered by the Manvantara to be the lowest point of humanity. The human race tries desperately to rebound from the spiritual atrocities of the previous age. (The allegory of Adam and Eve being cast from the Garden of Eden.)[83]

Right now, we are in the last of these four periods, the Kali Yuga, or the "age of darkness," which is said to have begun in the year 3102 B.C.E. with two ominous events. The first was the disappearance of the great warrior sage *Krishna*, the Christ of India, whose name literally means "Black One." The second event was the appearance, advance, and conquest of most of Europe and Asia by the Indo-European hordes who referred to themselves as the Hittites, Indo-Iranians, and Aryans, the latter being a name that means the "noble ones." Originating on the Eurasian Steppes circa 4000 B.C.E., the Indo-European advance became the mechanism to inaugurate the Kali Yuga. With superior weapons and steeds bred for speed (the Indo-Europeans introduced horses into Asia), these hordes converged on Europe and West and South Asia. They carried with them a propensity for extreme aggression and violence as never before witnessed in

25. Map showing the various branches which became part of the Indo-European cultural family.

our epoch. To the many nations that would gather to confront them, they must have seemed liked the legions of darkness, and they were. They traveled under the shroud of the age of Kali — the age of darkness, and they were undefeatable.

The Indo-Europeans who went West became the Greeks, Slavs, Germans, Celts, Thracians, Balts, and Illyrians. Those who invaded the eastern areas became the Anatolians, Phrygians, Armenians, Indo-Iranians, and Tocharians. There were other Caucasian populations, such as the Hurrians, Lydians, and Assyrians, who were conquered by the Indo-Europeans infiltrating the East, and who eventually succumbed to their cultural influence.

From the regions of Anatolia and Iran, the Indo-Europeans continued to push southward and eastward forcing their way into Mesopotamia, Canaan, and finally Northwest India. All of these geographical areas had for millennia been major centers of civilization for people of African descent. The formidable foe that encroached upon them brought a message of dire change. In India an epic poem of great antiquity, the "Ramayana," describes the battles and ensuing conquest of the Aryans' encounter with these ancient nations:

Ram saw his mission and the great destiny of his race. From that moment he no longer hesitated. Instead of igniting the spark of war among the peoples of Europe he decided to take the best of his race into Asia. Ram striving after divine science, had traveled into the southern countries where the priest of the black men had revealed part of their secret knowledge to him. Upon returning to the northern country he began to impart the knowledge of the sacred fire to his race in hopes of putting an end to the cult of human sacrifice which was increasing among his people, for he saw in this the ruin of his race.

Lighted fires kept burning for several months on the mountains where the signal for the mass migration of all who would follow Ram. The tremendous migration directed by the great shepherd of peoples slowly started to move departing in the direction of Central Asia towards the Caucasus Mountains where there existed several cyclopean strongholds of the black men which had to be captured.

He made friends with the Turanians, old Scythian tribes who inhabited upper Asia, and led them in the conquest of Sumer where he completely repelled the black men, for he intended that a people of unmixed white race would become a center of light for all others. Ram then pushed onward into India, the main center of the black men, ancient conquerors of the red and yellow races. He ordered the first attack and led the first thrust of this colossal battle in which two races contended for the scepter of the world.[84]

The "Ramayana" is a portion of a greater work known as the *Mahabharata*, which means the "great war." The colossal battle that it records began in the year 1500 B.C.E., in the northwest sector of India (now Pakistan) and is thought to have lasted for nearly 1,000 years as the indigenous inhabitants of India tried to repel the invaders. The Indians fought valiantly and many battles were won, but the war itself was lost to the Aryan intruders who conquered the Indus Valley descendants and renamed their land *Aryavarta*, "land of the Aryan." Though the aboriginal population of India managed to halt the eastward and southward advance of the Indo-Europeans, the cultural and religious influences they carried with them would incubate in the Northwest and, like a virus, eventually infect all of India.

This was a very pivotal period for the Earth and the families of humankind. The cultural mores and philosophical doctrines of the Indo-Europeans seemed diametrically opposed to those of the previous races. The Indo-Europeans indoctrinated the civilizations that they subjugated with values indicative of their peculiar mind-set. These values, which have endured to the present day, embrace (1) warfare or extreme and aberrant aggression; (2) racism and segregation by color; (3) the subjugation, disdain, inferiority, and impurity of women; and (4) absence of respect and understanding of the planet and its ecosystems. Although litanies have been written upon each subject, neither space nor time allow for great detail to be presented in this discussion. Each of these values, however, will be addressed briefly, to demonstrate the gravity of our present situation, and its significance within the cycle of the Kali-Yuga.

War

"Compared to war, all other forms of human existence shrink in comparison." – General George Patton

War is one of the primary contributions of the Indo-Europeans to contemporary world culture and civilization. Of the unique components that constitute Indo-European culture, warfare is a vital and integral part. The term *battle-ax culture*, which has been applied by anthropologists to the precursors of Indo-European

26. Fierce warriors, the Assyrians were unrivaled for centuries.

27. In this scene, Assyrian monarch Ashurbanipal strangles a lion with one arm while piercing its chest with his sword.

28A. Elamite citizens being escorted from their city by the Assyrians.

28B. Elamite warriors bound and shackled, marching to a fate worse than death.

culture, embodies the brutality and constant conflict among the various tribes of the Northern Cradle of Europe.[85] The oldest archeological evidence recently excavated from grave sites confirms what many historians had already postulated. Among the most sacred objects to the Indo-European were his weapons: "In a stone cut tomb was found a man accompanied by a stone battle-ax, copper daggers, an arrowhead and pot."[86] In the Po Valley of northern Italy were found other such burials. The large cemetery of the Remedello culture located in this area produced graves overrun with "metal daggers, halberds, axes, and awls."[87] J. Hawkes, writing of the Mesolithic and Neolithic battle-ax cultures, affirmed that "the battle axe cultures represent the roots of the Indo-European speaking peoples. . . . Though it may not have always been so, their character came in time to be dominantly pastoral, patriarchal, warlike, and expansive."[88]

In his book *In Search of the Indo-Europeans*, J.P. Mallory asserted that "The very fact that war-bands are by no means a uniquely Indo-European phenomenon should caution us. . . . Warfare is the product of environmental, economic and social circumstances that can be found anywhere, and there is no reason for assuming an inherently warlike character for the Indo-Europeans."[89] Mallory's observations are incongruent with the historical events of the period (4000–286 B.C.E.), chronicled by the many cultures overrun and decimated by the Indo-Europeans. The Indo-European proclivity toward war and violence is not only unrivaled in the ancient world, but is still zealously perpetuated in the present day. Since the appearance of the Indo-Europeans in the fifth millennium B.C.E., war has been such a common occurrence that, to many countries, it is a way of life and to all others, a tolerated and accepted cultural endeavor.

The Indo-Europeans' engagement in constant tribal warfare before their intrusive transcultural military exploits is evidenced in the verity that upon their arrival in West Asia, they remodeled the concept of war: "The influx of the Indo-European immigrants into the Near East during the second millennium B.C. revolutionized the art of war. The newcomers introduced the horse-drawn war chariot, which gave a swift striking power hitherto unknown in the Near East . . . the Indo-European . . . soon became a new aristocracy throughout the entire area including Egypt."[90] Wars were fought prior to the arrival of the Indo Europeans, but there were parameters to which most countries tried to adhere. No parameters contained the Indo-Europeans. Their battles were fought not only to defeat and subjugate, but to terrorize their victims into devout obedience. The invasion of West and South Asia by the Indo-Europeans was by no means a single major conquest. Most authorities agree that these invasions came in migratory waves over a period of 1,000 to possibly 3,000 years, from 2500 to the second century B.C.E. Other advances taking place in Europe began around 4000 B.C.E.

The Indo-Europeans ravaged and dismembered all those who dared to stand against them. Their main representatives in the Near East were the brutal and acrimoniously disposed Hittites. Overrunning the area of Anatolia in Asia Minor and northern Syria, the Hittites culturally indoctrinated the dominant group of the sector, the Hurrians (a group linguistically descended from the Caucasian family of languages). The Hurrians, in turn, infused the mores and traditions of the Indo-Europeans into another group, the Assyrians, who originally were Semitic: "From the beginning of the second millennium, the Assyrians were in close political and commercial contact with the Indo-European Hittites. Indo-European Hurrian princes appeared in various cities of northern Syria from that same time on. By 1500 B.C., Assyria was completely under control of the Hurrians."[91] The amalgamation of these two groups produced the most feared and destructive hegemony of West Asia, the Assyrian Empire. Though many of the Indo-European hordes were vicious and brutal — Kassites, Luwians, Phrygians — none could match the barbaric treachery of the Assyrians. As historian Cyrus Gordon so accurately described them, "The Assyrians were a ferocious violent people whose profession was war. To them life was war and their genius was concentrated on it."[92] Historically, the Assyrians were the first of the despotic empires to dominate the region of western Asia. Their nobles belonged to a warrior caste who introduced advanced tactical maneuvers and apparatus — battering rams and siege towers — into their fighting strategies: "The Assyrians elevated warfare to an exact science. They were not content to merely conquer peoples; they must completely destroy them."[93] They also employed the use of boiling fluids to scald and immobilize their adversaries while protecting themselves with heavy armor.

If the inhabitants of the besieged and conquered cities were captured alive, they faced a horrendous fate. They were skinned alive, then beheaded. The Assyrians would impale the corpses on stakes around the city and the skins of their victims would cover the homes and walls surrounding that same city. The personal proclamation of self-acclaim of the Assyrian monarch Ashurnasirpal substantiates this activity: "I marched from the Orontes . . . I conquered the cities . . . I caused great slaughter, I destroyed, I demolished, I burned. I took their warriors prisoner and impaled them on stakes before their cities. I settled Assyrians in their place . . . I washed my weapons in the Great Sea."[94] Runoko Rashidi, a scholar of West Asian history proclaims, "In all of the annals of human history, it is difficult to find any people with an appetite for bloodshed and carnage to rival that of the Assyrians."[95]

The Assyrians had many enemies, but none were as steadfast in their opposition to the Assyrian regime as the Elamites. Many of the bas reliefs and stelae uncovered in major Assyrian cities are of the battles fought against the Elamites. At one point the Elamites tried to yoke the combined strength of the kingdoms of Anatolia and the Levant with the Babylonians in the struggle to lay waste to the Assyrians. The battle was lost, and the Elamites were so viciously and vindictively punished that their ancient civilization literally vanished into oblivion. Their bones were exhumed and carried off to Assyria so that their souls would never be at rest.[96]

As stated previously, there were many Indo-European tribes notoriously inclined to extreme violence during war, but the only other group whose predilection toward unprecedented aggression that was analogous to that of the Assyrians were the Sythians. The term *Sythian* is the Greek equivalent of Aryan. What the Sythians lacked in military genius, arsenals, and tactical strategies, they compensated for in their moral transgressions concerning war. Of the various barbarous hordes that came from the Ukrainian Steppes, the Sythians are in some ways an anomaly. Master goldsmiths, their work is some of the best produced in antiquity. Refined, polished, and symmetrically aligned, their devotion to working in gold was only paralleled by their insatiable thirst for blood and war.

The Sythians constituted the last major wave of the great Indo-European warmongers. They were a dominant force in parts of

Europe, West Asia, and the northwest portion of South Asia, from the sixth to the first century B.C.E. In battle they were savage, and their vitality seemed inexhaustible. Upon conquest of their enemies they would immediately behead them, then proceed to drink their blood, usually from the skulls of other fallen foes. Like the Assyrians, the Sythians flayed their adversaries, fashioning from their dried skins pillow covers and capes. Herodotus recorded an annual tribal gathering at which warriors were disgraced if they had not killed anyone since the previous meeting. Since the appearance of the Sythian hordes, wars have been incessant.

Most of these wars have been fought and are still being fought or influenced by the European nations of the world—in civil wars and world wars alike, supplying weapons to other countries to engage in war, sending troops into countries to fight their wars, and politically instigating future wars. In fact, "It is a fair estimate that 100 million people have been killed by war since 1900. Responsibility for this mass slaughter rests directly upon the [European] male members of the species."[97] More than 57,000 Americans died in the Vietnam War alone. Gases and biological war devices annihilated all flora and fauna, rendering some land uninhabitable for the next 100 years.

Patricia Axelrod, a weapons analyst and associate professor at Johns Hopkins University, attributed the perpetuation of wars and weapons to the "military industrial complex," whose end is solely economic gain or profit. Axelrod went on to say that the concocted need for war is a "ruthless scam" and that 64.6 percent of the United States gross national product goes into wars and the manufacturing of weapons.[98] Social historian Charlene Spretnak, on the other hand, makes it clear that the European penchant for war involves more than gold-digging: "Destruction of the world by a small group of white men in order to achieve more wealth than they can ever possibly use does not make sense. We are talking here about a drive for power, a need for domination that must be examined . . . [Patriarchy] creates a culture that is destructive and death-oriented."[99]

When we confront the deplorable reality of warfare in the world, we see that most wars are begun by elite males of Indo-European descent, fought by men and women of lower status, and sanctioned by Western religious institutions. For example, in the fifth century C.E., Pope Innocent I proclaimed that God

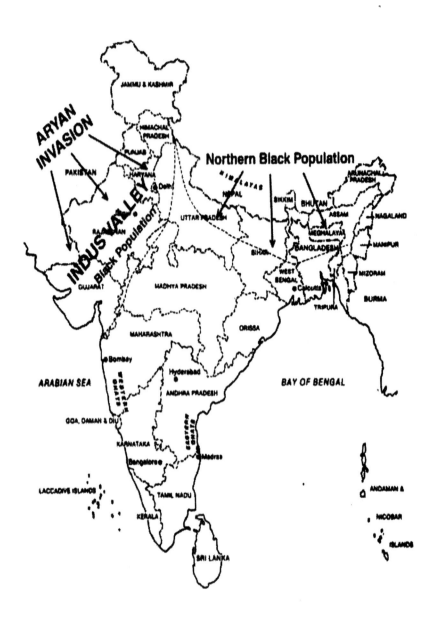

ARYAN INVASION

Northern Black Population

INDUS VALLEY

Black Population

JAMMU & KASHMIR

HIMACHAL PRADESH

PAKISTAN

PUNJAB

HARYANA

Delhi

RAJASTHAN

HIMALAYAS

NEPAL

SIKKIM

BHUTAN

ARUNACHAL PRADESH

UTTAR PRADESH

ASSAM

NAGALAND

MEGHALAYA

BIHAR

BANGLADESH

MANIPUR

GUJARAT

MADHYA PRADESH

WEST BENGAL

Calcutta

MIZORAM

BURMA

TRIPURA

ORISSA

MAHARASHTRA

Bombay

ARABIAN SEA

Hyderabad

ANDHRA PRADESH

WESTERN GHATS

BAY OF BENGAL

GOA, DAMAN & DIU

KARNATAKA

EASTERN GHATS

Bangalore

Madras

ANDAMAN &

LACCADIVE ISLANDS

TAMIL NADU

NICOBAR

KERALA

ISLANDS

SRI LANKA

29. Map of Aryan incursions as they converged on the Black Harappans of the Indus Valley civilization.

30. The great warrior sage Krishna in the form of Vishnu. Krishna was one of the key individuals in the historic battle, known as the Mahabharata, fought between the Blacks, or *Pandavas*, and the Aryans or *Kuravas* of India. Standing beneath the outstretched form of Krishna are the five *Pandava* warrior kings and their common wife, Draupadi. Dated 425 C. E.

gave the church the right to kill, and he permitted papal armies to employ the sword in their pursuit to punish those they condemned.[100] The founder of Italy's literary futurist movement, Filippo Marinetti (1876–1944) expressed best the philosophy of our time: "We want to extol the love of danger. . . . There is no beauty apart from conflict. There are no masterpieces without aggression. . . . We want to extol war — the world's only hygiene."[101]

Of course, war and conflict are not really the baseline issues before us. They are but the overt manifestations of a greater problem. If roles were reversed, and races other than the White race were playing the role of anthropologist, categorizing and ascribing characteristics to the many populations of our planet, how would they describe and categorize males of the European race? Would they show them to have a temperament that lends itself to aggressive and violent behavioral patterns? And if so, would such a mental predisposition constitute mental and moral instability? As it presently stands, there is no group influential enough to turn the mirror on the European male. There have been numerous books written and lectures given, but as the global condition worsens, we must ask, is the White male listening?

Westerners are indoctrinated with violent thoughts and actions from the moment of birth — the first unnecessary violent slap, the violent nursery rhymes told to us at bedtime, the violent and brutal cartoons we watch and eventually find humorous. These and other sociocultural phenomena condition us for the aggressive violent society and world in which we must live: "Power and order, pushed to their final limit, lead to their self-destructive inversion: disorganization, violence, mental aberration, subjective chaos. This tendency is already expressed in America through the motion picture, the television screen, and children's comic books. These forms of amusement are all increasingly committed to enactments of cold-blooded brutality and physical violence: pedagogical preparations for the practical use of homicide and genocide."[102]

"There is violence because we have daily honored violence. . . . A country where people cannot walk safely in their own streets has not earned the right to tell any other people how to govern itself, let alone to bomb and burn that people." – Arthur Miller

Racism and Segregation by Color

"I will say that . . . there is a physical difference between the white and black races which I believe will ever forbid the two races living together in terms of social and political equality. And in as much as they cannot so live, while they do remain together, there must be the position of superior and inferior, and I as much as any other man am in favor of having the superior position assigned to the white race." – Abraham Lincoln, 1864

The origins of the European attitudes of racial superiority and subjugation are rooted in the conquest of West and South Asia by the Indo-Europeans. A period of profound darkness and feudalism followed the destruction of India's great Indus Valley civilization. The year was 1500 B.C.E., and the Indian subcontinent was being ravaged by a series of devastating wars sweeping across the northwest and central sections of the country. These wars between India's indigenous Blacks and the invading Indo-Europeans, who, as previously stated, described themselves as the Aryans, would last close to a millennium.

As the great Aryan hordes pushed toward the eastern regions of the country, they were met with a gauntlet of formidable resistance by the Indians who occupied those areas. Finally, and inevitably, the Aryans began to succumb to the superior might of the indigenous population. As the millennium drew to a close, several nations were drawn into battle within the Indian interior, each siding with either the *Kuravas* (the White Aryans) or the *Pandavas*, whose legions constituted the Black or original inhabitants of the Indian subcontinent. These wars culminated in the early portion of the seventh century B.C.E. in the Mahabharata, the great and final battle between the two races. Fought on the plain of *Kurusetra* in the northwest of the subcontinent, this battle would decide geographical supremacy. Though India's legions halted the eastward advance of the Aryans, they would never again regain control of the northwestern portion of the country, once the very hub of their empire.

With the Aryan faction now dominating the cultural pulse of the northwest, severe and often destructive social devices were implemented to prevent intrusion from the more civilized and cultured Indians who had chosen to remain in that vicinity. This

31. Dravidian woman from South India born of Tamil extraction. The Tamil are the oldest of the four Dravidian groups which occupy South Asia. Harappan symbols have been found in the formative period of the Tamil script.

is the genesis of what Martin Bernal refers to as the *Aryan model,* the model that created the paradigm in which we presently exist in respect to race and racial attitudes. This factor becomes critical to acquire an understanding of the present, for the entire globe has been affected by it, especially the Black race.

The term *model* in this context signifies a simplified prototype, a precedent, frame, or mold from which more complex cultural idioms are derived. The term *paradigm,* for our purposes, means generalized patterns of thought that are culturally induced and communally applied to sociocultural reality. Thus, it is the model that in time, will create the paradigm, complete with its multitudinous complexities.

It is commonly agreed that with the Indo-Europeans arrived the cultural model that would ensure their longevity and survival. The issue of race, or more specifically color, seemed to predominate the Aryan mind-set, and created a central theme in their cultural prejudices: "historical, mythological and archaeological evidence suggest that it was these northern people who brought with them the concepts of light as good and dark as evil (very possibly the symbolism of their racial attitudes toward the darker people of the southern areas)."[103]

For a point of reference, we need look no further than India itself, the very hub of Indo-European racial iniquity instigated through the caste system. Though several cultures of the ancient world utilized a system based on caste, India's, as employed by the Aryans, was the first caste system founded on color: "The spread of the Indo-Aryan culture brought with it the origins and the concept of light-colored skin being perceived as better than darker skins. The Brahmins [*sic*], the priests of the lighter Indo-Aryans, were considered to be the epitome of the racial hierarchy."[104] In Sanskrit, the language spoken by the Aryans, the word for caste is *varna,* literally color.

The Aryan Brahmans professed that this system of human degradation was born from the God Brahma. They portrayed Brahma in human form, ascribing symbolic colors to the different regions of his body. The head of Brahma was white, reflecting the highest order of the caste, the Brahmanic or priest caste. The shoulders, arms, and torso of Brahma were red, representing the *kshatriyas* or warrior caste. The loins, hips, and legs of Brahma were yellow, which identified the *vaisyas* or merchant caste, responsible for the economic sanctity of the empire. Last

(and least), were the black feet of Brahma, designating the un-
holy abode of India's Blacks, upon whom the Aryan Brahma
would eternally stand. From this pre-Vedic period onward, the
title given to the original inhabitants of India is *dasya* or *dasa*,
which means servant, and *sudra*, which means slave.

As the Aryans began to saturate northwestern India, contact
with the conquered sudras proved unavoidable. The amalgamation of the Aryans with the indigenous population created, in
time, a mixed race: "In the course of five or six centuries the
Aryas [Aryans] had moved down from the Punjab to the fertile
valleys of the Ganges and set up powerful kingdoms—the Ku-
rus, Panchalas, Kasis, Kosalas, Videhas . . . the aborigines had all
been subdued and the Aryas had mingled with the civilized Indian peoples. . . ."[105] The union of the two races became an issue
of great consternation and dire concern for the Brahmans, who
envisioned the eventual demise of their race and culture. A revealing passage from the *Rg-Veda*, the Aryans' account of their
conquest of India (conservatively dated ca. 900 B.C.E.) states,
"We are surrounded on all sides by the dark-skinned Dasyus.
They do not perform sacrifices. They are unbelievers. Their
practices are all different. They are men! O! Destroyer of foes!
Kill them, destroy the Dasa race."[106] The children of these sacrilegious interracial unions became known as *untouchables*, and
the Brahmanic priests proclaimed them an abomination, the
lowest of the caste, falling even below the despised Dasas. In order to insure their racial purity, the Brahmanic priests created a
codex of statutes or laws to keep these castes distinct. In his book
India, Guiseppi Sormani revealed that "Much study has been
given to the real origin of the castes and the most dependable
authorities trace these back to the invasions of ancient times.
The white-skinned Aryans did not wish to mingle with the
dark-skinned Dravidians [sudras] who were the original inhabitants. . . The first measures towards dividing the populations
into castes were laws that forbade mixed marriages between
Aryans and Dravidians."[107] The Brahmans professed that these
laws were issued by the great lawmaker Manu, whom the Vedic
priests believed to be the progenitor of the human race, incestu-
ously begotten by the God Brahma upon his own daughter. The
priests decreed that the following standards be adhered to by all
those of Aryan or Indo-European origin in order to create racial
constancy and permanence:

THE LAWS OF MANU

1. He who weds a sudra [black] woman becomes an outcaste.

2. A Brahmana who takes a sudra to bed will sink into hell.

3. If a sudra mentions the names of the caste of the Brahmans or Kshatriyas, an iron nail ten fingers long shall be thrust red hot into his mouth.

4. If he arrogantly gives advice to the Brahmans, hot oil will be poured into his mouth and ears.

5. Food gets polluted by the smell of a pig, touch of a dog and the look of a sudra.

6. If a sudra hears the vedas [the holy and religious texts of the Aryans], his ears shall be filled with molten lead. If he speaks them, his tongue will be cut out; and if he memorizes them, his body cut to pieces.

7. A sudra must build his home outside the village, his wealth shall be dogs and donkeys, and their dress shall be garments of the dead, and they shall eat from broken dishes. Black iron shall be their ornaments, and they shall wander from place to place.[108]

Though these are but a few of the Laws of Manu, they convey the extreme conditions that India's Blacks were made to endure. Relegated to the bowels of socioreligious degradation, these people, known as *Harrapans,* were allowed to enter the towns and villages of the Aryans only at night when they could not be seen. They were forced to carry brooms with which to sweep away any remnant of their footsteps. The Aryan priests instituted laws that prevented the Blacks of India from entering shrines, temples, or any religious sanctuary because they believed that even their shadows would pollute the essence of God.

Thus, we see the origin of the Aryan model. The paradigm born from this was inevitable: When one throws a stone into still waters, the ensuing ripples are unavoidable. And so it was with the Aryan model, as it elevated the issue of race to society's most important, and gave birth to what we now call *Eurocentrism.*

Society, examined in its essential components, is a complex structure of interdependent elements and is no more than an organism intent on self-preservation. Thus, as humans become more sophisticated, the vital dynamics of society become more complex and pervasive. The integral units of the paradigm, which are resilient, adjust and conform to transformation, but do so without compromising the integrity of the cultural base, the Aryan model. It is this paradigmatic shift that allows the ethos, or spirit, of Indo-European culture to maintain, survive, and dominate the many cultures of the Earth. It embraces and indoctrinates the many host cultures it contacts, superimposes its ethos onto them, and makes them a parody of Aryan ways, dependent on European culture for their survival: "The socialist East and the underdeveloped South have nothing better to offer on any of the levels mentioned (wealth, democracy, or even social justice). On the contrary, these societies can only progress to the extent that they imitate the West. And this is what they are doing."[109]

Since its arrival, Indo-European racism has managed to survive historical transformation, retaining its original countenance. By the nineteenth century, the Aryan model had become the Aryan brotherhood: "A race, like the Old Aryans, scattered from the Ganges as far as the Hebrides, settled in every clime, and every stage of civilization, transformed by thirty centuries of revolutions, nevertheless manifests in its languages, religions, literatures, philosophies, the community of blood and of intellect which to this day binds its offshoots together."[110] The nineteenth century was the incubator of overt Eurocentricity, not the location of its birth, as Martin Bernal and sociopolitical economist Samir Amin believe it to be. Amin reported that "Eurocentrism is a specifically modern phenomena, the roots of which go back only to the Renaissance, a phenomenon that did not flourish until the nineteenth century."[111] The imposition of a Eurocentric world reality is not a recent occurrence. What is recent is its expression, perfected by nineteenth-century European intellectuals who found voice in the literature of the era, and who were able to once again espouse a doctrine indicative of an antiquated tradition. Where previously warfare was the construct that built the prior parameters for European cultural and global domination, now the pen, utilized in the new fields of psychology, Egyptology, history, and anthropology, would be used to indoctrinate the world with this more refined concept of racial superiority thereby making "the pen mightier than the sword." By the nineteenth century the African slave trade was beginning to wane, so it became imperative to have a social construct in place to ensure the preservation of the White race as it prepared for another encounter with a despised dark-skinned people. That construct became Eurocentrism. Apartheid appeared in Africa, and systematic and institutionalized segregation occurred in Europe and all of the Americas.

The new Eurocentricity, using the sciences to its advantage, professed that a race changed its form as it passed through different ages, but always retained an immutable individual essence. The quintessence that characterized the European race was pristine genetic superiority. Gustav Kossinna, the German archaeologist whose concepts would dominate the field in the early twentieth century, argued that the master races — the Aryans, the Finns, and the Sumerians — were of Germanic descent and were uncontaminated by race mixing, thereby creating the greatest civilizations. Kossinna and his ilk characterized European civilization as "the greatest in world history and as having been exclusively created by Indo-European-speaking Europeans."[112] In the area of linguistics, Friedrich von Schlegel testified that the Indo-European languages were of a spiritual nature, while others were animal. The idea that the Europeans were spiritual and that other races were material was pervasive throughout Germany by the late nineteenth century, and this same notion would become the basis of Nazi ideology.[113]

Bernal stated that it was during the nineteenth century that the Ancient model of history was replaced with the Aryan model. The racist architects of the Aryan model proceeded to rewrite world history. They omitted the contributions of those cultures and races they deemed impure, such as the African race, and found the ancient Greek historians and travelers fraudulent, their historical observations less than credible. Herodotus, who had been heralded as the "Father of History," became a character of dubious repute whose meandering accounts of his historical encounters were categorized as close to delusionary. German, French, and British Egyptologists painted Black Egypt White, while ethnologists and philologists purposely misread, misspelled, and misinterpreted the written chronicles of antiquity. Even the Moors, whose name literally means Black, became tawny and even White. It seems that "History has been transformed, within a hundred years in Germany, within sixty in France."[114]

Thus, Eurocentrism and all of its intellectual pretenses converged on humanity on a global scale, masked with the dregs of racial inequality. The result is illusion and subterfuge:

> Eurocentrism is therefore anti-universalist, since it is not interested in seeking possible general laws of human evolution. But it does present itself as universalist, for it claims that imitation of the Western model by all peoples is the only solution to the challenges of our time. This dominant culture invented an "eternal West," unique since the moment of its origin. . . . The product of this Eurocentric vision is the well-known version of "Western" history. . . . Eurocentrism is not, properly speaking, a social theory; it is rather a prejudice that distorts social theories. —Samir Amin, *Eurocentrism*

The Creation of Patriarchy

Origins of the Subjugation, Disdain, and Inferiority of Women

"Though destitute of virtue, or seeking pleasure elsewhere, or devoid of good qualities, a husband must be constantly worshipped as a god by a faithful wife. . . . If a wife obeys her husband, she will for that reason alone be exalted in heaven." – Law of Manu (900 B.C.E.)

In our present era, we have been relegated to what many feminists would call "his-story." For the past 3,000 years, women have, at the hands of men, suffered untold atrocities. Though few women, and even fewer men, are aware of these historical iniquities, their residual impact on our current society confronts us daily in the form of emotional and physical abuse: rape, social inequality, domestic subservience, assault and battery, and recreational licentiousness.

The organized struggle for women's equality in America began in the nineteenth century when several women's groups began advocating the abolition of slavery. In London in 1847, an international conference was held to discuss the issue of human bondage. The conference drew the attention of several women's groups, whose members attended in full number only to be thwarted by the American clergy. In 1848, a Woman's Declaration of Independence was drawn up, declaring womens' free-

32. Ethiopian Queen from Meroitic Cush known as "Candace," a Latin word derived from the Meroitic *ktke* or kentake meaning "Queen Mother." Ethiopia was and remained matriarchal for sometime—the empire being ruled by these queens.

dom in a patriarchal society and culture. This, a first foray into the male-dominated political arena, became the cause of much agitation, but would eventually set the stage for the widespread women's movement.

The media is constantly providing us with affirmations that women "have come a long way, baby." Until 1857, an English woman could not sue for divorce except by an act of Parliament, which of course was reserved for the aristocracy. Until 1881, a husband had the legal right to use physical violence to prevent his wife from leaving home; and until 1884, a married woman could be imprisoned for denying her husband the act of copulation. Using our existing historical time-line, it would indeed seem that women have come quite a distance, but this is only an illusion. It is difficult to imagine from our immediate historical vantage point that there was a period prior to our current epoch when women reigned supreme, in the sense that they did not have to beg for equality and a voice in the society. Women were held in high esteem and revered for their spiritual, social, and legislative insights and abilities. They were equal to men in all positions of power and authority, and quite frequently surpassed them with their ability to disseminate precise responsibility based on the moral merit of the individual, regardless of their gender. In fact, most of the world's great civilizations were at one time matriarchal. This was the era of the feminine, the time when the Goddess ruled.

When we peruse antiquity's record, we discover that "man's" greatest empires rest on foundations constructed and created by the genius of women. This has especially been the proven standard in African and African-derived civilizations: "Civilization itself was born, nurtured, and brought to maturity among the matriarchal African cultures of Kush and Egypt."[115] The principle cultures of western Asia—Sumer, Babylonia, and Akkad—were firmly matriarchal. Before the Islamic era of the seventh century C.E., even the Arabian Peninsula, which is at present culturally committed to the subjugation of women, was matriarchal for 2500 years. The Annals of Ashurbanipal state that Arabia was governed by queens for as long as anyone could remember.[116] The Islamic Allah was originally *Al-lat*, one part of a trinity of goddesses that included Kore or Q're, the Virgin, and Al-Uzza, the Powerful One.[117] Together they formed the triad known as *Manat*, the Threefold Moon. Furthermore, "Pre-

33. Ethiopian Kentake.

Islamic Arabia was dominated by the female-centered clans.
Marriages were matrilocal, inheritance matrilineal. Polyan-
dry — several husbands to one wife — was common."[118] The most
powerful of the dynasties to arise in southern Arabia, known as
Arabia Felix or "Happy Arabia," were the Sabeans, a strong matriarchal empire descended from Kush or Ethiopia.

By the eleventh century C.E., Arab explorers launched major
expeditions into the interior of the African continent only to find
the thriving remnants of a one-time powerful matriarchal influence still intact in many of Africa's kingdoms such as Ghana,
which still employs a matrilineal system of inheritance. While
the term *matriarchal* denotes a society or culture conceived, sustained, and governed by women, *matrilineal* refers to a society's
main principle of material inheritance, as in the acquisition of
property and other forms of identified wealth. Though matriarchal societies had all but disappeared in Africa by the ninth century C.E., many kingdoms still maintained a matrilineal social
structure.

In the region of the globe called the *southern cradle* by Cheikh
Anta Diop, matriarchy was in full flower from the most ancient
period. Dr. Charles S. Finch, III, reported that "the southern cradle was distinguished by agrarian societies in which the fe-
male/maternal role was dominate because . . . of intra-group
harmony, an intimate relationship with nature, and the central
place of the mother in family and social affairs [which] pro-
moted a co-operative, non-competitive social ethic . . . allowing
the elaboration of ever-more complex social systems."[119] Finch
drew attention to several elements that were not only exclusive
to matriarchal culture but literally intrinsic to its survival. Finch
continued,

> farming was almost certainly a female invention; it strengthened
> and amplified the matriarchy while materially and symbolically
> enriching it. . . . If the figure of the Egyptian goddess Sesheta is
> any indication, women may have even presided over the
> beginnings of writing. The attributes of this patron deity of
> writing powerfully suggest a female provenance for this
> profoundly important skill. . . . Though other forms of writing
> developed in Egypt . . . hieroglyphs were reserved for all
> ceremonial and sacred inscriptions. They are the surest keys to
> Egypt's psycho-mytho-historical ethos and we may presume
> that they were legacies of the matriarchate.[120]

34. Above is Queen Maya, mother of The Buddha, carved in the area of Northeast India during the Licchavi period, second century B.C. E. Prominent features, though mutilated, and cornrowed hair, present a commanding presence carved in stone.

35. The Egyptian Isis and Horus, dated to the Old Kingdom.

Though Finch treads somewhat cautiously in his assessments of the cultural pervasiveness of women's contributions to civilization, history clearly substantiates his claims. In the Babylonian tradition of West Asia, the noble art of tablet writing belonged to a select group identified as *mari-anu*. In ancient Egypt, a similar word, *mari-en*, was the title given to the scribes of old. Both words translate as "great one" or "mother." This title would later become the name of the Semitic Goddess Mari-Anna, whose other appellation was Ishtar, "the great goddess and mother who has borne the men with the black heads."[121] The Egyptian goddess Sesheta or Seshat, whose name means "lady of the builder's measure," is also heralded as the founder of the science of architecture.

In his voluminous *The Mothers*, Robert Briffault reported, "Woman was the creator of the primordial elements of civilization . . . the richer perceptions and interpretations that color the actualities of life, all art, all poetic sentiment, are irradiations of those extra-individualistic, racial interests of the female."[122] The East Indian text Brahmavaivarta Purana informs us that the goddess Savitri gave birth to the rhythms of the Ragas or love, the units of measurement of time, logic, and grammar. According to the universal creation myth, the world began in the womb of the Great Mother during her formless phase. She then took on the aspect of a vast, dark semi-liquid mass of potential energy and matter intermixed. The elements were so inextricably mixed in her that wet could not be distinguished from dry, nor hot from cold. This formless Mother was known as Temu in Egypt, Kali Ma or Maya in India, Tiamat in Babylon, Themis in pre-Hellenic Greece, and Tehom in Syria and Canaan.

When the oldest traditions are examined for the earliest mention of a creation myth, there is discussion of a Goddess' Mother-heart, shaping life, creating order, and bringing about cosmic organization. The ancient Egyptians called this Mother-heart principle, which unified all things, the *ab*. This Egyptian concept of the *ab* included not only the soul given each individual by her/his own mother's heart, but also the hidden heart of the universe. [123]

Frobenius (1873–1938), while in Kush (Ethiopia), was perplexed by the system and custom of women being the dominant class. Though he admired the social tranquility and the extremely organized communities he encountered on his sojourn,

144 Wayne B. Chandler

he was compelled to inquire about what to him was a bewilder-
ing cultural phenomenon: the matriarchate. He implored an
Ethiopian woman to explain this concept to him and she re-
sponded,

> How can a man know what a woman's life is? His life and
> body are always the same. The woman conceives. As a mother
> she is another person from the woman without child. She
> carries the fruit of the night nine months long in her body.
> Something grows. She is a mother. Something grows into her
> life that never again departs from it. She is and remains a
> mother even if her child dies. For at one time she carried the
> child under her heart. And it does not go out of her heart ever
> again. All this the man does not know. He knows nothing. He
> does not know the difference before love and after love, before
> motherhood and after motherhood. He can [know] nothing.
> Only a woman can know that and speak of that. That is why we
> won't be told what to do by our husbands.[124]

If we apply the axiom of correspondence to this statement, we
can understand the greater universal meaning of the feminine
creative force, which gives birth on all planes of existence.

Egyptologist Sir Wallis Budge reported that upon the funer-
ary stelae of the ancient Egyptians, the mother's name was in-
scribed, not the father's. Diodorus said that Egyptian queens
received more respect than the pharaohs.[125]

At the dawn of Chinese civilization, Blacks, as reported by
such scholars as Terrien de Lacouperie, James Brunson, and
Leonard Cottrall, instituted a culture that was unequivocally
matriarchal. The myths and legends of the formation of Chinese
civilization bear witness to this fact: "To the people of Shang
heaven ordered the 'black bird' to descend and to give birth.
Jiandi the mother of the Xia the progenitor of the Shang clan saw
a black bird drop an egg, she swallowed it. As a result she became pregnant and gave birth to the Xia."[126] As previously
stated, one of China's cultural heroes was Huang-ti (2698–2598
B.C.E.), also known as the "Yellow Emperor," yellow representing wisdom. He was responsible for teaching to the Chinese
the various skills of civilization, and ushering in China's Gold-
en Age. The most ancient manuals, as well as the spoken tradition of this culture, inform us that the Yellow Emperor sat at the
feet of a woman the Chinese refer to as Hsuan-nu (the Dark
Girl), the "peach of immortality." It was the Dark Girl who
taught the Yellow Emperor how to rule the kingdom with divine wisdom, and instructed him in military strategy, magic,

36. Venus of Willendorf. Europe, 30,000 B.C.E. Shown here exhibiting the characteristics common to Mother Goddess figurines in historical times. Possible Grimaldi influence created these artistic figures.

and the sixty-four sexual arts. Hua-Ching Ni informs us that "about five thousand years ago, Chinese society [was] a mother-centered society or Matriarchy. . . . The mother-centered society was the original way of human society."[127]

Thus, throughout Africa and West, South, and East Asia, there thrived from a very remote epoch a pervasive cultural concept based on a matriarchal belief system. Historians, anthropologists, and archaeologists have, for centuries, designated the southern cradle as the abode and origin of the matriarch, complete with many icons that reflect the goddess, or feminine aspect of universal order. By contrast, Europe, or the northern cradle, is considered the domicile of male-centered patriarchy, which has an inherent disdain for a matriarchal system. Extensive excavations in Europe during the 1960s, 1970s, and 1980s yielded significant archaeological data that may change this perception. Due in part to the immense undertaking of archaeologist Marija Gimbutas, impressive evidence of the existence of a matriarchal prehistoric society in Europe has surfaced, complete with goddess iconography. Gimbutas entered into this area of study with impeccable credentials (she is professor of European archaeology at UCLA and former curator of Old World archaeology at UCLA's Cultural History Museum), but her research and findings have been the center of ongoing controversy and debate. Backed by a preponderance of evidence, Gimbutas has described the dawn of the Neolithic age in European prehistory in several societies under the influence of a matriarchate. While she dates these cultures in southeastern Europe at 7000–3000 B.C.E. and in Western Europe at 4500–2500 B.C.E., much older artifacts have been excavated, some dating from the Lower Paleolithic (ca. 500,000 B.C.E.). Gimbutas' findings were not embraced with the kind of enthusiasm that she had envisioned. Many of her colleagues scoffed at the evidence, leaving Gimbutas dismayed by their reactions: "I absolutely never even thought that I shall be criticized. I am surprised that people are not for the truth. There is so much evidence of the existence of the Goddess and matristic culture. . . . It really is painful to hear from some people who are my former friends, painful because I see that they don't want to know."[128]

Gimbutas should not have been surprised by the reaction of her colleagues — all of whom were men. Riane Eisler, author of the best-selling book *The Chalice and the Blade*, provides a succinct explanation of the issue: "Marija's work threatens some of the established paradigms — namely, that male dominance has always been the way it is, that war has always existed. . . . Her critics are basically trying to dismiss the possibility that another alternative existed for humanity — a more holistic, more balanced beginning, not ideal by any means, but a different direction."[129]

Though the work of Gimbutas has opened a door to several possibilities concerning the presence of matriarchal societies in Europe, she is not the pioneer in this field. In fact, substantial evidence of a matriarchate was first postulated in the mid-nineteenth century by Swiss scholar Jakob Bachofen and American-born Lewis H. Morgan. Bachofen's book *Mother Right*, though controversial, laid the foundation for further investigation on the subject. *Mother Right* influenced Friedrich Engels, who found Bachofen's premise supportive of the Marxist concept of dialectical materialism, which was believed to be a force operating throughout history. Bachofen remarked, "The idea of motherhood produces a sense of universal fraternity among all men, which dies with the development of paternity. Ancient societies believed that those related by motherblood shared a common soul, so no member of the group could hurt another without doing injury to himself."[130]

The ideas of "motherblood" and "common soul" are concepts not readily comprehended by current historical and anthropological communities, which have compartmentalized the various cultures of the ancient world. The belief that cultures evolved independently of one another is fast becoming an absurdity. This form of tunnel-vision negates the acknowledgment of analogous culture traits, which indicate the diffusion of social, cultural, and biogenetic characteristics among societies.

There is no denying that the first cultures and civilizations in the southern cradle were matriarchal. The transmission of matriarchy from the southern cradle to the northern is extremely plausible when one considers humankind's exodus out of Africa into Europe, by way of a group of Homo sapiens known as the *Grimaldis*. The Grimaldis were identified by anthropologist Rene Verneau shortly after the discovery on June 3, 1901, of the Grimaldi caves, located in the Grotte des Enfants at Mentone. Scientists believe that the Grimaldis succeeded Neanderthals in

37A. Two Venus statuettes from prehistoric Europe—Morovia. Small breasts, thin waists, and *steatopygia* (extraordinarily large buttocks) characterize these carvings.

37B. South African Koisan woman characteristic of the many "Venus statuettes," obviously modeled from her form.

Europe, becoming a link between Neanderthals and the Cauca-
soid Cro-Magnons. The Cro-Magnon are regarded by paleon-
tologists as the most advanced culture of the Paleolithic Age.
Some postulate that the African Grimaldis entered Europe as
early as 40,000 B.C.E., and thereby on the evolutionary scale became the first human beings to occupy that continent. The
physical evidence was excavated by M. de Villeneuve, a French
archaeologist who discovered Cro-Magnon skeletal remains on
the upper two levels of the caves, while the African Grimaldis
occupied the much older caverns on the lower level. There is no
question that the skeletons found on the lower level were cere-
monially buried.

Further analysis on the skeletons was done by anthropologists
Marcellin Boule and Henri Vallois. Vallois and Boule became
the world's foremost authorities on the Grimaldis. After much
examination, both doctors published their conclusions in several journals and in their book, *Fossil Men*. It was at this point
that the statements of these two anthropologists initiated an ex-
plosive controversy: "When we compare the dimensions of the
bones of their limbs . . . these proportions reproduce, but in
greatly exaggerated degree, the characters [*sic*] presented by the
modern Negro. Here we have one of the chief reasons for regarding those fossils as Negroid, if not actually Negro. The Negroid affinities are likewise indicated by the characters [*sic*] of
the skull. These are large; the crania are very elongated, hyper-
dolichocephalic . . . the nose, depressed at the root, is very broad
(platyrrhinian). The floor of the nasal fossae is joined to the an-
terior surface of the maxillary by a groove on each side of the nasal spine, as in Negroes. . . . The majority of these characters [*sic*]
of the skull and face are, if not Negritic, at least Negroid."[131]

This discovery was the first in a series of such finds, with excavations in Brittany, Switzerland, Liguria, Lombardy, Illyria,
and Bulgaria. Dr. W.J. Sallas, a renowned anthropologist, came
upon a grave and commented that "it was filled with human
skeletons, mostly in the contracted position, and of all ages. . . .
There are the remains of 20 individuals, 10 of them in excellent
state of preservation . . . from the preliminary account and illustrations given by Dr. K. Absolon it would appear that they are
related to some Negroid race, and they recall in some respects
the Koranas of South Africa."[132] The next amazing find were
statuettes of several nude female figurines that came to be

38. The Norse god Thor. Indicative of the many Indo-European gods of lightening and thunder whose fathers were directly connected with the Sun. From ENCYCLOPEDIA OF THINGS THAT NEVER WERE by Michael Page and Robert Ingpen. Copyright (c) 1985 by Michael Page, text. Copyright (c) 1985 by Robert Ingpen, Illustrations. Used by permission of Viking Penguin, a division of Pegunin Putnam, Inc.

known as the Venuses. What makes these statuettes so extraordinary and archaeologically invaluable is that they are among the oldest sculptural forms rendered. The figurines are described as obese steatopygous women, with peppercorn hair: "These figurines are certainly mother figures modeled on the African Grimaldi women, the standard-bearers of Aurignacian culture in Europe. . . . This seems to be *prima facie* evidence of a pre-agricultural matriarchy, or proto-matriarchy, extending as Aurignacian culture did, from the Pyrenees to Siberia. . . . If we are correct, then at a time in fairly recent pre-history, the north was itself matriarchal, or at least proto-matriarchal."[133]

Three obvious factors follow from this data: (1) as previously shown by paleo-geneticists like Drs. Rebecca Caan and Stephen J. Gould, humanity had its genesis on the African continent; (2) with the migrations that ensued during the various epochs of the prehistoric era, cultural traits were carried with these groups, and transmitted to the populations in Europe that they encountered; and (3) the matriarchal concept not only began in the southern cradle, but with the spread of the African race, it indoctrinated almost all of humanity.

Thus, if we concede the cultural dominance of the female during the causal phase in the ascent of civilization, we must now entertain the reasons for its untimely demise. We find, comparatively speaking, in many cultures, especially those in West Asia, an abrupt and devastating transformation of the matriarchy to patriarchy, while other geographical locations such as Kush and southern Arabia retained this ethos for a longer time. Ancient Egypt was unique in its simultaneous expression of the two systems, combining them for political, social, economic, and religious equilibrium. The reasons for change are always multifaceted. What we perceive as the effect or transformative process depends largely on our understanding of how well we identify the causes that belie it. Often, the causes are undetectable to our five basic senses and deductive faculties. It is for this reason that everyone's perception of reality differs.

Erich Neumann, a student of Carl Jung, addressed this issue when he elaborated on what he sees as the cosmological inferences of the emergence of patriarchy. Neumann makes connections between the existing mother-cosmos and the radical change in the collective consciousness of "man"kind as it pertained to the emergence of solar symbology in the religious doctrines of the period.[134] When examining the ancient astrological and astronomical mythos of Egypt and Egyptian-influenced cultures, two possible phenomena are apparent: "The Afro-Kamitic cosmic mythos imperceptibly shifted over the millennia from stellar to lunar to solar orientation."[135] During the stellar phase, equality of the masculine and feminine principles was consummate as expressed in the spirit of the culture and society. This cultural period is identified as a *gylany* (*gy* from "woman," *an* from *andros*, meaning "man," and the letter *l* between the two for the linking of both halves of humanity), a term coined by Riane Eisler. It is in this environment where both sexes were socially equal.[136]

The lunar phase was ascendant after the stellar. In ancient as well as modern African tradition, the moon is a symbol of the Goddess. The moon is the embodiment of feminine mystique, power, and spiritual force. Upper Egypt was also known as *Khemennu*, "Land of the Moon." The ancients of Kush proclaimed that the moon was the source of all human souls and was therefore regarded as the realm of the dead and of rebirth because its influence was believed to be directly connected with the gestation of all mammalian life forms. Hence, the lunar phase would give birth to matriarchy in its many manifestations.

The solar phase symbolizes the preeminence of the patriarch. The Sun is the self, "I am" consciousness, the ego, the light of individuality. What was once the essential reality pertaining to the myth of creation, "that out of the primordial darkness came the light," transmutes into the never-ending triumph of "light over darkness."[137] The sun (light) becomes all that is right, and the world becomes color-coded.

In Egypt, this force takes the form of Ra or Horus, while in Aryanized Indo-European culture it is embodied in the God Brahma and marks an era of conquest and dominance. *Dev*, the Sanskrit word for *god*, literally means bright, glowing, or shining. Indra, one of the major war gods of the Indo-Aryans, murders Danu and her son, who both championed the socioreligious culture of the Goddess. Upon their death, "the cosmic waters flowed and were pregnant and this in turn gave birth to the sun."[138] The concept of the sun god emerging from the primeval waters appears in several Indo-European myths, and occurs in connection with two invasions that took place in prehistory. This obsession with the sun, light, and fire perme-

ates Indo-European culture, from their fire sacrifices to the light-
ning bolts of their storm gods. Consequently, with the advent of
the solar cosmological phase, the matriarchate eventually disappeared, and was replaced by the forbears of patriarchy, who carried with them an extreme hatred and disdain for women. With
the advent of patriarchy, the Great Mother was transformed
into masculine deities. In China, the primordial Mother NU-
KUA became Kuan-Yin. And though the literal translation for
Kaun-Yin was "the woman," she was represented as a man. In
India, Ma Nu or "Mother Nu" became the male Manu, war hero
of the staunchly patriarchal Vedic tradition. [139]

In tracing the perceptible or tangible impact of patriarchy, we
need only use the disciplines of history and archeology. Once
again we are led back to South Russia and the influence of the
Indo-European: "While European cultures continued a peaceful
existence and reached a true florescence and sophistication of
art and architecture in the fifth millennium B.C., a very different
Neolithic culture with the domesticated horse and lethal weapons emerged in the Volga basin of South Russia and after the
middle of the fifth millennium even west of the Black Sea. This
new force inevitably changed the course of European prehistory."[140] This new, yet despotic, culture has been labeled the *Kurgan*, a Russian term for *barrow*, the round receptacle in which
deceased males of high tribal standing were buried. Many historians, with evidence from archeological excavations, linguistic
research, and comparative mythology, believe Kurgan culture
to have originated during the seventh and sixth millennia B.C.E.
in the central Volga basin. The basic features of this culture were
patriarchy with rigid and harsh attitudes toward women, including the belief that women were born impure; patrilineality;
the domestication of the horse; and armaments such as the
mace, battle ax, spear, and dagger. For nearly 2,000 years, the
Kurgan culture flourished in the Volga basin, and then, without
warning, began overrunning all of Europe. What historians refer to as "old European culture" collapsed under repeated incursions by the Kurgans between 4300 and 2800 B.C.E., during
which the goddess-centered matriarchy was destroyed, and the
aggressive subjugation of women became the cultural norm.[141]

As the Kurgan (prototypical Indo-Europeans) engulfed
Europe, the matriarchy took its last gasp. Over several centuries,
Europe's matriarchal culture was conquered, amalgamated,

and finally absorbed, as the inhabitants of Old Europe were transformed into what would become the Indo-European.

With steeds fleet of foot, the Indo-Europeans began their exodus from Europe into West and South Asia, circa 2400–1300 B.C.E., conquering, obliterating, and establishing a new world order characterized by an obsession with racial purity, religious subjugation, and destruction of the matriarchal way of life.

When the Indo-European arrived in West and South Asia, the hierarchy of the goddess was firmly entrenched in the cultural matrix of these civilizations. Indo-European priests implemented what would become, and remain, a cultural construct for the view and treatment of women, which inevitably led to the ruin and abrogation of the female-inspired and governed matriarchate.

In South Asia, this sociocultural construct found expression in the ancient Laws of Manu:

1. The mind of woman brooks not discipline, for her intellect has little weight.

2. To kill women and sudras [Blacks] one need not worry, for it is not a sin.

3. A mother who remarries, a beautiful wife, and a disobedient son are enemies, and may be left with no sin.

4. We should always act with caution with fire, water, women, and snakes, for they may, if an occasion presents itself, at once put you to death.

5. One single object (a woman) appears in three different ways: to the man who practices austerities, she appears as a corpse; to the sensual man, she appears as a woman; and to dogs, as a lump of flesh.

6. Untruthfulness, rashness, guile, stupidity, avarice, uncleanliness, and cruelty are woman's seven natural faults.

7. Women have hunger two-fold, shame four-fold, inconsideration six-fold, and lust eight-fold more than man. [142]

In time these pronouncements became social attitudes chiseled into the very ethos of the cultures usurped by the Indo-Europeans. Thus, as the religious and philosophical doctrines began to be rewritten, this mind-set prevailed, tainting and in-

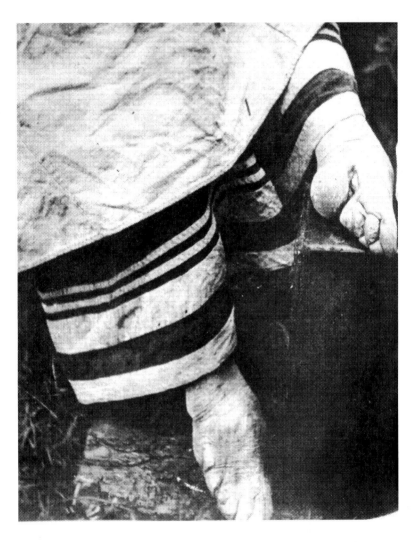

39. A rare photo of the lotus hook foot that Chinese men so avidly desired.

fecting the holy concepts of the Vedas, Judaism, Christianity, and Islam.

The *Catholic Encyclopedia* states, "The female sex is in some respects inferior to the male sex, both as regards to body and soul."[143] In 1 Corinthians 11:3, Saint Paul said, "The head of every man is Christ; and the head of every woman is man." Literature circulated by the Church proclaimed, "All wickedness is but little compared to the wickedness of a woman ... the natural reason is that she is more carnal than a man, as is clear from her many carnal abominations."[144] Martin Luther declared, "If women get tired and die of bearing, there is no harm in that; let them die as long as they bear; they were made for that."[145] Clement of Alexandria was quoted as saying, "Every woman ought to be filled with shame at the thought that she is a woman."[146] St.Thomas Aquinas insisted that every woman is birth-defective, an imperfect male begotten that way because her father was either ill, debilitated, or in a sinful condition at the time of her conception.[147]

With the consecration of subjugation in religious texts, the descendants of the Indo-Europeans found it easy to introduce laws oppressive of women into the very families and homes which were once female-centered, making impossible escape from the ensuing degradation. One of the oldest known documents of the Indo-Aryans, the Mahabharata (700–500B.C.E.), gives remarkable insight into what would eventually become the rigid standard for male/female relationships in Western and Western-influenced civilization. In the Mahabharata, Shiva, one of the great gods in the Indo-Aryan pantheon, in discourse with Uma,"Queen of Heaven," asked her to describe the duties of women. She replies thus:

> The duties of woman are created in the rites of wedding, when in presence of the nuptial fire she becomes the associate of her Lord [husband], for the performance of all righteous deeds. She should be beautiful and gentle, considering her husband as her god and serving him as such in fortune and misfortune, health and sickness, obedient even if commanded to unrighteous deeds or acts that may lead to her own destruction. She should rise early, serving her god, always keeping her house clean, tending to the domestic sacred fire, eating only after the needs of her god and guests and servants have been satisfied, devoted to her father and mother and the father and mother of her husband. Devotion to her Lord is a woman's honor, it is her eternal heaven.[148]

These ideas of what constitute a woman's duties, though written more than two millennia ago, are perpetuated into the twentieth century by the tangible stream of cultural consciousness identified by Bernal as the Aryan model. Fifty years ago, Western wedding vows contained these lines for the bride: "I take thee to be my wedded husband, to have and to hold, for fairer for fouler, for better for worse, for richer for poorer, in sickness and in health, to be bonny and buxom in bed."[149]

In India, the Brahmans, by way of subjugative convention, made women slaves for life, forever to be dominated by men.: "In her childhood a girl should be under the will of her father, in her youth under that of her husband, her husband being dead, under the will of her sons. A woman should never enjoy her own will. Though of bad conduct or debauched, a husband must always be worshipped like a god by a good wife."[150]

This same idea appeared in Western Europe, influenced greatly by the dictates of Christianity. Napoleon professed, "Woman is given us to bear children. She is our property.... She is our possession, as the fruit tree is that of the gardener."[151] According to Saint Thomas Aquinas, "a wife is lower than a slave because a slave may be freed, but woman is in subjection according to the law of nature, but a slave is not."[152] Clergy were infamous for their advice to female newlyweds, in which they echoed the sentiments of a sexist church: "Your duty is submission. ... Your husband is, by the laws of God and of man, your superior; do not ever give him cause to remind you of it." [153]

Upon examination of the aforementioned facts, it is obvious that sociocultural transformation for women has been slow in coming. The ancient model of sexism has endured for almost 5,000 years without recess. Men in a patriarchal society cannot imagine the psychological, physical, and spiritual horrors that women have borne for these last 5,000 years. Believing in the sanctity of patriarchy, men's nefarious historical conduct includes slavery, battery, torture, murder, and rape.

Rape was an anomaly in the Eastern cultures of antiquity prior to the arrival of the Indo-European; when it did occur, it was not tolerated for any reason. The matriarchal populations that dominated the areas of West Asia during this epoch had strict laws regarding this abominable action: "In *Eshnunna* (in Sumer) at about 2000 B.C., if a man raped a woman he was put to death. In the Old Babylonian period ... before the major incursions of the Indo-Europeans . . . the same punishment was given."[154] In the laws of Assyria, which are dated between 1450 and 1250 B.C.E. (when Assyria was under Indo-European control), we read that if a "man rapes a woman, the husband or father of that woman should then rape the rapist's wife or daughter and/or marry his own daughter to the rapist."[155] According to the law of the ancient Hebrews, a woman, upon being the victim of a rape, was forced to marry the rapist provided she was single; if she was betrothed or married, she was stoned to death for having been raped.[156] Such ludicrous logic has created the unwritten and silent acceptance by men of this sinister and debase plague, which is perpetrated in streets, on college campuses, in the work place, and is virtually forgiven by our legal system.

What becomes obvious is that the ancient model, created by the Indo-Europeans, is the foundation of the norms and mores that comprise the infrastructure of our sociocultural beliefs. These beliefs may be likened to a cancer that expands daily, gradually devouring the organism it has infected. The cultural cancer of patriarchy reached its pinnacle on three different continents between the sixth and nineteenth centuries C.E.

In China, life for women changed when the practice of feet binding began, circa 583–588 C.E. This practice, which persisted in China until the beginning of the twentieth century, entailed crippling the feet of Chinese girls around the age of five or six. Foot-binding was a lifelong process of imposed torment and affliction that slowly and methodically broke and deformed the woman's foot until the desired appearance was achieved. The four smaller toes of the atrophied three-inch foot were folded completely under the sole; and the whole foot was folded in half so that the underside of the heel and toes were brought together. The name given to this aberration was the *lotus hook foot*. Once the process was complete, the feet had to remain bandaged for life; if the foot ever began to spread the pain would be unbearable. Many women died of gangrene and suppuration before the desired transformation was achieved. In his book *Chinese Footbinding*, Howard S. Levy explored the many cultural peculiarities of this custom: "Chinese men were conditioned to intense fetishistic passion for deformed female feet. Chinese poets sang ecstatic praises of the lotus foot that aroused their desire to fever pitch. The crippled woman was considered immeasurably charming by reason of her vulnerability, her suffering, and her helplessness — she couldn't even escape an attacker by running away."[157]

In Europe, the maniacal expression of patriarchy reached its zenith in the twelfth century, as it began the five-hundred-year reign of the Inquisition. The Inquisition served a two-fold purpose: it brought wealth to an unscrupulous Catholic Church, and by its mass annihilation of the female sex, it suppressed a growing concern of the resurgence of feminine power in medieval Europe. The Inquisition was technically consecrated on May 15, 1252, by the authority of Pope Innocent IV. The most elaborate extortion racket ever devised, its initial purpose was the confiscation of property, imprisonment, torture, rape, and death. For centuries, the Church had aspired to keep the European populace sedated with a religion that was obviously corrupt and immoral. Despite the Church's efforts to keep its patrons in ignorance, many of its members with strong economic and political influence began to see their investments as futile and the Church as no more than a leech. The eleventh century saw a Church desperate for support from its one-time loyal congregation, and it embarked upon a massive building spree of several cathedrals to reinstall a measure of blind faith in its flock. This effort seemed to be aimed at the female population, for the edifices that were constructed were temples of "Our Lady," replacing the Mother-shrines previously destroyed.[158] Unfortunately for Europe, its population did not fall subject, leaving the Church no recourse but violence.

Wealthy land owners and merchants were targeted, falsely accused of heresy, and imprisoned. While incarcerated, their property and all valuable belongings were confiscated and auctioned for the benefit of the Church. Italian inquisitors in the fourteenth century became extremely rich off the blood of its wealthy victims. Inquisitor Heinrich von Schultheis wrote, "When I have you tortured, and by the severe means afforded by law I bring you to confession, then I perform a work pleasing in God's sight; and it profiteth me."[159] To add insult to injury, accused individuals were expected to pay for their own imprisonment, food, and torture.

When the Church had substantially filled its coffers, it turned its attention to the women of the land. Most authorities estimate that millions died during the Inquisition, eighty-five percent of whom were women.[160] The persecuted women were labeled

40. Obviously humiliated, this woman stands before bartering business men as she is auctioned at a Roman slave market.

41. European woman being sold to a North Arabian sultan, who carefully examines her teeth.

witches or heretics, and their trials were mockeries of justice. Accused women were never told the nature of their charges, and they had no right to legal counsel. Evidence supporting their condemnation was accepted from witnesses such as criminals and children as young as two years old. No favorable evidence or character witnesses were permitted; and if anyone stepped forward to speak on the accused's behalf, they too were accused as a heretic, which resulted in their arrest. Most important, no accused woman was ever found innocent.

Henry Charles Lea, one of the foremost authorities on the Inquisition, remarked, "The only punishment recognized by the Church as sufficient for heresy was burning alive."[161] Hours, days, and sometimes months, of torture preceded being burned. Furthermore, "Torture was officially sanctioned in 1257 and remained a legal recourse of the Church for five and a half centuries."[162] Even if the woman confessed, she was tortured. The Inquisition's handbook, *Malleus Maleficarum*, or *Hammer of Witches*, was written in 1484 by the Reverends Kramer and Sprenger, the sons of Pope Innocent VIII. This book stated that the accused witch must be "often and frequently exposed to torture."[163] There are reports of some women being tortured as many as fifty times with an array of salacious gadgetry. Lea stated, "It can hardly be doubted that a major driving force of all witch hunts was sadistic sexual perversion. Torturers liked to attack women's breasts and genitals with pinchers, pliers, and red hot irons. Under the Inquisition's rules, little girls were prosecuted and tortured for witchcraft . . . at nine and a half years."[164] Inquisitors forced condemned women to recite a pledge absolving the men of any wrong doing: "I free all men, especially the ministers and magistrates, of the guilt of my blood; I take it wholly upon myself, my blood be upon my own head."[165] Parame stated that more than 30,000 women were executed in the fifteenth century.[166] The chronicler of Treves reported that in the year 1586, the entire female populations of two villages, with the exception of two women, were wiped out by inquisitors.[167] Two other villages were destroyed and completely eradicated from the map.[168] In 1589, 133 women were burned in one day in the village of Quedlinburg. In 1524, one thousand women died at Como. Strasburg burned five thousand in a period of twenty years, and the Senate of Savoy condemned eight hundred so-called witches at one event.[169] Nicholas Remy boasted of personally sentencing eight hundred

42. A Moorish bath in North Africa. Most European women captured by Christian and Jewish slavers eventually ended up in such a facility. Here they were groomed, fed, and bathed until they were ready for market.

women in fifteen years, and in one year alone forcing sixteen witches to commit suicide. A bishop of Bamburg claimed six hundred women in ten years; a bishop of Nancy reported eight hundred in sixteen years; a bishop of Wutzburg, nineteen hundred in five years. Five hundred women were burned alive within three months at Geneva, and four hundred in a single day at Toulouse, while the city of Treves burned seven thousand women.[170]

The list of dates, places, and numbers is almost endless, and there is no justification for such monstrosities. The Inquisition flourished until 1835, especially in Central and South America where Native Americans were tortured, raped, and burned for being unbelievers of Christianity. Anthropologist Jules Henry said, "Organized religion, which likes to fancy itself the mother of compassion, long ago lost its right to that claim by its organized support of organized cruelty."[171]

Slavery, as it pertains to women, had far-reaching consequences. Prior to the advent of the Indo-European, servitude did abound in many areas of West Asia, and it bore a close resemblance to later systems in Africa, where subjugated individuals could and many times did rise to levels of social equality, and even prominence. Slavery, as imposed by the Indo-European, was a vastly different system in philosophy and intent because it was connected to the establishment of a market economy, hierarchies, and the state. There was no prospect of social integration on any level, and all lived under barbaric conditions. Women, categorically, were the first slaves: "Historical evidence suggests that this process of enslavement was at first developed and perfected upon female war captives."[172]

Slavery originated as a substitute for death by execution, commutation of a death sentence to vassalage. In the initial Indo-European conquest, only women were spared, for they were not regarded as a physical threat. The systematic killing of males went on for centuries. To deploy a detachment of male slaves, many of whom were former warriors, into fields with copper hoes or sickles was to arm them with potential weapons. Until Indo-Europeans could find a means of safely working male labor into the society, they executed them. The women of the conquered districts were incorporated, as captives, into Indo-European households and society. With their male companions and relatives slaughtered or severely mutilated, these women had no hope of rescue or escape. Being totally isolated and devoid of help increased their captor's sense of power, which led to mass raping of captive women: "There is overwhelming historical evidence for the large-scale enslavement and rape of female prisoners . . . . The practice of raping the women of a conquered group has remained a feature of warfare and conquest from the second millennium B.C. to the present."[173] That such practices have continued in this era is easily verified by the recent mass raping in Bosnia by the Christian Serbians of Muslim women. What would make such diabolic and intolerable acts not only tolerable, but excusable in our present world? University of Wisconsin historian Gerda Lerner has provided us with a sobering perspective into this social-cultural malady:

> [Rape] is a social practice which, like the torture of prisoners, has been resistant to "progress," to humanitarian reforms, and to sophisticated moral and ethical considerations. I suggest this is the case because it is a practice built into and essential to the structure of patriarchal institutions and inseparable from them. It is at the beginning of the system, prior to class formation, that we can see this in its purest essence.[174]

Globally, little has changed regarding this crime. In 1993, in Bangladesh, a fourteen-year old girl and her mother were sentenced to one hundred lashes. The crime charged to this couple is as follows: The girl had been raped by a village elder; but since there were not four "good Muslim" male witnesses to the assault, as required under Islamic law, he was exonerated for lack of proof. The rape had left the teenager pregnant for which she was judged and found guilty of sex outside of marriage. Sex outside of marriage is referred to as *zina*. In Pakistan, seventy-five percent of women in jail are there on charges of zina. Many, if not most, are reported to be rape victims.[175]

With the arrival of Indo-Europeans into Greece, rape in literature became rampant: the rape by Zeus of his own mother Rhea, the rape of the Sabine women, Apollo's innumerable rapes of the nymphs, not to mention the rape of his own sister, Artemis. Homer's *Iliad*, written in the eighth century B.C.E., makes constant reference to the era of Indo-European invasions in Greece, circa 1200 B.C.E. In Book One, Homer mentions the socially accepted practice of enslaving captured females and distributing them among the warriors to be used sexually in the context of the spoils of war.[176] There are numerous accounts in Greek history of the Greek policies toward women captives. In earlier periods, they were mauled and raped by soldiers; in later periods, with the acknowledgment that women could be marketed as a viable commodity, they were parceled as slaves and sold throughout the Mediterranean. Describing Greek slavery in the ninth and tenth centuries B.C.E., M.I. Finley remarked, "The place of the slave women was in the household, washing, sewing, cleaning, grinding meal. . . . If they were young, however, their place was also in the master's bed."[177]

White slavery, the bondage of women (particularly non-Black women) for sexual and other purposes, was pervasive for millennia. Historian T.B. Irving stated that between 786 and 1009 C.E., "Franks and Jews traded Slavs and Germans who had been taken prisoner . . . on the Frankish territories. Thus 'slav' and 'slave' became interchangeable terms. . . . They [the Franks and Jews] made young boys into eunuchs at Verdun. . . . The slaves were driven from France to Spain in great herds like cattle. When they reached their destination, the men were purchased as servants or laborers, the women as household help or concubines. . . . Many women were also imported from Galacia, for their blonde appearance attracted the Arab gentlemen."[178] For the next several centuries, European women were in great demand in Spain, West Asia, and North Africa. During the Moorish occupation of North Africa and Spain, Moorish baths were commonplace. Most of the female slaves captured by the Franks, Jews, and Christian slave traders ended up in these facilities. The bathhouses were immense and luxuriously maintained, and the women kept there were well-groomed, fed, and bathed until they were ready for market.

With the approach of the fifteenth century and the overthrow of the Moorish empire in Spain, European slavers turned their covetous eyes to the "Dark Continent." Though the Arabs and Portuguese had begun the exploitation of men and women in Africa centuries earlier, northern Europeans would bring the rapacious industry of slavery to an all-time low. In its 3,500 year history, slavery had become an institution based on an applied science. In antiquity, the practice of enslavement was largely expressed through war, the conqueror over the conquered, transcending racial barriers. In the European slave trade in Africa, unlike previous institutions of slavery, Africans were regarded as bestial, or less than human. This perception, as well as the accompanying propaganda, allowed unspeakable and inhuman practices to become commonplace. And once again it would be women, Black women (the embodiment of the intersection of race and gender), who would be twice-victimized.

The first of these atrocities was forced breeding. Black women were sexually abused in two respects: they were used as concubines for their White slave masters and as breeders to produce future merchandise for the slave market. As breeders, enslaved women were forced to participate in various experiments, never before attempted.

The Black woman's position as a sexual slave laid the groundwork for one of the features of race and class oppression that would survive the abolition of slavery well into our present era. Her position was also a device that "dishonored the women and by implication served as a symbolic castration of their men."[179] Enslaved Black men existed within circumstances in which they could not protect their sisters, wives, or even their female children. These circumstances rendered many Black men psychologically impotent. Furthermore, "By subordinating . . . captive women, men learned the symbolic power of sexual control . . . and elaborated the symbolic language in which to express dominance and create a class of psychologically enslaved persons."[180] This issue is at the center of a long history of debate, notably argued by Daniel Moynihan and others, over the value and extent of the impact of American slavery on the lives of contemporary Black Americans. It is not my intention here to resolve that debate, but rather to highlight perhaps the only truth we can take from it: Slavery is a part of the collective memory of both Black and White Americans, and it is this memory that contains the potential for mental, moral, and spiritual debilitation.

Using Black women as breeders was a diabolically innovative advance in the field of institutionalized slavery. There is much controversy surrounding this issue, even today. Most apologists and White American historians of slavery still try to deny this painfully obvious fact. Frederick Law Olmstead believed that slave breeding was common: "Most gentlemen of character seem to have a special disinclination to converse on the subject. . . . That a slave woman is commonly esteemed least for her laboring qualities, most for those qualities which give value to a brood-mare."[181] The prevalence of this practice is further confirmed in a letter written to Olmstead by a slaveholder: "In the states of Md., Va., N.C., Ky., Tenn., and Mo., as much attention is paid to the breeding and growth of Negroes as to that of horses and mules. Further south we raise them both for use and for market. . . . A breeding woman is worth from one-sixth to one-fourth more than one that does not breed."[182] Being forced to conform to an existence of constant terror resulting from perpetual physical and emotional abuse, Black women intent on survival adjusted, making it possible for their spirit to thrive and develop into its current expression.

As slavery in America approached the mid-nineteenth century, the twilight years of physical bondage, many new developments were taking place. The need for slave-owners to maximize the investments in their women breeders was becoming of paramount importance. Due to incompetent White physicians on plantations, countless women were mutilated in childbirth from a condition known as *vesicovaginal fistula*, an opening between the bladder and the vagina that occurs as the result of instrument damage sustained by the woman during delivery. Those that did not die were rendered infertile, making them worthless as breeders.

One physician, Dr. James Marion Sims, decided to rectify what was fast becoming an economic calamity. Sims became interested in a particular woman named Anarcha, who developed a vesicovaginal fistula while Sims was delivering her child. Since she was no longer valued as a breeder, Sims decided to experiment on this woman to discover a surgical remedy for the condition. He built a hospital/laboratory and secured the service of an unused jailhouse in which Anarcha and several other Black women were detained for surgical exploration. Between 1845 and 1849, Sims performed hundreds of operations on these women and others, exploring various techniques to close their fistulas. "Sims made them his guinea pigs, performing hundreds of experimental and exploratory operations on them until they died off one by one and were replaced by fresh victims."[183] Sims performed all of his operations without the use of anesthetics, keeping the women heavily dosed with opium to combat resistance and struggle. In effect, Sims finally perfected the procedure, curing vesicovaginal fistula during his thirtieth operation on Anarcha.[184]

Dr. Sims went on to perform thousands of such operations on innumerable Black women. Surgical procedures such as clitorindectomies and ovariotomies were most common. At the end of Sim's career, he was honored as the "father of gynecology." When he died, the *Journal of the American Medical Association* declared, "His memory the whole profession loves to honor, for by his genius and devotion to medical science he advanced it in its resources to relieve human suffering as much, if not more, than any man who has lived within this century."[185]

Patriarchy includes an explicit and destructive misuse of power. Since the arrival of the Indo-European, women have been victimized by men who advocate violence in its most extreme measure. Because of the cultural pervasiveness of Indo-European civilization, most men, regardless of race, have been infected with an inherent disdain for or misunderstanding of women. We would like to think that the world has changed, that the examples previously presented are obsolete and invalid. But is that reality? Because male children are preferred in contemporary India, four out of every ten Indian female infants are killed at birth using various methods—suffocation with a wet towel over the face, various poisons that take from ten to twenty minutes to take effect, or head bashing. In Rajasthan, up until fifty years ago, every woman was systematically killed, and all wives imported. Such deeds of violence have left India deficient in its female population by twenty-five million women. India is the last existing concentrated hub of Aryan influence, and therefore is the most extreme example, but Europe, Africa, Asia, and the Americas retain some degree of blatant female subjugation. Here in the United States, sixty-nine percent of all women raped are between the ages of nine and sixteen years. Every twelve minutes, somewhere in this country a woman is being abused by a spouse, boyfriend, father, or casual acquaintance. The Center for Mental Health Services reports that in the United States ten women a day are killed by their husbands. Every fifteen seconds a woman is beaten and every six minutes a woman is raped. The top three professions that foster domestic violence on females are law enforcement, medicine, and law. Ironically, when a woman is physically abused, the first person she sees is a law enforcement agent, then a doctor, and last her lawyer. [186]

More than 100 million women in Africa, Asia, and the Middle East have suffered and will continue to suffer genital mutilation. The most common of these procedures are clitoridectomies, where the clitoris or entire external genitalia is eliminated. These operations are performed by untrained men and women

43. Young Kaiapo boy of the Brazilian jungles whose environment is being threatened. Once the most feared warriors of the central Brazilian rainforest, these people now live in harmony with other tribes to combat a common enemy — The Corporations.

using village knives and razors and no anesthesia. Demonstrating the obvious drawbacks of patriarchy does not necessarily condone a complete expression of matriarchy as a means to a more enlightened end. Some historians revel in the fact that, in antiquity, many parts of West and South Asia were under a matriarchate characterized by goddess sects that degenerated into decadence and savagery, blood rituals, and fiendish sacrifices. Though this may be factual, it is important to understand the reasons for matriarchy's demise. The penetration and absorption of external elements, rather than a natural expiration brought about by time or self-inflicted cultural disintegration, ended matriarchal systems.

It is imperative to understand the catastrophic effects Indo-European culture had on the matriarchate from the very outset. Patriarchy, as expressed through Indo-European culture, has always been the antithesis of female-dominated society. In ancient societies, the matriarchate not only represented life in the most mundane sense, it represented a cultural and religious ethos that was unrecognizable by the northern invaders who would conquer and eventually destroy it. The matriarchy had been firmly entrenched in West Asian culture for millennia, thus its destruction was an arduous process. Altering religious symbology, blood and fire sacrifices, which were a vital component of all Indo-Iranian and Indo-Aryan religious rites, and lascivious behavior in worship that lead to the conversion of the goddess to whore contributed to destroying the matriarchate. As the ichumen fly larvae feed on the cecropia caterpillar, which acts as the larvae's unsuspecting host, so did Indo-European belief slowly eat away at the spiritual abundance of these matriarchal societies.

This is not to say that matriarchal culture in Europe and West and South Asia was perfect, but that it is unjust to assess its merits based on the historical perversion bequeathed to it by the Indo-Iranians, Hittites, Assyrians, and Aryans. If we must measure society and culture on the basis of gender, then let us say that the ideal situation would be a gylany, where both men and women approach life and living on equal status.

> The enmity toward the Mother extends to nature, which is seen as an antagonistic force to be conquered and exploited. Her secrets are turned against her by rampant technology and the foundation of life

crumbles before our eyes. . . . This is the outcome of the mass wars characteristic of an age dominated by masculine archetypes, each war stepping up the scale of destruction a notch higher than the previous one. Finally, the attempt to dominate nature has bred a weapons technology that threatens to annihilate all history, all humanity at a single stroke. It is the masculine archetype run riot, threatening to rend all that exists asunder. — Charles S. Finch, III, M.D.

Humanity and Earth's Ecosystems

"Faced with the threat of an untamed nature primitive humanity had two choices, blend into nature or deny it. . . . Judaism and its later Christian and Islamic heirs proclaimed the original separation of humankind and nature. The superiority of humankind made in the image of God and the submission of nature, soulless and reduced to the object of human action." — Samir Amin

The preceding quotes by Amin and Finch provide a current account of humankind's confused perception of nature. The Indo-European mindset has always seen nature as something to be conquered and controlled. This is evident in the desire to control weather patterns, natural courses of rivers, the animal species of the world, and the human organism with the use of artificial drugs and devices. The severity of these actions are expressed in various global customs that have pushed humanity to the brink of environmental catastrophe.

Though science has made astounding advances, there is a fundamental misconception of what allows the inhabitants of this world to coexist harmoniously. In 1854, Native American Chief Seattle delivered this address to an American Congressional Committee, whose European constituency had overrun the country, decimating animal and plant life:

> This we know, all things are connected, like the blood which unites one family, all things are connected. Teach your children that the Earth is our mother. Whatever befalls the Earth befalls the sons and daughters of the Earth. Man did not weave the web of life; he is merely a strand in it. Whatever he does to the web he does to himself.[187]

Unfortunately, this advice has gone unheeded. The human need to control nature has become warped into a god complex, which disguises itself as scientific exploration. There can be no better example than genetic engineering. In 1972, five scientists in the state of California began experimenting with the fusion of genetic material from diverse subjects to create "new and different" life strains. This radical genetic technology is known as recombinant DNA, and eventually allowed scientists to create anything, from viruses to oil-devouring microbes to fruits and vegetables with genetic material from animals for longer shelf life. Like so many prior experiments, these were fated to go awry, mainly because of a lack of compassion for any life. The geneticists who acknowledged the deprivation of compassion within the scientific community saw this work as dangerous and began voicing their concerns about the ethics of such radical genetic engineering. Much of their distress was based on previous experiments done in the 1950s and 1960s in the field of cancer research. Most of the cancer viruses used were *simian* or monkey viruses, and the most popular was the SV40. Though SV40 was a relatively uncomplicated viral strain, it still proposed a perplexing problem to researchers. Though harmless to monkeys, it caused cancer when injected into mice, hamsters, and human cells. This set the stage for a national catastrophe when millions of Americans were injected with SV40, in what was declared "an altogether unsettling biological experiment and systematic . . . silent, man-made epidemic."[188] The virus was a contaminant of the Sabin/Salk polio vaccines given prior to 1962. Though a spokesperson for the institutes that manufactured the vaccine claimed it was an inadvertent contamination, independent private investigations proved otherwise.[189]

This incident and others created deep-seated consternation among many in the scientific community regarding forays into genetic manipulation. Unfortunately, their concerns went unheeded; the proponents of the new science triumphed, and laboratories experimenting with recombinant DNA were constructed the world over from Japan to the National Institutes of Health outside of Washington, D.C. With unbridled fervor, scientists began to create new and dangerous life forms, which some profess gave birth to incurable epidemics such as AIDS, which was recognized by the world medical establishment in the 1980s.

Attention was first drawn to the possibility that AIDS is a man-made virus when virologists confirmed that it takes at least a decade for a virus to mutate into another strain. There are currently six mutated strains of the AIDS virus — sixty years of mutative development in less than eighteen.[190] AIDS itself is a riddle to science. The stories concerning its origin are inconsistent and misleading. The first official explanation was that the virus originated in Africa in the indigenous Green Monkey. Many doctors, such as Robert Strecher, now say that "the disease in Africa began in the cities, and not in the jungles. And the most important point of the matter is that the genetic makeup of the AIDS virus does not exist in man or primates . . . the virus does not grow in monkeys in Africa. It has not been associated with pygmies in Africa, who have daily contact with the monkeys. . . . So not only is it improbable that the virus came from monkeys, it's virtually impossible."[191] The AIDS virus erupted almost simultaneously in the United States, Haiti, Brazil, and Central Africa. Dr. Strecher also informs us that HIV–I is the combination of two unrelated retroviral strains: the sheep visna virus and the bovine leukemia virus.

Other doctors, for example, William Campbell Douglas, claim to have pinpointed the very institution that allowed the virus to incubate in various so-called Third World locations (Brazil, Africa, Haiti, India, and Southeast Asia), all occupied by people of color. In an article titled, "WHO Murdered Africa," Douglas asserts that the National Cancer Institute (NCI), in collaboration with the World Health Organization (WHO), produced the virus in their laboratories at Fort Detrick (now NCI). The 1972 bulletin of WHO, Volume 47, page 251, stated, "An attempt should be made to see if viruses in fact exert selective effects on immune function. The possibility should be looked into that the immune response to the virus itself may be impaired if the infecting virus damages, more or less selectively, the cell responding to the virus."[192] What is being described sounds eerily like AIDS. Creation of such a destructive organism seems to be a peculiar goal for a health organization.

More recent developments around AIDS have been just as controversial. Peter Duesburg, a professor of molecular biology at the University of California, Berkeley, was given a substantial grant to prove that HIV is the cause of AIDS. Duesburg reported the following: "Human immunodeficiency virus (HIV) is not the cause of AIDS because it fails to meet the postulates of Koch and Henle, as well as six cardinal rules of virology. . . . In contrast to all pathogenic viruses that cause degenerative diseases, HIV is not biochemically active in the disease syndrome it is named for. . . . Under these conditions, HIV cannot account for the loss of T cells, the hallmark of AIDS. It is paradoxical for a virus to have a country-specific host range and risk group-specific pathology. In the United States, ninety-two percent of AIDS patients are male, but in Africa AIDS is equally distributed between the sexes, although the virus is thought to have existed in Africa not much longer than in the United States."[193] Peter Duesburg released this report to the public in 1991.

The quest of science to play the role of God in genetic engineering climaxed with the October 1993 *Time* magazine report that the first laboratory duplication of a human embryo (cloning) had been accomplished. Since 1993, the science of cloning is close to being mastered. The University of Wisconsin has successfully cloned several cows, and in Europe the Scottish sheep Dolly is also seeing double. Using genetic engineering, science has effectively fused fish and animal genetic material with fruit and vegetables to give the latter longer shelf life for consumers. These forays into manipulating the genetic code—the building block of life—have triggered numerous debates and fierce controversy world wide. The crusade for genetic mastery has become a frightening obsession in Western science. The secrets of life have been revealed to an arrogant, irresponsible, and destructive child; it is comparable to making an arsonist chief of the fire department. How will this information be processed and used? For the benefit of all humanity, or for domination over the various populations of the world? And what of Hiroshima and Nagasaki—have we really matured since then?

Deadly viruses other than AIDS have been discovered, all in Third World countries. There are the ebola and hunta viruses, which scientists claim arose "out of nowhere." The trademark of these viral forms is the complete dissolving of veins, arteries, capillaries, and organs, causing extensive internal hemorrhaging and painful death.[194]

Extensive devastation of the ecosystems is also taking place. The persistent disintegration of the planet's ozone shield by the industrial complex is creating environmental havoc. Two enormous holes that span miles are now evident in the Earth's ozone layer and ionosphere, one over North America and the other over Europe. Joe Farman, the British scientist credited with the discovery of the Antarctic ozone hole in 1985, stated that seasonal losses of ozone over North America could reach twenty to thirty percent in the next four years. Not only are new weather patterns forming because of this disruption, but deadly diseases are resulting from it. The Australian government reports that there are 140,000 new skin cancers in that country because of ozone depletion. Global warming and air, river, and lake pollution have become far too common. Mariner Jacques Cousteau, in a 1982 diving expedition to the deepest, most unexplored oceanic regions, found beer cans and bottles on the sea floor. This prompted Cousteau to claim that the Earth's seas and oceans were dying. In 1990, eight years later, Jacques Cousteau's comments were confirmed. Aquatic explorers in the scientific community released reports verifying that eighty-five percent of the marine life (plankton, phytoplankton, and seaweeds included) in the Mediterranean Sea was dead or dying, with the Atlantic not far behind.[195]

And what of the tropical rainforest? What once comprised four percent of Earth's surface has been reduced to only half that. In the northern timberlands, thousands of acres of old-wood trees are being obliterated daily by the logging industry. Tropical rainforest with landmass equal in size to the state of Florida is lost each year. That is approximately eighty acres every minute. What are the ramifications of such environmental upheaval? When forests of such magnitude are sacrificed for amusement parks, office buildings, and shopping malls, the complex ecosystems that were maintained by that flora are destroyed. Animals, insects, and microorganisms that were sustained by the forest become extinct. Botanists estimate that twenty to forty animal and insect species survive on just one plant variety. What is the future of life on Earth when entire jungles are being destroyed? Current statistics estimate that 100 to 150 animal species vanish each day.[196]

A report dramatizing our dire situation was released May 28, 1996. It stated that the oxygen count of the Earth's atmosphere, which has been a consistent twenty-one percent, though down from thirty-eight percent, has been reduced to a mere eighteen percent, and the oxygen count for cities is only between twelve and nine percent. This reduction is due to the vast annihilation of flora and fauna that comprise the Earth's forest and jungles. The exchange of gases critical to the survival of all biospheric life — oxygen from plants and carbon dioxide emitted from humans and animals — has been jeopardized; if we continue on the course we have charted for ourselves, we too will be extinct as a species. And extinction is forever! In September 1991, CNN reported that, by the year 1998, half of all known animal species on Earth will have perished. And the human beings who reside in locations in which this destruction is being wrought are being driven from their land or brutally killed. Thirty-seven thousand children under the age of five are starving to death daily, adding to the starvation of millions of human beings who cannot survive because of our ecological condition. David Pimentel, an ecologist at Cornell University, remarked that Earth's land, flora, water, and cropland are disappearing so rapidly that the world population must decrease by 2 billion by the year 2100 in order to avoid "an apocalyptic worldwide scene of absolute misery, poverty, disease and starvation."[197] Even now, the world population at 6 billion is at least three times what the Earth's battered natural resources and depleted energy reserves can handle comfortably. Pimentel stated, "If people do not intelligently control their own numbers, nature will. That we can count on."[198] Vice President Al Gore, who authored the best-selling book *Earth in the Balance*, remarked, "In our relationship with this planet, we have become like the unfaithful servant — even as we witness environmental vandalism on a global scale, we are implicitly preparing to say we were asleep. . . . Human civilization and the natural world are on a collision course."[199]

This collision course is due, in part, to the fact that humans see Earth as dirt, stone, wood, fire, and water. We push the planet to its limit, never thinking that it will defend itself to survive. We do not think of the rainforest as the lungs of the Earth that allow the critical exchange of atmospheric gases so that all life may be sustained. Though humankind likes to see itself as master of Earth, we are to Earth what insects are to us. It is humans who have become the virus to this planet, and the planet's immune system is preparing to defend itself.

Earthquakes and other natural calamities have increased tenfold over the last twenty-three years. *The Washington Post* reported that segments of coastline along the West Coast are rising faster than normal, a strong indicator that the area is due for a massive earthquake, according to a University of Oregon study. A team of scientists compared highway and railroad surveys and changes in tidal levels and found that each year many areas of coastline from Cape Mendocino in northern California to Newport on the Oregon Coast are rising almost ten times faster than expected. Sections of the coast in Washington state also are rising quickly. Clinton E. Mitchell, coauthor of a study published in the 1994 *Journal of Geophysical Research,* said "We're talking about millimeters per year rather than tenths of millimeters." According to the study, the rapidly rising coastline indicates that pressure is building underground, a sign of an imminent earthquake.[200]

The Hermetists teach that all things are endowed with mind. When we recognize this planet as a composite organism, we will see that it too has self-defense and maintenance capabilities. When its equilibrium is destroyed, Earth will fight to regain it. Tehuti/Hermes stated, "*For if the world was and is and will be a living thing that lives forever, nothing in the world is mortal. . . . So if the world must always live, the world must be completely full of life and eternity. . . . The world itself dispenses life to everything in it and it is the place of all things governed under the sun. The world's motion is a twofold activity: eternity enlivens the world from without, and the world enlivens all within it, [this] is divine law.*"[201] To push this planet to the point of retaliation is asinine; to allow the existing Indo-European mindset to dictate our relationship with the Earth is a reckless death-wish. All ancient populations prior to the arrival of Indo-European culture knew how imperative it was to maintain a harmonious accord with this planet; Native American, Chinese, African, West and South Asian, and older European cultures were attuned to Earth's natural scheme. Our situation is perilous; and if we stand by idly, Earth will act for us:

> Nature alone is waking folks up. We done had three hurricanes or so in the last year or two. The ground is shaking in California; its shaking in Missouri. They had a tremor in South Carolina the same day or the day after the hurricane in Florida. Something's happening, man, and its happening in America.
> —Denzel Washington, *Rolling Stone,* 1993

The four major categories that have been discussed indicate characteristics that can be regarded as hallmark qualities of Indo-European society. It is essential to present both the ancient and modern models of Indo-European culture in order to dramatize the "stream of cultural consciousness" that is intrin-

sic to European behavior, specifically that of the men who advocate and insure its survival.

Through analysis of these cultural idiosyncrasies, we may understand the pivotal role played by the Indo-European mindset
in maintaining and perpetuating the Kali Yuga, the present cycle. The paradox is that in the Kali Yuga, or Age of Darkness,
Indo-European culture must prevail in order to perpetuate the
savage temperament of this debased period. Subsequently, in
order for the human race to insure its survival and see to fruition
its spiritual aspirations, it must thwart and contest Indo-European culture at all cost. It is this eternal struggle between the
forces of light and dark, good and evil, that continues to inspire
the human race to achieve greater levels of awareness and
higher states of consciousness. The greater our awareness of all
the dimensions of history, the greater our craving to act.

The ancient ancestors of the human race predicted our dilemma millennia ago, simply by understanding the nature of
the Law of Rhythm. Though they were compliant to the universal rhythms of the Earth, they were, because of their understanding of the cycles, cognizant of their position in history.
This is verified in some of the documents left to us by those who
inhabited these civilizations during that ancient epoch. The first
of these chronicled prophecies was an oral consignment given
to a descendent of the Harrapans in Northwest India. His name
was Vyasa, which means "one who expands or amplifies," a
general term applied in days of old to the highest gurus in South
Asia. There were several of these great men in ancient India (the
Puranas lists 28), and they were acknowledged as amazing seers
or prophets. One of them is credited with compiling the Mahabharata and the Puranas of India. His date, as assigned by Orientalists, is 1400 B.C.E.; many believe, however, this date is too
recent. The more accepted date assigned by Western historians
more recently (and thus, less accurate), is between 700 and 400
B.C.E. The following excerpt is an enlightening and provocative
examination of our future:

> The barbarians will be masters of the banks of the Indus.... There
> will be contemporary monarchs reigning over the earth, kings of
> churlish spirit, violent temper, and ever addicted to falsehood and
> wickedness. They will inflict death on women, children, and cows;
> they will seize upon the property of their subjects, and be intent
> upon the wives of others; they will be of unlimited power, their lives
> will be short, their desires insatiable.... People of various countries

intermingling with them, will follow their example; and the barbarians being powerful in the patronage of their princes while the purer tribes [of the earth] are neglected. . . . Wealth [spiritual] and piety will decrease until the world will be wholly depraved. Property alone will confer rank; wealth [material] will be the only source of devotion; passion will be the sole bond of union between the sexes; falsehood will be the only means of success in litigation; and women will be objects merely of sensual gratification. . . . External type will be the only distinction of the several orders of life; . . . a man if rich will be reputed pure; dishonesty (anyaya) will be the universal means of subsistence, weakness the cause of dependence, menace and presumption will be substituted for learning; liberality will be devotion. He who is the strongest will reign; the people unable to bear the heavy burden, khara bhara (the load of taxes), will take refuge among the valleys. . . . Thus, in the Kali age will decay constantly proceed, until the human race approaches its annihilation. . . . When the close of the Kali age shall be nigh, a portion of that divine being which exists, of its own spiritual nature shall descend on Earth. . . . [They] will re-establish righteousness on earth. . . . The men who are thus changed...shall be the seeds of human beings, and shall give birth to a race who shall follow the laws of the Krita age, the age of purity.[202]

The second document that foresaw our present era comes out of ancient Egypt from Hermes himself. In the Book of Asclepius (the Greek name for Imhotep), Hermes related this foreboding tale to his apprentice Imhotep, whom Hermes declared was like the Sun:

It befits the wise to know all things in advance, of this you must not remain ignorant: a time will come when . . . divinity will return from earth to heaven. . . . O Egypt, Egypt, of your reverent deeds only stories will survive, and they will be incredible to your children! Only words cut in stone will survive to tell your faithful works, and the Scythian or some such neighbor barbarian will dwell in Egypt. For divinity goes back to heaven, and all people will die, deserted, as Egypt will be widowed and deserted by god and human. . . . Whoever survives will be recognized as Egyptian only by his language; in his actions he will seem a foreigner.

[Imhotep], why do you weep? Egypt herself will be persuaded to deeds much wickeder than these, and she will be steeped in evils far worse. A land once holy, most loving of divinity, by reason of her reverence the only land on earth where the gods settled, she who taught holiness and fidelity will be an example of utter unbelief.

*In their weariness the people of that time will find the world
nothing to wonder at or to worship.... People will find it oppressive
and scorn it. They will not cherish this entire world, a work of god
beyond compare.... They will prefer shadows to light, and they will
find death more expedient than life. No one will look up to heaven.
The reverent will be thought mad, the irreverent wise; the lunatic
will be thought brave, and the scoundrel will be taken as a decent
person. Soul and all teachings about soul (that soul began as
immortal [and] expects to attain immortality) as I revealed them to
you will be considered not simply laughable but even illusory... They
will establish new laws, new justice. Nothing holy, nothing
reverent nor worthy of heaven or heavenly beings will be heard of
or believed in the mind.*

*[They will be driven] to every outrageous crime – war, looting,
trickery, and all that is contrary to the nature of souls.... When all
this comes to pass Asclepius [Imhotep], then the master and father,
the god whose power is primary . . . will take a stand against the
vices and the perversion in everything, righting wrongs, washing
away malice in a flood or consuming it in fire or ending it by
spreading pestilential disease everywhere. Then he will restore the
world to its beauty of old so that the world itself will again seem
deserving of worship and wonder.*[203]

The parallel between the two stories is uncanny, suggesting
that we are presently living these passages. The legacy of Indo-
European culture is only beginning to unfold. As our current cycle progresses, in keeping with the dictates of the Manvantara,
there will be sudden diverse changes in our environment, as
well as in the evolution of human consciousness. The Manvantara reflects that within the dominant cycles of the Earth are
smaller ones, which are also indicative of transformation.
Smaller cycles appear in the Kali Yuga, which elevate humanity
to more ethical plateaus of sociocultural understanding and interaction. Such periods may endure for several millennia,
gradually deteriorating as the darkness of the Kali Yuga once
more engulfs the human race. Though the general condition of
the race worsens, what was achieved in these more enlightened
cycles is retained by various groups, which towards the end of
the Yuga, will survive and start anew as they enter a different
age. [204]

The Kali Yuga, which began in 3102 B.C.E., just completed its
first minor cycle in 1898, almost one hundred years ago. The
Manvantara informs us that we are now in a stage of transition

to a new minor cycle, due at the beginning of the twenty-first century. The Manvantara decrees that it is within this period of transition that telluric changes, such as severe seismographic activity, may occur on a global scale, along with radical deviations in Earth's weather patterns. We may also experience an elevation of consciousness through spiritual awareness, bonding the human family together on levels yet unexplored.[205]

Every ancient culture has recorded, prior to these great changes, geophysical calamities, usually a great flood that swept over and destroyed life on Earth. Westerners are familiar with this event in the Christian Biblical account of Noah and the ark, which is no more than an interpretation of a much older tradition from the Akkado-Sumerian tablets discovered in the demolished library of Ashurbanipal, monarch of the Assyrians from 668 to 626 B.C.E. These twelve fragmented tablets, written in Akkadian cuneiform and known as the Gilgamesh Epic, tell a story of a great flood that enveloped Earth. Several accounts of the flood myth have been unearthed in West Asia, in the vicinity of Mesopotamia. The Assyro-Babylonian texts were discovered first, then the Sumerian. The Babylonian account reads as follows:

> By our hand a rainstorm . . . will be sent to destroy the seed of mankind. . . . All the windstorms of immense power, they all came together. And when for seven days and seven nights the rainstorm in the land had raged, the huge boat on the great waters by the windstorm had been carried away. . . .[206]

The Sumerian account is combined, in part, with a list of eight *antediluvian* (meaning "before the flood") kings or family dynasties, who ruled the five great cities of Eridu, Badtibira, Larak, Sippar, and Shuruppak. It speaks of a period immersed in virtue before and after the flood: "After Anu, Enlil, Enki, and Ninhursag had fashioned the blackheaded people, Vegetation burgeoned from the earth, Animals, quadrupeds of the plain, were brought artfully into existence."[207] The account continues, saying, "There are five cities, eight kings ruled them for 241,000 years. Then the Flood swept over the earth. After the Flood had swept over the earth and when kingship was lowered again from heaven, kingship was first in Kish [Mesopotamia]."[208]

There are other accounts of the deluge that are equally compelling. In Africa, the people of Unyoro say, "God, infuriated at the arrogance of human beings, threw the firmament to earth and thus completely destroyed the first human race."[209] The annals of China state that during the time of an Emperor named Yahou, "The sun did not go down for ten days. The world was in flames, and in their vast extent the waters over-topped the great heights, threatening the heavens with their floods. The water of the ocean was heaped up and caste [sic] upon the continent of Asia; an immense wave that reached the sky fell down on the land of China. The water was well up on the high mountains, and the foothills could not be seen at all. The water was caught in the valleys between the mountains, and the land was flooded for decades."[210] The Mexican Zapotec recorded, "They say that it rained so much once that all the lowlands and all men were submerged except a few who managed to take refuge on the high mountain ranges. They covered the small entrances of the caves so the water would not enter, and put within them provisions and animals."[211] In India, it was written,

> Bhagwan had created out of earth two washermen: male and female. From this brother and sister the human race had its birth. The maiden would always visit the river to draw water, carrying rice with her to feed the fish. Then one day the great fish Ro asked her, "Maiden, what reward do you desire?" She answered, "I know of nothing." Then the fish said, "Through water the earth will be turned upside down." The rains began to fall, slowly at first, then in ever greater torrents. It was as if earth and heaven had merged into one. Then God spoke, "Thus have I turned the earth upside down."[212]

The geological disturbances recorded in antiquity are so numerous and comprise such a substantial part of the mythological legacy of Earth's many civilizations that we may need to reevaluate our theories on this matter. Often, we are content to dismiss these accounts as products of overactive imaginations. But could people throughout time and across cultures have been in a state of psychotropic delusion?

In the British Museum, there is a document written by the Mayans of the Yucatan, known as the Troano Manuscript. Dated circa 650 C.E., this manuscript was discovered and translated by one of the first European archaeologists to decipher the Mayan glyphs, Augustus Le Plongeon. It too speaks of a disaster of global proportions:

> In the year six Kan, on the eleventh Mulac in the month Zac, there occurred terrible earthquakes which continued without interruption for thirteen Chuen. The country of the "hills of mud," the land of Mu, was sacrificed. Being twice upheaved, it

suddenly disappeared during one night, the basin being
continually shaken by volcanic forces. Being confined, these
caused the land to sink and to rise several times in various
places. At last the surface gave way and ten countries were torn
asunder and scattered. Unable to stand the force of the
convulsions, they sank with their sixty-four million
inhabitants.[213]

There can be no doubt that this account is a recapitulation of
an earlier incident passed on to them from earlier civilizations
that flourished in the region long before the Maya.

In examining the many stories and legends of tremendous telluric disasters, one cannot help but wonder if there is scientific
evidence that points to the possibility of such changes having
taken place. In the words of Berkeley Professor, Don Cameron
Allen, "we must remember that the flood myth is a special case
in the formal study of myth. For no other myth has been examined so meticulously from the point of view of its being reconciled with the findings of science."[214] The deluge description that
quotes God as having said, "thus have I turned the earth upside
down," suggests the idea of pole reversal, an ever-growing field
of study. In calculating the direction of Earth's magnetic field,
geologists look at igneous rock to see exactly how to determine
shifts in the poles. Lava contains iron minerals such as magnet-
ite, ilmenite, and hematite, which become magnetized at formation. By studying the direction in which these minerals form,
geologists are able to confirm that Earth's magnetic field has
changed many times. Pole reversal is said to take about 2,000
years, a figure based on pure conjecture. Allan Cox, a Stanford
University geophysicist, stated in his book *Plate Tectonics and
Geomagnetic Reversals*, "If we turn farther back into earth history
we find that the poles have been reversed, not once, but many
times. So we assume that such a reversal is possible in the future."[215] No one knows what causes this reversal, or more importantly, the planetary repercussions once it has taken place.
All current geophysical theories regarding the phenomena of
polar reversal are based on the research of Dr. Charles Hutchins
Hapgood. Hapgood, a graduate of Harvard University where
he taught the history of science and anthroplogy, was born in
1904 and became renowned for his inquiry into polar shifts,
what was in his time a controversial subject. So profound were
the scientific theories of pole reversal advanced by Hapgood,
that he eventually drew the attention of one Albert Einstein. Fas-

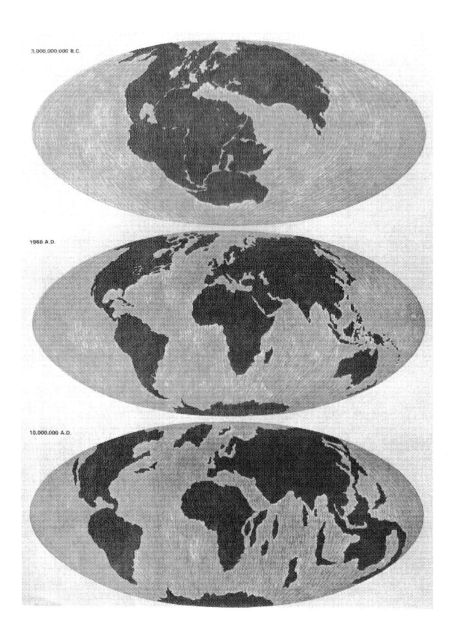

44. As shown by this map, the Earth has changed many times to acquire its present appearance. Theories abound as to how this process of global transformation occurs, but it amounts to little more than speculation. Geomagnetic reversals may play a substantial role in how our continents divide and the drastic changes which have taken place on the surface of our globe.

cinated by Hapgood's calculations regarding the subject, Einstein was impelled to write the foreword to Hapgood's book, *Earth's Shifting Crust*. Charles Hutchins Hapgood's calculations led him to believe that the last polar shift was between 17,000 and 12,000 years ago, and that the North Pole would have been in the Hudson Bay area of Canada.[216] Scientists would like to think the process of polar shifting a gradual one, but at this time, they may only speculate, and their speculative approach is filled with error. Let us not forget the several mammoths discovered frozen solid on the tundras of northeast Siberia. These animals were so well-preserved that the sled dogs consumed their flesh without incident. In the stomachs of these mammoths and between their teeth was undigested grass and leaves. When the vegetable matter in their stomachs was analyzed to determine the species of plant, it was discovered that the plants did not grow in the regions where the animals died but far to the south, as much as a thousand miles away. This clearly shows that the shifting of Earth's poles was amazingly sudden and rapid, for if the animals had not been frozen as soon as they died, there would be evidence of decomposition.[217] The oldest of these antediluvian beasts, the Adams mammoth, is dated at 36,000 to 40,000 B.C.E. and was discovered in Siberia in 1799. Since the discovery of the first mammoth, several more have been found around the perimeter and interior of the arctic circle. The Beresovka mammoth was such a find, carbon dated between 33,000 and 36,000 B.C.E. The latest of these finds was in 1977, and is also dated circa 36,000 B.C.E. A mammoth discovered in 1948 was well-preserved, and was carbon dated to 12,500 years ago. If we use these frozen mammoths as indicators regarding pole reversal, we see that the poles have shifted at least two times over the last 36,000 years, the last shift occurring a mere 12,500 years ago, which is a date consistent with the recorded flood myths of antiquity. This can be substantiated by the research of two field scientists, Fred Wendorf and Fekri Hassan, who found impressive data regarding agricultural ventures in Paleolithic Egypt circa 16,000 to 10,000 B.C.E. They discovered that between 11,000 and 10,000 B.C.E. these efforts ceased "due to a great flood in the land." This flood that swept over ancient Egypt coincides with the dawn of the Age of Leo in Egyptian cosmology and the commencement of a new cycle called the "Great Year" inaugurated between 10,617 B.C.E. and 10,858 B.C.E., approximately 12,500 years ago. In examining the Egyp-

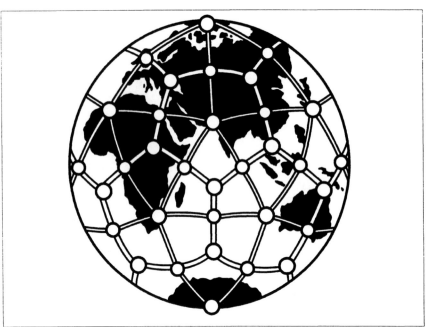

45A. The planetary energy grid that envelopes our Earth. The circles are major vortexes of energy where in this epoch, Earth's greatest civilizations were born and evolved. *David Kennedy.*

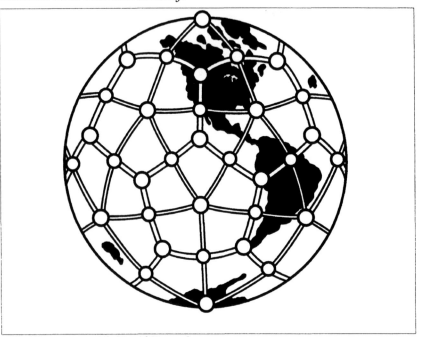

45B. Planetary grid. *David Kennedy*

tian zodiac of Denderah, which some authorities have proven was originally constructed in 1600 B.C.E. (as opposed to 100 B.C.E.), we find in the Age of Leo, the lion in a "boat" surrounded by the major entities or gods who symbolize Egypt's creation myth or new beginning. There is Tefnut who represents the principle of moisture, water, the primeval fluid, and Shu, who signifies the space between earth and heaven and who creates the firmament by separating the two. These symbols reflect a language telling us not only of a new world cycle, but telling of what telluric events happened to create that new beginning. During the last several years, there have been countless individuals in the scientific community who have tried to predict catastrophic/transformative events. One of the most famous of these predictions came in the mid 1970s from two scientists, John R. Gribbon and Stephen H. Plagemann, in a book entitled *The Jupiter Effect*. The book was a countdown to a 1984 doomsday that was to be characterized by massive earthquakes, tidal waves, changes in Earth's atmosphere, and a gradual slowing of Earth's axial rotation, and was to be caused by the alignment of several planets perpendicular to the Sun. Needless to say, none of these events materialized, and both scientists were labeled as frauds. However, that such a doomsday event is plausible is found in the commentary of both Herodotus and Plato. Herodotus, one of the more inquisitive Greeks, who ventured into Egypt in the fifth century B.C.E., discovered through conversations with an Egyptian priest that "four times in this period (so they told me) the sun rose contrary to his wont; twice he rose where he now sets, and twice he set where he now rises."[218] Plato, in his dialogue *Politicus* or *The Statesman*, wrote,

> I mean the change in the rising and the setting of the sun and the other heavenly bodies, how in those times they used to set in the quarter where they now rise, and used to rise where they now set. . . . At present periods the universe has its present circular motion, and at other periods it revolves in the reverse direction. . . the motion of the earth is changed by "blocking of the course" and [goes] through "shaking of the revolutions" with "disruptures of every possible kind," so that the position of the earth became at one time reversed, at another oblique, and again upside down, and it wandered "every way in all six directions. Of all the changes that take place in the heavens this reversal is the greatest and most complete."[219]

As it happens, the same planetary configuration identified by Plagemann and Gribbon will appear once again on May 5, 2000 in the sign of Taurus. This alignment could possibly (though this is only conjecture) cause many of the changes predicted for 1984. The angle of this configuration will be unlike that of the 1984 alignment, which astronomically could be a critical differ-ence. As beings whose civilization has but a mere five-thou-sand-year recorded history, we have no way of knowing the dynamic mechanisms of our solar system and how it works.

One thing is certain: For the last several years, Earth's mag-netic field has been changing, fluctuating in frequency. Several theories attempt to explain what this means to Earth and its in-habitants but science has yet to provide a satisfactory answer or even address the subject publicly.

Hermetists of ancient Egypt have always believed that our Earth and all matter that resides upon it, whether "living" or "non-living," is but a result of energy transformation. Various branches of science are now substantiating this concept, with physics in the vanguard. One of the most intriguing theories presently being advanced is that of the planetary grid, said to be the very cornerstone of science and evolution.

The grid's fundamental structure is thought to have been dis-covered in the 1960s by Ivan T. Sanderson, who headed an or-ganization that investigated the unexplained. Sanderson was a biologist and prolific writer, having authored eighteen books, ranging in scope from language and mathematics to zoology and botany. Though Sanderson identified the grid, the main body of research was later initiated in the early 1970s by three Russians of diverse historical and scientific background. They were Nikolai Goncharov, an historian enthralled by the ancient world, Vyacheslav Morozov, an engineer, and Valery Makarov, a specialist in electronics. Together, after several years of re-search, they created by the late 1970s the first scientifically based hypothesis for their case of a grid or web of energy that embraced the Earth. Their work would eventually find its way into Russia's most popular science journal, *Khimiya Zhizn* (Chemistry and Life), where their theory was met with great en-thusiasm. Drawing from an assortment of disciplines such as ar-chaeology, meteorology, ornithology, and geochemistry, the three researchers advanced a hypothesis that the earth projects from within itself to the surface a dual geometrically regular-ized grid. The first part of this grid forms twelve pentagonal slabs over the sphere which, the researchers believe, indicated the original shape of the planet—a dodecahedron. They went on to say that the remaining portion of the grid causes the sphere to gather from twenty equilateral triangles, making the planet geometrically an icosahedron. By superimposing the dual grid over the entire planet, the researchers professed the discovery of Earth's energy structure or skeleton.

This energy structure that surrounds our planet seems paramount in the maintenance, preservation, and evolution of all biospheric exchanges. The *biosphere* is that plane or part of the Earth and the atmosphere in which all organisms live. The researchers found that at the junctures of these slabs or plates is where volcanic and seismic activity proliferates and that at the nodes of the grid were global centers of maximal and minimal atmospheric pressure distribution that coincided with the origin of hurricanes and monsoons. Goncharov, Morozov, and Makarov also discovered that the paths of these hurricanes, as well as those of the Earth's prevailing winds and water currents, follow the ribs of the grid.

The most profound discovery the three made was with respect to culture. They postulated that all of Earth's earliest and greatest civilizations were born at the very intersections of their respective grids. This should come as no surprise that our ancestors were well aware of our planetary grid. It is certainly known that Pythagoras studied in Egypt for twenty-two years. Pythagoras also advanced the theory to the Greeks that Earth was constructed of geometric patterns which emanated a web of energy. Plato, a staunch adherent to the Pythagorean school of thought, wrote that the Earth viewed from above, resembles a ball sewn from twelve pieces of skin. Plato, like Pythagoras, was a pupil of Egyptian thought.

The intersections of the planetary grid are literally energy vortexes, and we can only guess how our ancestors utilized such power, or for that matter, the impact the vortex had on the evolution of their civilizations. When the locations of the grid intersections are examined, we find that they correspond to the cultures of Kush (Ethiopia), Kmt (Egypt), Mesopotamia, the Indus Valley in India, the Khmer of Cambodia, the Xia and Shang Dynasties in China, Mongolia, Australia, the United Kingdom in Western Europe, Easter Island, Peru, and the Ife and Benin cultures of Nigeria. Can we logically relegate these correlations to pure coincidence? The Russian team also stated that by using

46. Comparative photograph of the planet Jupiter and Earth.

the location of the pyramids at Gizeh as Intersection 1, they could construct the entire grid system and identify what they interpret as the major cultural pulse of civilization—for example, the flow of cultural information from one geographic region to another.[220]

Scientists may ask what this has to do with electromagnetism, pole reversal, and planetary deluges. The natural situation for a planet is to be in unison with its grid. The grid poles should align themselves with the Earth's axial poles. Our planet's magnetic poles are the effect of specific grid relationships, meaning that it is believed the grid maintains the polar stability of the globe's current northern and southern polar caps. Therefore, if an axial pole-shift is to take place, the two axial poles that result from this shift will be two of the energy grid's master nodes that lie 180 degrees apart. The planetary grid of the Earth is presently in a stage of realignment—it is changing its current position to our globe. The effect of this will be a shift of the Earth's poles, meaning that the energy which sustains our immediate polar stations will cease to exist. One may ask what would be the consequences of such a deviation? Rodolfo del Valle, a geologist of the Argentine Antarctic Institute released a report in March 1995 exclaiming that a vast section of ice is breaking away from the northern tip of Antarctica which could speed up global flooding. A chunk of ice measuring forty-eight miles by twenty-two miles has broken off the Larsen Ice Shelf. Farther north, a three-hundred-foot-deep ice shelf has collapsed, leaving only a plume of fragments in the Weddell Sea. Scientists reported that the Larsen cracking was caused by a regional warming trend that they have been unable to explain. Dr. de Valle stated that the melting ice is exposing rocks that will absorb heat and cause the icecap to melt more: "Recently I've seen rocks poke through the surface of the ice that had been buried under 2000 feet of ice for 20,000 years. If conditions remain unchanged this could cause catastrophic flooding all over the world. We thought the flooding would occur over the course of several centuries, but the whole process has been much quicker than we anticipated. Last November, we predicted the barrier would crack in 10 years, but it has happened in barely two months."[221] The statements made by de Valle clearly demonstrate the gravity of our situation. Scientists are also acknowledging an acceleration in the melting of the Arctic ice cap. They assert that we are entering an era of climatic changes unprecedented in the last 10,000 years.[222] These are signs that our poles are preparing to shift. Polar shifting does not necessarily indicate a reversal of the poles. Polar reversal is an event that creates ice ages, frozen mammoths, or a planetary deluge. Most advocates who watch and map the changes in the grid patterns feel that this shift will be six or seven degrees. However, some, such as John T. Sinkiewicz and Christopher Bird, have predicted as much as a forty-five-degree shift, which would cause all that is frigid to be tropic and all that is tropic to become barren wastelands of ice.[223]

It is obvious, even to the neophyte, that we are in a period of transformation or profound change. If we adhere to the dictates of rhythm as espoused by the Hermetic Philosophy, we understand that there are no arbitrary incidents. All things follow a pattern that leads to a greater end, which is but a beginning for another drama to be played. Hidden within the shadows of Indo-European culture are the ancestral keys to comprehending our tomorrow. One such key is to be found in what the ancients called the *Great Year*.

The Great Year was known to all civilizations of the ancient world, though we may say conclusively that it was discovered and utilized first in Kmt and India. The Egyptians employed it as a great celestial time table, predicting events long before they unfolded. Like so many universal phenomena locked into the mythos of ancient wisdom, the Great Year expresses itself macro- and microcosmically. Microcosmically, the Great Year is determined by what is called the *Precession of the Equinoxes*, which operates in accord to the 23.5 degree tilt of the Earth's axis. This 23.5 degrees of tilt gives the illusion of unsteadiness to the Earth as it rotates and revolves around the sun. As a result of the illusion of a reeling Earth, the magnetic north pole portrays a slow, retrograde circle around the north pole of the ecliptic. The positions of the equinoxes gradually change to a counter-clockwise motion and the pole-star is supplanted for another. The time given for the Earth's axis to complete this cycle is 25,920 years. The Egyptians divided this astronomical event into twelve partitions, each represented by a constellation usually symbolized by an animal. From these constellations we derive the twelve signs of the zodiac, originating from the Greek word *zoion*, which means *animal*. Each zodiacal constellation governs thirty degrees. Moving through a constellation at the rate of seventy-two years per degree, we find the precessional

47. Pleiades star cluster. *The Colorado Astronomical Observatory.* The Pleiades loom prominently in the myths and legends of several ancient cultures. Most notably are those cultures of the African continent and West Asia. Astronomer Gabriele Vanin says the Pleiades has been the most frequently observed and recorded star cluster since time immemorial. The Pleiades are mentioned in the texts and in the oral legends of many civilizations of the world. Some have regulated their civil life according to their seasonal positions. Different cultures have given them various names: the Seven Sisters, the little eyes, the Jewel Chest, the Old Wives, the Seven Doves, and the Chariot and the Company of Maidens.

circle represents one month of 2,160 years in the Great Year and each month constitutes an age. When 2,160 is multiplied by twelve, one arrives at 25,920 years.

The macrocosmic manifestation of the Great Year synthesizes the astro-mythos with the essential dynamics of human evolution, both physically and spiritually. The Great Year, in its microcosmic expression, concerns itself with ages of planetary as well as individual change, creating geologic, social, and religious tribulations of the period or age; it sets the stage for the drama in which humanity must endure.

In its macrocosmic expression, the principal focus of the Great Year is the spiritual evolution of all humankind. As human beings, we are by design genetically coded to the unremitting rhythms of this grand cycle. The following example will show how intrinsically bound the human race is to the astro-biological sequences of the Great Year: The average rate of respiration in human beings is 18 breaths per minute. In an hour, the average of course is 18 times 60 minutes, which equals 1,080 breaths. In a period of twenty-four hours, one day, the average is 1,080 times 24, which equals 25,920 the time period of the Great Year! As we breathe 18 breaths per minute, our average pulse rate is 72 times a minute; seventy-two is also the time it takes to transit one zodiacal degree in any of the twelve constellations. Seventy-two pulses per minute equals 4,320 an hour. As stated at the outset of this chapter, the number of years in the Kali Yuga, our current epoch, is 432,000. Though these correlations are fascinating, the indispensable theme is that all of the numbers when added equate to 9. In the science of ancient Egyptian numerology and "sacred geometry," the numeral 9 was regarded as one of four omnipotent primordial numbers. It represents humanity, the end of cycles and how these two aspects of creation engage one another.

The macrocosmic inferences of the Great Year in our existing period is that the age of darkness will give way to an age of light. That it is the end-time of the prophecies; those prophecies foretold by the visionaries of ancient Kush, India, Egypt, and the Americas. This was the higher significance of the Great Year as understood in antiquity; that it was a cosmic trigger to shift humanity from separation into oneness, the union of star light with matter, and the marriage of spirit with self. But if indeed this is a possibility, what would be the mechanics that could initiate such transformation?

Earlier we spoke of ancestral or ancient keys to access the information we so desperately need at this moment in history. The beings of antiquity were always aware of their tomorrow and devised precise devices or oracles to furnish those necessary revelations. To scientifically authenticate the mythos of traditions deemed archaic, is to literally establish a new perspective of reality. The ancients avow that humanity's principal engagement with transformation begins with our interaction with Earth's electromagnetic energies. The exchange of biodynamic force between human beings and our planet has become an ever increasing field of study. Scientists have confirmed beyond reasonable doubt that the Earth's electromagnetic emanations have profound impact on all substance within the biosphere of our globe, regardless of its organic or inorganic composition. Science has also been made aware of the electromagnetic content of individuals. Victor R. Beasley, Ph.D., documented in his book *Your Electro-Vibratory Body: A Study of the Life Force as Electro-Vibratory Phenomena*, the relationship of physics and the human body. Beasley chronicled the findings of such pioneers as Nikola Tesla, Humphrey Osmond, George De La Warr, and others, who have postulated that humans are both receivers and transmitters of electromagnetic frequencies. Though the current research done in this field is quite impressive, what looms more prominently is that these bioelectric interchanges were known by the ancient Egyptians, Akkadians, Shang, and Ancient Indians of South Asia. Examples of an understanding of electrical force abounds in ancient Egypt, from the ability to electroplate jewelry with gold and silver to the foraging of iron so pure it prompted Egyptologist Chiekh Anta Diop to remark that such a purity of iron would require the type of sophisticated processes used in modern electrolytic refinement. In ancient Akkad, Elam, and later China, we find evidence of this awareness of electromagnetism in the oracle which has come to be known as the I-Ching.

To many, ideas such as these seem far-fetched, but there are interesting correlations with the binary oracle of the I-Ching. The Akkadians of ancient West Asia, originators of the I-Ching, divided this oracle into two aspects: the upper portion, which pertains to Heaven and records the various fluctuations in the

magnetic field, and the lower, which relates to Earth, and records the biopsychic or electro-vibratory field that envelops all
humankind. (See the chapter on polarity for diagrams.) These
ancestors of the human race postulated that there is continuous
interplay between the two fields; and when Earth's electromagnetic field is sufficiently modified, it directly impacts the biopsychic field of humankind with the potential to alter the state of
consciousness on a global scale: "The binary code [as found in
the I-Ching] not only underlies the code of life—the genetic
code—but all electrical, electromagnetic, and neurological functions as well [which] also points to the binary nature of the most
primordial functions of the human psyche."[224]

Dr. Patricia Newton, a psychiatrist with Johns Hopkins Medical Institute, has given a biochemical analysis of patients she has
worked with who have exhibited paranormal behavior resulting from alterations in the Earth's electromagnetic field: "Increase and change of the electromagnetic field has a profound
effect upon the melanin centers of the brain. Melanin centers in
the brain are also precursory, at least melatonin is precursory in
the foundation and development of adrenaline, serotonin, and
norepinephrine, the neurotransmitter peptide which have to do
with altered states of consciousness and brain function."[225]

Melanin is a pigment produced by melanocyte cells and stored
in the epidermal tissue of all humans in varying quantities. It is
also found internally in the brain, especially the *substantia nigra*,
our central nervous system, heart, liver, and other glands and
organs. It is important to understand that the ration of melanin
found in the surface tissue has no bearing whatsoever on the
amount of melanin found in brain and glandular tissue. A
chemical analysis of melanin reveals that

> melanocytes are neuron-like cells which produce melanin and
> numerous proteins in response to electromagnetic radiation.
> The production of melanin starts with the conversion of
> tyrosine by the enzyme tyrosinase to 56-iodole quinone. . . .
> Tyrosinase is a copper containing enzyme which catalyzes the
> conversion tyrosine (an amino acid) and stabilizes the
> conformation of the melanin structure. The metal ion acts as
> backbone for the polymer structure of melanin, resulting in a
> metal-organic complex. The amino acid forms peptide linked
> formations with the metal ions. The ligands are attached at the
> nitrogen atoms . . . the interactions occurring between the
> central Cu [copper] ions. This complex metal compound is the
> only substance in the body that qualifies as an "ORGANIC

SEMICONDUCTOR"... Melanin granules form a large neural network structure, whose function is to absorb and decode "electromagnetic waves."[226]

With melanin as the body's organic receiver, the absorption of electromagnetic frequencies is constant in all humans. If we factor in the steady change of electromagnetism on Earth, and its impact on biochemical programming, especially as it pertains to increased levels of extrasensory perception, we may begin to identify a universal scheme or strategy for human evolution through higher consciousness. When we observe the universe beyond, we cannot help but be overwhelmed by its grand design. What we fail to realize as compartmentalized human beings is that we too are a part of that design and astronomical occurrences impact human beings just as they impact the Earth.

On July 16, 1994, astronomers excitedly witnessed the collision of the planet Jupiter with the comet Shoemaker-Levy 9, the comet believed to be similar to one that hit Earth and destroyed the dinosaurs.[227] The Associated Press released a report on April 27, 1998, which suggested that on November 17, 1998, the earth's atmosphere would be hit with the most severe meteor shower in 33 years, a bombarment of debris that could damage and destroy some of the nearly 500 satellites that provide worldwide communications, navigation, and weather watching. The report stated that the debris consists only of particles—some thinner than a strand of hair and most no larger than a golf ball, but these particles are hurtling through space so fast that they can have the destructive power of a .45 caliber bullet.[228] The ancients, by the decree of the Great Year, revealed through their prophetic writing that the Earth and all who reside upon it are silently being prepared for another astronomical event—one of the most important events in this epoch.

Every 25,920 years Earth, along with the rest of our solar system, completes one orbit around the central sun of the Pleiades known as Alcione. The Pleiades is a constellation at a distance of approximately four hundred light years from Earth's Sun. In 1961, Paul Otto Hesse, an investigative astronomer, discovered a photon belt that encircles the Pleiades at a right angle to its orbital planes. Hesse reported that the belt was *torroid* ("doughnut" in shape) with a thickness of approximately 2,000 solar years or 759,864 billion miles. There are those who believe Our Earth is presently completing this cycle of 25,920 years. They state that the Sun, along with this planet, is entering this photon belt between the year 2000 and 2011. Technically, a *photon* is a collision between an anti-electron or positron and an electron. The split-second collision between these two particles causes them to explode, destroying themselves. The ensuing impact and destruction of positrons and electrons creates a brilliant burst of light energy we refer to as *photonic*. When this process is placed within the category of stellar phenomena, we have one of the greatest astronomical events conceivable—an enormous mass of pure light energy. Several astronomers have been observing this field of light energy for at least thirty-six years and their observations have led them to several conclusions. Around the perimeter of the belt exist what investigators refer to as the *null portion* of the photon belt. This seems to be an area of extreme density or compression and is that part of the belt that Earth will initially contact. These astronomers estimate that it will take five to six days to pass through the null zone of the photon belt and that there is potential for extreme transmutation. Because the various energy fields within the zone are so compact or dense there is the possibility that Earth's electric, electromagnetic, and gravitational fields will be significantly altered. Staying within the parameters of science, we know that these three fields of energy have much to do with how form and mass are determined and manifested on our planet. Modification of these three forms of energy means change takes place on an atomic level and effects all terrestrial matter regardless of its composition. Consequently, the human organism could be biochemically, physiologically, or even genetically transformed. Those investigating this phenomena have also acknowledged what appears to be gamma radiation emanating from the perimeter of the belt. They speculate that due to unusual configurations of stellar alignment, there is the possibility that Earth will enter an area of the null zone where it will be engulfed in darkness, without light or heat energy from the Sun for a period of two and one half to three days. If this is correct, the profound outcome of such integration could result in a series of chain reactions that would impact the entire human race. When electromagnetic energy is exposed to photonic energy, which is the carrier of electromagnetism, the terrestrial field of electromagnetism is vastly altered. Thus, as the Earth passes through the photon belt, its electromagnetic field could be significantly amplified; which in turn would generate an extreme increase in frequency of our own biopsychic/electro-vibratory field, causing rapid escalation in the biochemical neurotransmitting peptides, which increase levels of awareness or extra-sensory perception. Therefore with respect to humanity, we are potentially speaking of a simultaneous transformation of consciousness, on a global scale.

News agencies around the globe are beginning to report strange astronomical phenomena directly related to gamma-ray spaceburst. The phenomena described seem to have the characteristics of the approaching photonic belt. In a report titled "Galactic Object Puzzles Astronomers," NASA astronomers announced that they have discovered a new object in our galaxy stationed between the constellations Scorpio and Sagittarius that exhibits a combination of behaviors never before seen in the 35-year history of gamma-ray astronomy.[229] The new object is being called the brightest source of hard X-ray/gamma rays in our galaxy. It emits repetitive bursts of light radiation at a rate and duration vastly different from other pulsars in the universe.[230] One group of scientists have stated that the bursts emanate from a relatively close "spherical halo" of objects enclosing Earth's home galaxy.

Whatever the outcome, we can be assured that any changes will be for the benefit of the human race as a whole and for the preservation of Earth. Dr. George Wald, a Harvard University Nobel Prize winning scientist, sees our future as foreboding. A vision for change for the greater good has eluded him based on our current global reality. Wald declared with deep conviction, "I think human life is threatened as never before in the history of this planet. Not just by one peril, but by many perils that are all working together and coming to a head at about the same time. And that time lies very close to the year 2000. I am one of those scientists who finds it hard to see how the human race is to bring itself much past the year 2000."[231] The date 2011 seems pivotal in the history of humankind. The Dalai Lama feels that the twenty-first century will be a time of peace and tranquility. Having survived recent history, which he calls "great misery and destruction," the Dalai Lama anxiously awaits this period of renewed hope and spiritual awareness.[232]

As we approach the twenty-first century, we find ourselves morally bankrupt and spiritually destitute. Our current social expression via Indo-European culture has run its course and, if we are to survive, massive reformations must take place. The axiom of rhythm is moving us, and as it transforms our present age, it will be rhythm that also determines the transformation of the human race. Though it is said that there will be many who will suffer in this period, it must be understood that these are merely growing pains for Earth and humanity, and we must embrace the changes that bring light to such a dark era. It has happened before and will happen again, for change is the only constant in the universe. Tehuti stated, *"The world is time's receptacle; the cycling and stirring of time invigorate. Yet time works by orderly rule: order and time cause the renewal of everything in the world through alternation. Nothing in this situation is stable, nothing fixed, nothing immobile among things that come to be in heaven and earth: the lone exception is God. . . ."*[233]

With respect to rhythm and the Manvantara, we must try to keep in perspective references to time. In geological time an instant can be ten million years—because ten million years is but 1/450 of Earth's accepted history. A thousand years is an interval so short that it is all but undetectable to geologists, and is so treated as a passing moment, just as it is treated by the Manvantara. Naturalist Loren Eiseley described how little we know about Earth's history: "With our short memory, we accept the present historical climate as normal. It is as though a man with a huge volume of a thousand pages before him decides to read only the final sentence on the last page and pronounce it history."[234]

It would be less than fair to neglect one of the most studied and controversial figures in recent history. His prophecies resound the ancient mythos and predictions of past civilizations, and have been analyzed by scientists and historians alike. Born Michel de Notre Dame in St. Remi, France, in 1503, he rose to prominence as the royal physician, counselor, and confidant to King Charles IX. He studied humanities at Avignon and medicine at Montpelier University, the top medical school in Europe. His knowledge and reputation as a healer were unrivaled, even in the midst of the black plague and other abominable afflictions ravaging Europe. He also believed that he was of the lost tribe of Istar, whose characteristic was that of seer or prophet. He began publishing predictions at a time when others were brutally murdered for the mere utterance of the sort; for it was the time of the Inquisition, and prophecy was considered a sign of witchcraft. In 1540, he published an almanac based on astrological predictions, and in 1555 he printed his first series of quatrains, which prophesied the future from Louis XIV to the year 3797. We have come to know this man as Nostradamos, and he had much to say about this period in Earth's history:

> When Saturn is in Aquarius and Sagittarius is ascendant, disease, famine, and death by war as the century approaches renewal. Neptune will shake fire from the Earth's center causing a great earthquake in the "New City." Two great rocks will make war a long time. The sound of a rare bird will be heard on the pipe of the highest story—death and cries are heard within the great circle and the bushel of wheat will rise so high that man will eat his fellow man. The blood of religions will flow freely in great abundance, like water. Woe ruin and hardship to the clergy. [In time] the divine word will bring mystic deed, body, soul, and spirit having all power. Within the circle will be a great and sudden flood—one has no place or land to go to. Humane realm and angelic offspring causes lasting peace and unity. Peace is maintained. Long awaited he will never come in Europe he will appear in Asia, one issued from the Great Hermes. He will be over all the Kings of the East. Saturn again late, will come back and dominion will be changed to the black nations.[235]

CHAPTER 7

The Principle of Causation

"Every Cause has its Effect; every Effect has its Cause;
everything happens according to Law; Chance is but a name
for Law not recognized; there are many planes of causation,
but nothing escapes the Law." – Kybalion

The Law of Causation is the seventh and final Hermetic axiom, espousing the truth that nothing in the universe happens by chance, that *chance* is merely a term indicating cause existing but not recognized or perceived. Hermes, once more giving instruction to Imhotep stated, *"What we call Heimarmene, [Imhotep], is the necessity in all events, which are bound to one another by links that form a chain. She is the maker of everything, of all things in heaven and earth made steadfast by divine laws."*[236]

This principle, known to many as the law of cause and effect, was enunciated by Hermetic teachers and aspirants in the earliest periods of Egyptian history. The principle is presently expressed in virtually all philosophies and religions. Westerners have come to identify superficially this law with sayings such as, "as ye sow, so shall ye reap," and "what goes around comes around." Copernicus, Galileo, and Newton all recognized this law; Newton expressed it as, "for every action, there is an equal and opposite reaction."

The ancient Egyptian concept of *maat*, which signifies justice, truth, and righteousness or correct action, embodies causation on its many levels. Morally, causation maintains universal equilibrium through this process of correct action. If one commits a beneficial deed, there is a reaction that enhances the positive potential of his or her life. Consequently, if one initiates base actions, the result will be a lesson of equal severity, which the wise will take advantage of to enhance their growth and maturity. People who do not understand why they continuously encounter the same obstacles, are doomed to repeat the lesson until it is learned.

Musician and poet James Marshall Hendrix gave insight into this cyclic experience of cause and effect in the following verses:

48. Bronze statue of Guatama Buddha, Thailand, eighth century C. E. The Buddha was born in the Northeast sector of India that had historically been the abode of several great Black dynasties such as the Nanda, the Mauryan, and Gupta. He espoused a doctrine of unity and non-violence, an essential component of Indian tradition.

49. Buto, the hawk-headed Soul of Pe. Made of bronze and dated ca. 600 B.C.E.

Machine gun, tearing my body all apart—Evil man makes me
kill you, Evil man makes you kill me, even though we're only
families apart. . . . Same way you shoot me down, you'll be
going just the same, only three times the pain, you've got your
own self to blame. . . . I ain't afraid of your bullets, I ain't afraid
no more—after awhile your cheap talk don't even cause me
pain, so let your bullets fly like rain—because I know you're
wrong and you'll be going just the same—Machine gun,
tearing my family apart.[237]

Hendrix spoke authoritatively, using our present sociocultural condition as an example of causation. This law makes known
that there is continuity between all events precedent, conse-
quent, and subsequent. In physics, this idea of cause and effect
constitutes a major pattern of change or transformation in the
universal order: "Energy and momentum are transferred over
spatial distances only by particles, and . . . this transfer occurs in
such a way that a particle can be created in one reaction and destroyed in another only if the latter reaction occurs after the former."[238]

Examples can illustrate this axiom. A boulder atop a mountain
is dislodged and crashes through the roof of a cabin in the valley
below it. Initially, it may seem that this occurred by chance, but
close examination exposes a chain of causes that led to this disaster. Throughout the year, there had been periodic rain that
caused erosion of the soil around the rock. The erosion caused
trees to fall, trees that may have prevented the rolling of the
stone, even after it was displaced, not to mention the incline of
the mountain and the force of gravity, and so on. Another example can be seen in disease. Doctors now know that the consump-
tion of denatured foods can cause numerous vitamin and
mineral deficiencies, which in turn cause debilitation of various
organs and glands, thus inhibiting the necessary chemical and
glandular secretions for maintenance of the body's immune system, which when impaired subjects the body to destructive
maladies such as colds, influenza, sclerosis, cancer, and so on.
These mundane examples of causation illustrate the simplicity
of this concept.

The Law of Causation, when combined with other axioms of
Hermetic Philosophy, provides an understanding of why things
work or happen the way they do. It is one thing to know *how* the
universe works, and quite another to know *why*. It is differenti-
ating the mechanics from underlying causes as they pertain to

personal as well as universal conditions that leads to understanding. Without the equation to comprehend this law in its
entirety, the human race is left to view life as a relative condition. Earth moves relative to the sun, but the whole solar system
moves relative to the galaxy, and the galaxy moves relative to
the rest of our universe. Science is astute enough to know that
the universe is moving also, but relative to what? Tehuti would
simply reply, "relative to the All," for what else could there be?
The world is full of starvation, disease, malice, greed, and oppression. Noticeably, the human family is not at peace with itself. According to the Law of Causation, we must eat the fruit
from the seeds we sow ourselves; obviously we must be plant-
ing the wrong seeds. It is not causation that creates the woes and
sorrow of the world; it is us, existing without "correct action."
The following is an outline of cause and effect, also known to
many as *karma*. We may see in these truths the cause of humankind's afflictions.

The Buddha of ancient India bequeathed to the human race the
Four Noble Truths, in which he identified the cause of human
suffering, avowed that this condition may be rectified, and pre-
scribed a cure. The First Noble Truth declares that humankind's
frustration arises from our refusal to accept that all things are
transitory and impermanent, that flow and change are basic
features of nature. Mental sickness, frustration, and suffering
arise when we resist this principle of change, attempting to root
ourselves in permanence. Time does not go by, or pass, or get
spent, or wasted. Change happens and time is our way of making sense of the realness of change. Change, too many times, results in pain, sadness and grief, as we long for permanence in a
fluid world. Time helps to remedy this pain. Its apparent tangi-
bility calms us; it posits stability where there is fluidity. Time is
spatial, based as it is on prepositions (*before, over, at, between,
about, by, during, on*). The concept of time allows us to predict, remember, plan, and give order to the world and universe around
us.

The Second Noble Truth is about our clinging to the illusions
that we create. These illusions reflect an improper view of life,
resulting in profound obliviousness. Out of this ignorance human beings compartmentalize and dissect the world, inhibiting
the natural continuity of universal rhythm by putting our finite
realities in fixed categories created by the mind: "We are trapped

in a vicious circle where every action generates further action and the answer to each question poses new questions. . . . This vicious circle is driven by *karma*, the never ending chain of cause and effect."[239] Thus, humans repeatedly find themselves generating actions that do not lead to realization, and posing questions that never yield answers.

The Third Noble Truth assures that the pain and suffering of humanity can be ended, that the vicious cycle of cause and effect can be broken through acknowledging the oneness of life, the interconnectedness of all things. The attainment of this state of mind is known by Buddhists as *nirvana*, or liberation through transcendence.

The Fourth Noble Truth leads to the path of transformation via discipline, study, and austerity. Because of the cultural structure of Indo-European society, we are forever engaging in lifestyles that lead to constant frustration and immeasurable anxiety. Many of us lead lives dependent on neurodepressants such as valium, lactrocane, excedrine, and alchohol, or stimulants like ritalin and prozac, which numb our sociocultural discontent.

Like time and space, causation can be transcended. We are bound by it only because of our ignorance of how to escape it. Cause and effect is an idea that is limited to a certain experience of the world, an experience that has been the essence of our existence for the past three thousand years. The principle underlying cause and effect is that we create our own reality; it is not imposed upon us. If our present situation is brought about by our past actions, thoughts, and desires, we can transform this environment through our present and future actions. We are too quick to blame others for our personal predicaments. Once we begin to move with awareness, we see how our actions create reactions in others, both desirable and undesirable. It is also imperative that we not allow ourselves to react without clarity to situations created by others. Learning not to react is the hardest lesson of all; maybe the lesson is not that one should never react, but that the proper reaction can bring about change. Lao Tse said, "When one does not contend, who is it that may contend against him?"[240] Obviously, Indo-European culture is constructed on contention. The cultural attitudes of subjugation, inequality, and disdain create the social arena in which we endure daily. "Does not contend" does not necessarily mean turn the other cheek. We may also take the route of the peaceful warrior, yielding as blows are delivered, and redirecting their force. Through observation, study, and nonattachment, we may avoid being pulled into automatic reactions to social provocations. We must draw from another source, a higher source that is unattainable to many in our present culture.

Every reaction that leads to anger, insult, assault, debauchery, or deceit is a battle lost before it has begun. Such reactive responses are not only expected and obvious, but they are systematically welcomed, since they will create and maintain the mental–emotional imbalance that imprisons us. We have set in motion for ourselves a cycle of cause and effect that must be broken if the human race is to reach new elevations:

> *But the Masters, knowing the rules of the Game, rise above . . . placing themselves in touch with the higher powers of their nature, and dominate their own moods, characters, qualities, and the environment surrounding them; and, thus, become Movers in the Game instead of Pawns – Causes instead of Effects.*[241]

CONCLUSION

The Seven Hermetic Laws of Ancient Egypt can teach us several things. They give us a comprehensive look at how universal order operates on its many levels. All life as we know it is subject to these laws, for these laws constitute timeless order and knowledge. But the possession of this knowledge in itself is of no value. Knowledge must be accompanied by proper action. The laws of Tehuti provide vast information, insights, and eventually wisdom, about the self, the Earth, and the universe. They also reveal the inextricable connection among all things. Hermetists who diligently work to master understanding of these principles know that the principles are never destroyed, only manipulated. We overcome one law by nullifying or counterbalancing it with another, to maintain stability.

The knowledge contained in these laws can be culturally transformative and spiritually liberating. Information that can potentially remove the social blinders of our present culture can be considered menacing, for it leads to autonomous thought. People have been led to question the validity of independent thought, conditioned instead to believe in Disneyland, McDonalds, Saturday morning cartoons, and the herd instinct, where the many are led by the few.

We are approaching an era that will reverberate with the frequency generated by the laws of Tehuti/Hermes. Legend tells us that the temples of ancient Egypt once emitted vibrations of such intensity that in order to enter them, one's personal vibratory frequency had to coincide with those of the temple, or madness would ensue. Prophetic tradition informs us that in the twenty-first century, only those who are harmonious with the century's expression of peace, tranquility, and higher mind will survive it without loss of sanity. Though we have been inculturated with innumerable distractions to ensure our ignorance, we must now put forth concerted effort to dissolve our mental manacles and push forward. Historians have before them an immense task, for an understanding of the past is a glimpse of the future. The problem confronting them is that the custodians and scribes of these ancient temples, sanctuaries, and libraries maintained impeccable records, and they give a vision of history that contrasts sharply with what Western civilization holds dear. Though some historians fight valiantly to uncover the truth of these periods, the greater part of this information, which cannot be substantiated by Western academia, is dismissed as fable or fantasy. Unfortunately, historians succumb to this method of analysis, and many times disregard their own ancestral legacies. On one hand, they fight to uncover data that authenticates the anthropological or physical presence of a group, while on the other, they dismiss the directory of events recorded by the inhabitants of that civilization.

This type of historical scholarship not only prevents a complete comprehension of these ancient empires, but forces the omission of the spiritual, philosophical, and mythological components so valuable in the understanding of cultures such as African/Egyptian, Indian, Sumerian, Olmec, Mayan, Akkadian, and Chinese. Unlike our present culture, the spiritual/mythological verities we choose to disregard in these civilizations comprised the very hub of their existence, and were inseparable from all other ingredients of society. The academic dissection and compartmentalizing of these civilizations makes it impossible for us to understand their experiences; yet this type of historical scholarship is the trademark of investigative research in our current era, primarily because we are unable to fathom the aspects of ancient culture that we dismiss as invalid.

Therefore, we must question our sources. Who tells us that the so-called legends, myths, philosophies, and legacies of the ancients are illogical and insupportable? Why do we comply with standards of investigation that do not accurately represent history? Now, more than ever, we must put these questions in perspective.

There are particular groups in historical academia, specifically those labeled *Afrocentric* and *revisionist,* who argue the geographical origin of philosophy. They identify an African genesis in the area of what is now modern Ethiopia and Egypt. While others applaud Greece as the dawn of philosophical tradition, the revisionists adamantly assert such an idea is blasphemous. The reality, albeit a harsh one, is that philosophy as known and expressed in Western civilization is primarily of Greek origin. Even the word from which it is derived, *philosophos,* meaning lover of wisdom, is unquestionably Greek. Thus, the truth before us is that a comprehensive philosophy was corrupted in ancient Greece. There it incubated and was born anew, contaminated with an Indo-European mindset or belief system. Philosophy, as it is presently employed, is no more than an intellectual exercise and has been this way in the Western world since being redefined in Greece. For the last several centuries, Western philosophers have sat, while sipping the finest wines, and pondered the meaning of life. They pose questions that never yield answers nor lead to self-realization, therefore never creating solutions to the problems that we create in the world around us. The entire field of academia is based on this premise. Debates are forever being waged, but no decisive resolutions are ever reached. Life's ideas are thrown onto a battle ground of conjecture, and truth, always illusive, becomes unattainable. Academia professes to be in the vanguard of conceptual innovation, but in reality academics only speak, write, and lecture to one another. The masses or common people never reap the rewards of their ongoing dialogue. This type of philosophical meandering not only allows the continued disintegration of society but literally encourages it. Many of today's youth have no compassion for life. Schools and family, once the fount of information and knowledge, are failing in creating the moral foundation so essential in developing thinking, responsible, benevolent children. Society as an institution for the preparation and preservation of life is inept, sending all the wrong messages. The youth of today mirror this void in our society, emulating the images they receive; and lest we forget, they are our tomorrow, our future.

It was Imhotep who said the philosophy of the Greeks is an inane foolosophy of empty speeches without action. We, in this culture, lack proper knowledge, proper action. Currently in academia it is vogue to proclaim everyone's historical viewpoint as authentic because one cannot possibly know what transpired historically. Therefore, your story is just as relevant as the next. Such perceptions are based on deception, for though this idea is parceled throughout the academic world, the books on historical events read by most never change. Thus, our historical perceptions or views never change keeping the human race, or what academics call *popular culture*, entrenched in the quagmire of ignorance — truth being illusive and unattainable. History is filled with truth, but one must diligently search for it. The truths that are heralded by our culture are always based in the tangi-

214 Wayne B. Chandler

ble, but this is not the only abode of real truth. We must never forget that in the West, ignorance is bliss.

Academia has much to offer humankind. Though the field is changing, and constantly being infused with new vision and spirit, academia must begin to embrace the broader realities of life in the world in which we exist, creating a more holistic approach to popular culture as well as to the lives of individuals in scholarly positions. It is within so-called popular culture where change must take place because the individuals that comprise this strata constitute the very heartbeat of Earth's civilizations. Thus academics must begin to explore that body of intelligence that transcends a purely intellectual approach to learning and knowledge, thereby creating a dynamic synthesis of mind–body expression, which was so evident in many of Earth's older cultures.

In contrast, the love of wisdom in the ancient civilizations of Egypt, India, and China was a living dynamic process. That which we refer to as *philosophy* comprised the guidelines to which they intellectually adhered. But their ever present reality was that true transformation is not possible through development of the intellect alone, regardless of the amount of information consumed. Therefore, special practices, such as meditation to quiet and expand one's mental faculties; breath control, which allowed the development of one's internal and physical energy; and specific movement techniques, which gave one the ability to actually express this energy and power were used, bringing about true metamorphosis and integration of body, mind, and spirit. We still see this expression of life in China through the science of *Taoism*, which means "the way," in India via *yoga*, which means to yoke or unite, as in mortal to God, and the Sufis of Islam, who incorporate many Hermetic precepts in their disciplines. This missing factor or element in Western philosophy has given way to a superficial means of self-realization: It only exists in our ego and nowhere else.

If the prime universal axiom expresses the need for constant change then we must examine, with extreme scrutiny, those individuals and doctrines that influence what and how we think. Our cultural rhythm is dramatically influenced by those who voice severe conservative perspectives regarding our existence. Conservatives feel the need to impede change at all cost. This being the case, we are constantly immobilized with cultural inertia within our minds, our societies, our civilization. We acknowledge this verity daily through news media in the never-ending battle between the "liberal" and "conservative," both of which are just two extremes of the same expression — conservative!

We have studied Darwin's theory of evolution and though it contradicts every ancient codex on the subject, we still insist that it is a valid model of how human and animal evolved. Darwin, in his book *Descent of Man* (1871), stated on page 911, "We thus learn that man is descended from a hairy, tailed quadruped . . . an inhabitant of the Old World. . . . The higher mammals are probably derived from an ancient marsupial animal . . . and this from some amphibian like creature, and this again from some fish-like animal."[242] Darwin's theory then and now lacks convincing evidence. The preponderance of new and old data in the fields of paleontology, genetics, and geology are telling the human race a different story about its past. Science would like us to think that the term *ancient* equates to *primitive,* but this is incorrect. Too many artifacts, documents, and standing monuments give testimony to a pervasive genius that engulfed the ancient world. The Hermetic Philosophy is evidence of this genius, as it opens a doorway into the minds of these individuals and tells us a story of a time when humans walked in harmony with God and Nature. They were truly advanced beings.

In studying the sciences of the Old Kingdom of ancient Egypt, particularly astronomy, we see that the ancients had developed an accurate calendar by 4241 B.C.E. Since it takes millennia of astronomical observation to create a calendar, it is obvious that their civilization is much older than the West admits. Even Plato insisted that the ancient Egyptians had been keeping abreast of planetary cycles for at least ten thousand years. The Egyptians understood the equinoxes and could calculate their apparent retrograde movement through various astrological constellations over a period of 25,920 years. We know this as the Great Year.

We also know, by mathematical examination of the Great Pyramid, that the Egyptians had a precise understanding of longitude and latitude, and had calculated the shape, density, and size of the planet. The Piri Reis map, reputed to have been removed from the Great Library of Alexandria prior to its burning, gives a clear example of latitudinal and longitudinal coordinates. The Moors, who removed an ancient astronomical document from an Indian monastery in South Asia in the seventh century C.E., gave this picture of the Earth as seen by these brilliant astronomers:

> The world is round as a sphere, of which the waters are adherent and maintained upon its surface by natural equilibrium. It is surrounded by air and all created bodies are stable on its surface, the earth drawing to itself all that is heavy in the same way as a magnet attracts iron. The terrestrial globe is divided into two equal parts by the equinoctial line. The circumference of the earth is divided into 360 degrees . . . the earth is essentially round but not of perfect roundity, being somewhat depressed at the poles. [243]

Western science did not arrive at these geodetic conclusions until the advent of satellite technology in the early to mid-1970s. Ancient Europe (the Greeks) did not develop a calendar until several millennia after the Egyptians, which Herodotus in 500 B.C.E. reported as inferior to that of the ancient Egyptians. The Greeks had no understanding of the Great Year, latitude, or longitude. In 450 B.C.E., Empedocles of Agrigentum taught that Earth was made of meal, cemented together with water. Almost six thousand years after the inception of the first Egyptian calendar and eight hundred years after Moorish science computed the geodetic measurements of the Earth, Europeans still thought that if they sailed too far East, they would fall off the edge of the world because it was believed to be flat. The Kushites and Egyptians, the mariners of antiquity, sailed from the eastern to the western hemisphere as early as 1200 B.C.E. Yet European historians would have us believe that these people who built pyramids, none of which have been duplicated in our era, could not build a mere boat and sail the seas. In the later part of the seventeenth century, Galileo advocated the idea that the planets revolved around the sun. He was accused of heresy and subjected to house arrest for the rest of his life. A November 1993 article in *The Washington Post* reported that after 359 years, the Catholic Church has finally exonerated Galileo, and accepted that the Earth does indeed revolve around the sun. The irony in this is that in the fifth, fourth, and third centuries B.C.E., Greeks, as well as other European aspirants, were pouring into Egypt by the hundreds. Several were taught the higher sciences, which they later tried to impart to their countrymen, who scoffed, ridiculed, or condemned, through violence, their instruction. Pythagoras is a classic example, burned alive for the things he taught. Aristarchus, writing in the third century B.C.E., professed that the Earth was a spinning object, along with other planets that revolved around a central sun. He, too, was found guilty of heresy, and paid dearly for his transgressions. It would be almost two thousand years before this concept would be resurrected by Copernicus and others.

The previous examples are accurate historical accounts, given only to dramatize a point and gain clarity regarding our present condition. Indo-European culture, compared with the older more erudite cultures and civilizations of the world, still has a great deal to learn and it is the task of everyone concerned to create the cultural balance that we, at this time, so desperately need. If we adhere to the redating of the Egyptian Sphinx to 10,000 B.C.E., the recent carbon dating of the Indus Valley to 7000 B.C.E., and the historical mythos of West Asian civilization to circa 5000 B.C.E., most of the world's civilizations had reached their pinnacle and were in a state of decline when the Indo-European appeared on the historical stage. They came as conquerors, taking the liberty to interpret the philosophical and spiritual traditions of the cultures they destroyed as they so desired. It is ironic that we sit at the feet of a culture, historically reckless and morally undisciplined, to learn the lessons of life, and that we are content with what is espoused as truth.

Revelation is to be found in the very truths that are hidden. The axioms of Tehuti/Hermes or Thoth have endured since the beginning of time, for they comprise the very fabric of the mental universe. These principles that we in the West have only recently discovered and are still learning were created to bring about cultural, social, and spiritual transformation. They are the cornerstone of true civilization, in that they provide a scientific method for spiritual ascension. These axioms contain within them the "flower of our race" and the "seed of civilization." They emerge from the primal abyss to destroy the barbarous and in so doing, eternally defend the spirit of humanity. It will be the laws of Tehuti that will eventually lead us to the ultimate frontier of the twenty-first century.

Notes

1. Wade Nobles, "African Psychology," in *Egypt Revisited*, ed. Ivan Van Sertima (New Brunswick, N.J.: Transaction Publishers, 1989), p. 39–40.

2. Brian P. Copenhaver, *Hermetica* (London: Cambridge University Press, 1992), p. 58.

3. Ibid.

4. Deepak Chopra, *Ageless Body, Timeless Mind* (New York: Harmony Books, 1993), p. 195.

5. Ibid., p. 220.

6. Peter Tompkins, *Secrets of the Great Pyramid* (New York: Harper Celapnon Books, 1971), p. 3.

7. "The Divine Pymander," *Collectanea Hermetica*, trans. Dr. Everard, ed. William Wynn Westcott (1623; London: Kessinger, 1992), pp. 21–31.

8. *Kybalion*, Hermetic Philosophy (Chicago: The Masonic Publication Society, 1940), p. 26.

9. Ibid., p. 28.

10. Ibid., p. 30.

11. Ibid., p. 31.

12. Ibid., p. 39.

13. Ibid., p. 35.

14. Ibid., p. 38.

15. Ibid.

16. Salomon Reinach, *Orpheus* (New York: Horace Liveright, Inc., 1930), p. 295.

17. Homer Smith, *Man and His Gods* (Boston: Little, Brown & Co., 1952), p. 253.

18. Henry Charles Lea, *The Inquisition of the Middle Ages* (New York: Citadel Press, 1954), p. 60.

19. G.G. Coulton, *Inquisition and Liberty* (Boston: Beacon Press, 1959), p. 177.

20. Barbara Tuckerman, *A Distant Mirror* (New York: Alfred A. Knopf, 1978), p. 522.

21. Lea, *The Inquisition of the Middle Ages*, p. 643.

22. Ernest Becker, *The Denial of Death* (New York: The Free Press, 1973), p. 178.

23. Charles Guignebert, *Ancient, Medieval and Modern Christianity* (New York: University Books, 1961), p. 287.

24. Max Weber, *The Protestant Ethic and the Spirit of Capitalism* (New York: Charles Scribner's Sons, 1930), p. 115.

25. Becker, *The Denial of Death*, p. 178.

26. Sigmund Freud, *Civilization and its Discontents* (London: Hogarth Press, 1949), pp. 23–24.

27. Gottfried Wilhelm von Leibniz, *Basic Writings: Discourse on Metaphysics* (New York: Open Court Classics, 1902), pp. 5–6.

28. Mary Baker Eddy, *Science and Health with Key to the Scriptures* (Santa Clara, Calif.: Pasadena Press, Inc., 1934), p. 626.

29. Ibid., p. 116.

30. Ibid., p. 117.

31. Ibid., p. 120.

32. Kybalion, *Hermetic Philosophy*, p. 56.

33. Copenhaver, *Hermetica*, p. 78.

34. Kybalion., p. 53.

35. Wayne B. Chandler, "Of Gods and Men," in *Egypt Revisited*, ed. Ivan Van Sertima (New Brunswick, N.J.: Transaction Publishers, 1989), p. 143.

36. Kybalion, *Hermetic Philosophy*, p. 59.

37. Kamau R. Johnson, *Beyond the Watch: A Survey of Human Time Perception* (University of Florida: Unpublished Ph.D. diss., 1987), pp. 9–11, 13. Western science and its academic disciplines perceive time within a number of distinct patterns. All humans are bound by many manifestations of time in daily life. Every human being has, at some point, manipulated time and perceived its fundamental impermanence. When we are in a hurry, time is fleeting; when we are awaiting an expected event, time seems to drag; and when we are enjoying ourselves, time moves with a regrettable rapidity. In the words of artist Marti Klarwein, "I waited for one hundred years, all I did was wait all day everyday. Now when I look back, it seems like I waited for only one day; a day that lasted one thousand years." Time perception can vary with age: "until their first year, infants live in the continual present, experiencing no sense of time. . . . The child continues to develop in his time sense and becomes more sophisticated in his early teens." Time perception can also vary with mental state. The use of some chemical substances, such as marijuana, opium, and mescaline, can alter perceptions of time.

38. Ibid., p. 14. Why is it then that, even in the face of so much practical evidence, Westerners are unable to comprehend the fact that time is insubstantial? "Another mode of human time experience besides the present, and duration, is what is termed as temporal perspective. Our temporal experience of time is determined by the type of culture, society, and environment that we inhabit. Thus our perception of time is influenced by personal, cognitive and cultural factors. . . . Temporal perspective relates to our cultural beliefs and constructions of the world, and their effect on how we interpret time experience."

It is of note that Newton remained firm in believing cyclical time was intrinsic to nature. However, others, such as Leibnitz, Barrow, and Locke were strong advocates of a linear orientation. This orientation gathered momentum in a short three centuries after Huygen's pendulum clock.

To the surprise of many, there is no rational basis for "real" time apart from events and their moment. "The way in which change is measured and standardized is merely an arbitrary convenience, depending upon one's values and one's worldview." All quotes are from Marti Klarwein, *God Jokes* (New York: Harmony Books, 1987), p. 36.

39. Chopra, *Ageless Body, Timeless Mind*, p. 164. It has only been in the last twenty years that the interest in the science of applied meditative technique has grown in America. Prior to the 1970s, it would have been ludicrous for someone in a "scientific" or medical field to express serious interest in this subject, identified so strongly with the radical flower children of the 1960s. Lately, it has become obvious that the so-labeled cultural deviants of the 1960s have left their philosophical mark on the generations to come.

40. June D' Estelle, *The Illuminated Mind* (Cotati, Calif.: Alohem Publishing Company, 1988), pp. 13-14.

41. Ibid., p. 14.

42. Rene Descartes, *Discourse on Method and Meditations on First Philosophy*. Trans. Donald A. Cress (Cambridge, MA: Hackett Publishing Company, 1980), p. 89, 90

43. Stan Tenen, *Geometric Metaphors of Life* (San Anselmo, CA: Merv Foundation, 1990).

44. Kybalion, *Hermetic Philosophy*, p. 75.

45. Ibid., pp. 75–76.

46. Barbara Walker, *The Woman's Dictionary of Symbols & Sacred Objects* (San Francisco: Harper & Son, 1988), p. 69.

47. Kybalion, *Hermetic Philosophy*, p. 114.

48. Copenhaver, *Hermetica*.

49. Ibid., p. 63.

50. Kybalion, *Hermetic Philosophy*, p. 115.

51. Peter Tompkins, *The Secret Life of Plants* (New York: Harper & Row, 1973).

52. Kybalion, *Hermetic Philosophy*, p. 123.

53. Ibid., p. 141.

54. William Walker Atkinson, *Practical Mental Influence* (Pasadena, Calif.: Walker Publishing, 1971), p. 14.

55. Ibid., p. 15.

56. Ibid., p. 16.

57. Ormond McGill, *The Mysticism and Magic of India* (London: A.S. Barnes and Company, 1977), p. 174.

58. Rudolf Ballentine, and Allan Weinstock, *Yoga and Psychotherapy* (Chicago: Himalayan Institute, 1976), p. 131.

59. Chukunyere Kamalu, *Foundations of African Thought* (London: Karnak House, 1990), p. 31.

60. Ibid., p. 36. Chinese historians state that, like Ifa, the I-Ching was once designed in a rectilinear fashion. It is not known exactly when, but the forerunners of Chinese civilization later discovered that these trigrams could be rearranged into a circular form. The oracle of Ifa, like the I-Ching, is said to connect the genetic patterns of DNA and RNA, linking the past of the human family to its current expression. Ironically, geneticists have just recently established this fact known to West African culture for

millennia. But Ifa, again in line with the I-Ching, professes to go beyond the physical and connects the race with a "road of energy" and "power" that is available to those who know and practice the oracle. This road in I-Ching is the ever present interplay between the Earth's electromagnetic field and the biopsychic field of the human race. Ifa, like the I-Ching believes these patterns of energy are established prior to our birth in the world but does not lend itself to predestination. Through the divination of Ifa, the cultures of West Africa believe it is possible to know something about our future and "the outcome of all our undertakings." Ifa, as the I-Ching, tells one of a potential future if we do not act to change our present circumstances. Thus, the older features which comprise the Ifa oracle can arguably be said to have comprised the basis of thought now identified in the I-Ching.

61.Paul Carus, *Chinese Thought* (New York: Open Court Press, 1907), p. 34. Considering the possible antiquity of Ifa and its geographical point of origin, it is plausible that this Tablet of Destiny, now referred to as the I-Ching, evolved out of the older system of Ifa. If we examine the biblical Table of Nations, we are informed that, "The sons of Ham: [father of the Black race] were Cush, Mizraim [Egypt], Phut, and Canaan. Then Cush begot Nimrod; he became a mighty one on the earth. The beginning of his kingdom was Ba'bel, Erech, and Accad, all of them in the land of Shinar [Mesopotamia]." This is the biblical lineage of the Black race; its dawning rooted in the soil of the African continent, originating from a common point, and eventually spreading to West Asia. There is no denying the cultural and linguistic affinities that show a cultural interconnectedness. There are also those parallels that pertain to the systems of writing between the cuneiform and Egyptian. Thus, it is probable in my opinion that the Ifa oracle was taken into West Asia and expounded upon and refined by the Akkadians of Accad thus creating, in time, the Book of Changes, known as the I-Ching. This common point of origin and diverse cultural expression is substantiated by current archaeology. The findings of the UNESCO International Scientific Committee states that circa 20,000 B.C.E., most of West to East Africa was an inland sea, which began to recede and drain, leaving by 10,000 B.C.E. large lakes, streams, rivers, and swamps. The various cultures and people that inhabited this area used these waterways as a mode of travel and cultural exchange, and became known as the "Aquatic civilization."

This civilization, which once lived around the perimeter of the inland sea, then inhabited an area that spread across the continent, from the Atlantic coast to the Nile Basin. Numerous archaeological sites have been unearthed in the Saharan highlands and the southern fringe of the desert from the upper Niger, through the Chad Basin, to the middle Nile, and south as far as the East African Rift Valley. These aquatic people of West and East Africa varied in their physical type but skeletal remains recovered indicate that they were most certainly a Negroid people, harmoniously living and trading with one another. Evidence shows that they were master ship builders and traveled the lakes and rivers from one part of the continent to the other. This civilization thrived for several millennia until adverse climatic conditions began to dehydrate and reduce the aquatic size and productivity of the region. I believe it was at this point in history, ca. 5000–4000 B.C.E., that extensive migrations took place out of Africa into West Asia carrying with it the vestiges of West African culture as seen with the Ifa.

Some of the Ifa principles are as follows: There is one God, and there is no devil except that which we make for ourselves; except for birth and death, there is no single event in our lives that cannot be forecast and changed; we grow and obtain wisdom through life and are reborn through life's revelations; what we call Heaven is home and Earth the proving ground or a marketplace where we learn the lessons of life, and we are in constant passage between the two; we are part of the Universe in a literal, not figurative way; we must never initiate harm to another human being or the Universe of which we are a part; temporal and spiritual capacities must work together for we are born with a specific path and it is our goal to travel it.

62. Ibid., p. 34. Taoist master Chee Soo states in his book *The Chinese Art of T'ai Chi Ch'uan* that Taoism came into being in China between 10,000 and 5,000 B.C.E. He refers to those that instructed the Tao as the 'Sons of Reflected Light,' a sect of people the Chinese annuls claim were over seven feet in height, and wore a type of clothing that had never been seen in China before. Chee Soo goes on to say that where they came from is still a mystery. What is significant in Chee Soo's pronouncement is that those that introduced the Tao to China came from a place foreign to the Chinese people. These 'Sons of Reflected Light' are also responsible for introducing silk weaving, glass and pottery making, metal working, and the manufacturing of gun powder. Historically, all of these cultural elements can be traced to the Shang Yin Dynasty (1766–1100 B.C.E.),which is documented as China's first historical empire.

63.Terrien de Lacouperie, *The Yh-King and its Authors* (London: Davit Nutt, 1892), p. 106.

64.Terrien de Lacouperie, *The Language of China Before the Chinese* (1887; reprinted by Che'eng-wen Publishing Company, Taipei, 1966), pp. 14–15.

65. Ibid., p. 15.

66. de Lacouperie, *The Yh-King*, p. 96.

67. Ibid., pp. 100–101.

68. Helena Petrova Blavatsky, *The Theosophical Glossary* (Los Angeles: Cunningham Press, Inc., 1982), p. 81.

69. Jose Arguelles, *Earth Ascending* (Boulder and London: Shambhala, 1984), p. 21.

70. Ibid., p. 42.

71. Nik Douglas and Penny Slinger, *Sexual Secrets* (New York: Destiny Books, 1979) p. 1.

72. Copenhaver, *Hermetica*, p. 79.

73. Douglas and Slinger, *Sexual Secrets*, p. 34.

74. Kamalu, *Foundations of African Thought*, p. 36.

75. Merlin Stone, *When God was a Woman* (New York: Dial Press, 1976) p. 67.

76. Kybalion, *Hermetic Philosophy*, pp. 202–203.

77. Ballentine and Weinstock, *Yoga and Psychotherapy*, pp. 70, 85.

78. Ibid., p. 88.

79. Joan Armatrading, *The Shouting Stage* (Hollywood, A & M Recordings, 1988).

80. S. Shankaranarayanan, *The Ten Great Cosmic Powers* (Pondicherry, India: Dipti Publications, 1972), p. 31.

81. George Feuerstein, David Frawley, and Subhash Kak, "A New View of Ancient India," *Yoga Journal* (1992):64–69.

82. Westcott, *Collectanea Hermetica* (London: Kessinger Publishing Company, 1992), p. 109.

83. P.K. Manikkalingam, *The Divine Science* (Madras, India: Paari Nilayam, 1924), p.18. Though the author feels the Manvantara is the most complete scientific canon that addresses the cycles of humankind and the Earth, it is most assuredly not the only one. The Etruscans of ancient Etruria recorded that there were *seven elapsed ages* of which great men appeared at the end of each epoch. The Greek traditions by way of Kmt, speak of the *supreme year* at the end of which the Sun and all the planets return to their original positions. Aristotle said the supreme year had a great winter called *kataklysmos* and a great summer called *ekpyrosis*. The ancient Maya divided their ages by the names of their consecutive suns. These were the *water sun, earthquake sun, hurricane sun,* and *fire sun*. (See Immanuel Velikovsky, *Worlds in Collision*, pp. 46, 50, and 51). The idea that Earth's ancient civilizations identify humans (Homo Sapiens) millions of years into our past seems somewhat far fetched. Ironically, there is a great body of evidence to substantiate this, thereby authenticating these cyclic historical periods addressed in the Manvantara and other doctrine's of the ancient world. *Forbidden Archeology: The Hidden History of the Human Race,* by Michael A. Cremo and Richard L. Thompson is an outstanding source of information that documents such evidence. Dr. Michael Cremo is a researcher who specializes in the history and philosophy of science. Richard Thompson is a doctor of mathematics and evolutionary biology. Together they compiled a book of almost 1,000 pages of archeological finds that give the human race a much longer history than ever thought possible. Because of the extensiveness of the text it would be impossible to give it proper representation. Some of the items unearthed in excavations do deserve mentioning, for I believe eventually, these artifacts will institute a new era in research. A shoe print in shale has been found in Utah dating back to the Cambrian Period of 590 million years ago. An iron cup from Oklahoma was discovered in a coal mine. The cup was dated to the Carboniferous Period of 360 million years ago. Metallic tubes from France dated to the Cretaceous era, 144 million years ago, have also been found. Several human footprints have been found as far back as the Jurassic Period, 135 to 195 million years ago. With respect to human remains, Cremo stated that in the 19th and early 20th century quite a number of scientists found human bones in early Tertiary and early Quaternary formation. He says although these bones attracted considerable attention they are now practically unknown. Both Cremo and Thompson feel this evidence has been and will continue to be dismissed because it does not fit the dominant paradigm that pertains to Darwinism and the evolution of humankind.

One of the most profound discoveries was by Arizona geologist Clifford L. Burdick. Three decades ago Burdick was doing research in Texas around the Paluxy River bed. There he discovered a set of human footprints in rock that dated to an extremely remote prehistoric era. The prints were described as belonging to a human being of "formidable dimensions." The length of the foot was 16½ inches long and, judging by the depth of the impression this human stood at least 8 feet in height. Though this was a remarkable discovery, what would prove to be even more incredible was that along side and 18 inches apart from these human footprints, were dinosaur prints made at the exact same time. The two sets of tracks continued on together for about 4 feet then disappeared beneath layers of sedimentary rock aligning the river bed. Burdick slowly removed the striated layers of stone and found the continuation of the prints, which proceeded for another several feet, side by side, man and beast walking together. This astonishing discovery proved that man and dinosaur were contemporaneous. Burdick would eventually send these prints to the most reputable geologic labs and paleo-scientists the world over. All would substantiate the authenticity of these prints which dated to the Jurassic period. Burdick is now an elderly gentleman, holding on to one of the greatest finds of the last two thousand plus years and has yet to see science or his colleagues try and change the historical record regarding the evolution of man.

84. Eduard Shure, *The Great Initiates* (San Francisco: Harper and Row Publishing, 1882), pp. 63–65. This account given of the Ramayana is Shure's interpretation which the author found interesting and amazingly accurate. Recently, historians have advanced the theory that Ram did not appear until the third century B.C.E., marching his armed legions to the south of India, conquering all of Dravidia and spreading the Brahmanic or Aryan faith. This is inconsistent with what is known of South Asia at that period. Most of the kingdoms in the south as well as the northeast and southwest were under the influence of Buddhism, having been dominated by the powerful Mauryan dynasty, or Buddhism's religious predecessor, Jainism. It was not until the fall of the Mauryan dynasty and the later rise of the Gupta empire (330 C.E.) that we begin to see the northern influence of Brahminism being pushed upon the southern kingdoms by the Brahmanic Guptas, whose cultural influence lasted well into the ninth century C.E., although their dynasty lasted only three centuries. Though Shure's account is an accurate portrayal of the event and period, the legendary warrior Manu, the lawgiver and Aryan savior, may be substituted for Ram.

85. J.P. Mallory, *In Search of the Indo-Europeans* (London: Themes and Hudson, 1989), p.70.

86. Ibid., p. 93.

87. Ibid.

88. Stone, *When God was a Woman*, p. 63.

89. Mallory, *In Search of the Indo-Europeans*, p. iii.

90. Cyrus Gordon, *The Ancient Near East* (New York: W.W. Norton, 1962), p. 45.

91. Stone, *When God was a Woman*, p. 58.

92. Gordon, *The Ancient Near East*, p. 66.

93. Runoko Rashidi, "Africans in Early Asian Civilization," in *African Presence in Early Asia,* edited by Runoko Rashidi and Ivan Van Sertima (New Brunswick, N.J.: Transaction Publishers, 1985), p. 21.

94.Werner Keller, *The Bible as History* (New York: Bantam Books, 1956), p. 257.

95. Rashidi, "Africans in Early Asian Civilization," p. 21.

Notes   225

96. D.D. Luckenbill, *Ancient Records of Assyria and Babylonia Volume 2* (Chicago: University of Chicago Press, 1927), p. 309–312.

97. Helen Block Lewis, *Psychic War in Men and Women* (New York: New York University Press, 1976), p. xiii.

98. Author's personal interview with Patricia Axelrod, Washington, D.C., 1995.

99. Charlene Spretnak, ed., *The Politics of Women's Spirituality* (New York: Anchor/Doubleday, 1982), p. 401.

100. Vern L. Bullough, *The Subordinate Sex* (Urbana: University of Illinois Press, 1973), p. 122.

101. Geoffrey Wolf, *Black Sun* (New York: Random House, 1976), p. 258.

102. Lewis Mumford, *Interpretation and Forecasts* (New York: Harcourt Brace & Jovanovich, Inc., 1973), p. 385.

103. Stone, *When God was a Woman*, p. 66.

104. Ibid., p. 71.

105. Dharma Theertha, *History of Hindu Imperialism* (Madras, India: Dalit Educational Literature Center, 1941), p. 25.

106. Ibid., p. 32.

107. Stone, *When God was a Woman*, p. 71.

108. G. Buhler, *The Law of Manu* (New Delhi, India: Motilal Banarsidas, 1979), p. 401.

109. Samir Amin, *Eurocentrism* (New York: Monthy Review Press, 1989). p. 107.

110. Kwame Anthony Appiah, "Race," in *Critical Terms for Literary Study*, edited by Frank Lentricchia and Thomas McLaughlin (Chicago: University of Chicago Press, 1990), p.284.

111. Amin, *Eurocentrism*, p. vii.

112. Martin Bernal, *Black Athena Vol. II* (New Brunswick, N.J.: Rutgers University Press, 1991), p.67. The issue of race is quickly moving into the forefront of academia. Much work has been done by various researchers, but the most dominant scientist in the field would have to be Luigi Luca Cavalli-Sforza. Cavalli-Sforza is Professor Emeritus of Genetics at Stanford University Medical School. In 1984, Cavalli-Sforza, along with two other colleagues, published the massive text *The History and Geography of Human Genes*, a book containing fifty years of genetic research. The book was an exhaustive analysis of human genetic data gathered over a fifty-year period and new data reflective of the recent advanced techniques currently utilized in the field of molecular genetics. The three scientists were able, with obtained genetic material, to map the worldwide distribution of hundreds of genes. From this map, they have inferred the lines of descent and expansion as they pertain to the populations of our planet.

Most geneticists, from Cavalli-Sforza to Stephan J. Gould, profess with great adamancy that there is no such thing as race outside of the human race. That the idea of compartmentalized races in the human species serves no purpose and, with respect to genetic science, does not exist. Over the years, historians and anthropologists have identified from three to sixty different pseudo-races. Presently, a recent survey (Kathryn

Barrett-Gaines, *Defining Race: A Historical Look at Race and Law in South Africa and the United States*) reported that only fifty percent of all physical anthropologists and twenty-nine percent of cultural anthropologists believe in the concept of race. Genetic research currently affirms that human life began on the continent of Africa and from there, in successive migratory waves beginning as early as 150,000 years ago, populated the world as we know it, creating, with climate as a factor, the various physical expressions of the human family.

Cavalli-Sforza has stated that there are no "pure races" due to the extensive overlapping or grafting of one population on another. Blacks for example have mixed with Chinese, Whites, Indians, etc. The Mongols and Huns who conquered much of eastern Europe, have left their genetic imprint upon the modern populace. Racially associated genetic imperfections cross race lines as well. While sickle cell anemia, usually associated with African people, is not found in some South African communities such as the Xhosa, we do find it diffused among many White Mediterranean groups. This mixing, though elusive to the naked eye, is revealed through genetic mapping. Therefore the whole issue of "racial purity" is a fabrication serving those who created it. Race is a social construct built to suit or give validity to other social beliefs. There can be no doubt that the conception of race as we understand it, leads directly to the practice of racism. Many authorities, such as bell hooks, agree that patriarchy and White racism are inextricably linked.

Kathryn Barrett-Gaines, an African historian and anthropologist at Stanford University, has advanced a theory explaining some aspects of race relations in this culture via two factors: One is *factors of distance* and the other is *distance from purity*. Barrett-Gaines stated that in factors of distance, physical appearance and color of skin are indeed important to the project of racial classification. But if one looks at race in South Africa, it is clear that it was never predicated on just color, or just any one factor. Neither simply economic nor biological factors are completely explanatory. That there is something about being Black in a capitalist democracy, of which the United States and South Africa are examples, along with Britain, Australia and New Zealand. Barrett-Gaines asked the question, in light of the evidence, what is African or American about "Blackness" and what is capitalist about it?

With respect to distance from purity, Barrett-Gaines professed that there is no color line per se, only relation. Race is less about otherness and more about difference and distance. The metaphor of a color line implies two-ness and a sharp, prohibitive, definitive distinction between peoples. She feels, as is obvious from the South African and American cases, that this image is not useful for analyzing and explaining historical phenomena. The notion of "distance from purity" creates polar parameters from purity to lack of. Whiteness she said, has been made the closest to purity while that which denotes savage/primitive, by means of Western perspective, has been fundamentally representative of lack. The notion of distance from purity is more congruent with the way people position others in relation to themselves. Barrett-Gaines says that metaphors like *half White and half Black* are actually references to purity. The "one-drop" metaphor is structured on distance from purity, not on a color line. What Barrett-Gaines was expressing here is something we all have encountered in some form or fashion. Individuals like Michael Jordan, Michael Jackson, Denzel Washington, Lena Horne, and Oprah

Winfrey are closer to what we could call *cultural purity* as it transcends race. They are looked at as being more than Black. But individuals such as President Clinton, John Wayne, Charlton Heston, and Margaret Thatcher are held by many as quintessential examples of what constitutes purity. Facing the incongruence of a color line and the material world forces a rethinking of policies based on two groups, two races, multiculturalism, and pluralism. Barrett-Gaines' theories are interesting and worthy of examination.

113. Ibid., p. 75.

114. Appiah, "Race," p. 284.

115. Charles S. Finch, III, *Echoes of the Old Darkland* (Decatur, Ga.: Khenti Publishers, 1991), p. 58.

116. *Assyrian and Babylonian Literature: Selected Translations* (New York: D. Appleton & Co., 1901), p. 120.

117. Amaury de Riencourt, *Sex and Power in History* (New York: Dell Publishing Co., 1974), p.193.

118. Ibid., pp. 187–89.

119. Finch, *Echoes of the Old Darkland*, p. 59.

120. Ibid., pp. 61, 78.

121. Terrien de Lacouperie, "The Blackheads of Babylonia and Ancient China," *The Babylonian and Oriental Record* (1891):233.

122. Robert Briffault, *The Mothers, Vol. 1* (New York: Macmillan, 1927), p. 432.

123. Barbara G. Walker, *The I Ching of the Goddess* (San Francisco: Harper & Row, 1986), pp. 1–7.

124. Carl Jung and C. Kerenyi, *Essays on the Science of Mythology* (New York: Bollingen, 1949), pp. 141–42.

125. Wallis Budge, *Dwellers on the Nile* (New York: Dover Publications, 1977), p. 20.

126. As Quoted from the Shi-Jing (Book of Odes), 900 B.C.E., and the Sima Zian, 90 B.C.E.," in Wayne B. Chandler, "Trait-Influences in Meso-America, in *African Presence in Early America*, ed. Ivan Van Sertima (New Brunswick, N.J.: Transaction Publishers, 1987), p. 278. The presence of Blacks in Ancient China has long been recognized. In defining the Chinese term *K'un-lun*, Leonard Cottrell in *The Concise Encyclopedia of Archaeology* (1960) informed us that "This word, found in Chinese texts . . . seems to apply to a number of peoples characterized by a 'black' skin and frizzy hair. . . . Their geographical location and their maritime skills made them important contributors to the cultural history of south-east Asia and south China."

127. Hua-Ching Ni, *Mystical Universal Mother* (San Diego, Calif.: College of Traditional Healing, 1991), p. 44. It is interesting to note that in the original I-Ching, or Book of Changes, *K'un*, the receptive or feminine energy, was the hexagram or gate that led to the other 63 hexagrams, its position being at the apex of the oracle. It established the teaching of the gentle path of the universal virtue of femininity, which was reflective of the matriarchal way of life. Upon the overthrow of the Black Shang and, thus, the matriarchate, King Wen of the Zhou (1134 B.C.E.) reversed the

order placing the masculine power of the patriarchate, *Chyan* on top and *K'un* on the bottom. (Hua-Ching Ni, p. 3)

128. Marija Gimbutas as interviewed by Mirka Knaster, "Raider of the Lost Goddess," *East West Journal* (1990):39.

129. Ibid., p. 40.

130. J.J. Bachofen, *Myth, Religion and Mother Right* (Princeton, N.J.: Princeton University Press, 1967), p. 80.

131. Legrand Clegg, II, "The First Invaders," in *African Presence in Early Europe*, edited by IvanVan Sertima (New Brunswick, N.J.: Transaction Publishers, 1985), pp. 24–25. Though primary attention is given to the Africoid Grimaldis, all of the skeletal remains excavated in the Grimaldi caverns bear this title. My point is that the Africoid Grimaldis were the first and by far the oldest-known of these populations that migrated out of Africa.

132. Ibid., p. 1.

133. Finch, *Echoes of the Old Darkland*, p. 61.

134. Erich Neumann, *The Origins and History of Consciousness* (Princeton, N.J.: Princeton University Press, 1973), pp. 92–96.

135. Finch, *Echoes of the Old Darkland*, p. 99.

136. Marija Gimbutas, *The Language of the Goddess* (San Francisco: Harper & Row, 1989), p. xx.

137. Stone, *When God was a Woman*, p. 70

138. Ibid.

139.Barbara G. Walker, *The I Ching of the Goddess*, pp. 1–7.

140. Gimbutas, *Language of the Goddess*, p. xx.

141. Ibid., p. xxi.

142. The Laws of Manu as quoted in the Chanakrya Pandits Maxims. Acquired in India. In the private collection of the author, pp. 1–2.

143. Bergen Evans, *The Natural History of Nonsense* (New York: Alfred A. Knopf, 1965), p. 180.

144. Heinrich Kramer and James Sprenger, *Malleus Malefricarum* (New York: Dover Publications, 1971), p. 44.

145. de Riencourt, *Sex and Power in History*, p. 258.

146. Wolfgang Lederer, *The Fear of Women* (New York: Harcourt Brace & Jovanovich, Inc., 1968), p.162.

147. de Riencourt, *Sex and Power in History*, p.227. Ironically, modern genetic research purports that the XY chromosome that produces the male is physiologically an "incomplete" female chromosome. The female brain not only has a finer texture and more complex organization than that of the male but, relative to body weight, is one-fourth heavier, which geneticists state is indicative of superior intelligence. It has been estimated that the female brain develops from birth at four times the rate of a male. Research also shows that women display keener intelligence, are superior conversationalists, think and speak faster, and exceed the male when it is a question of native mental capacity, rather than social opportunity, in professional life. (Amlak Gabree, *The Superior Aspects of Women: A Tribute to Feminine Nobility*, (Washington, DC: Universal Church of Christ, 1991)

148. Ananda K. Coomaraswamy, *The Dance of Shiva*, (New York: Noonday Press, 1957), pp.98–99.

149. W. Carew Hazlitt, *Faiths and Folklore of the British Iles* (2 Vols.) (New York: Benjamin Bloom, Inc., 1965), p. 447.

150. Briffault, *The Mothers, Vol. 1*, p. 345.

151. Emily Taft Douglas, *Margaret Sanger: Pioneer of the Future* (New York: Holt, Rinehart and Winston, 1970), p.137.

152. de Riencourt, *Sex and Power in History*, p. 219.

153. Barbara Ehrenreich and Deirdre English, *For Her Own Good* (New York: Doubleday, 1978), p. 7.

154. Stone, *When God was a Woman*, p. 59.

155. Ibid.

156. Ibid., p. 60.

157. Howard S. Levy, *Chinese Footbinding: The History of a Curious Erotic Custom* (New York: Walton Rawls, 1966), p. 4.

158. Joseph Campbell, *The Mask of God: Creative Mythology* (New York: Viking Press, 1970), p.395.

159. Rossell Hope Robbins, *Witchcraft and the Inquisition* (New York: Crown Publishers, 1959), p.451.

160. Barbara Ehrenreich and Deirdre English, *Witches, Midwives, and Nurses: A History of Women Healers* (New York: Feminist Press and SUNY/College at Westbury, 1973), p. 8.

161. Lea, *The Inquisition of the Middle Ages*, pp. 231–32.

162. Robbins, *Witchcraft and the Inquisition*, p. 269.

163. Kramer and Sprenger, *Malleus Maleficarum*, p. 226.

164. Lea, *The Inquisition of the Middle Ages*, p. 99.

165. Robbins, *Witchcraft and the Inquisition*, p. 105.

166. G.G. Coulton, *Inquisition and Liberty* (Boston: Beacon Press, 1959), p. 263.

167. Ibid., p. 7.

168. Robbins, *Witchcraft and the Inquisition*, p. 219.

169. Walter Scott, *Letters on Demonology and Witchcraft* (London: George Routledge & Sons, 1884), p. 170.

170. Homer Smith, *Man and His Gods* (Boston: Little, Brown, & Co., 1952), pp. 292–93.

171. Jules Henry, *Pathways to Madness* (New York: Random House, 1965), p. 422.

172. Gerda Lerner, *The Creation of Patriarchy* (New York and London: Oxford University Press, 1986), pp.78–79.

173. Ibid., p. 80.

174. Ibid.

175. *The Human Rights Watch Global Report on Women Rights* (New York: Women Human Rights Project, 1995), pp. 9–27.

176. Richmond Lattimore, ed., *The Iliad of Homer*. (Chicago: University of Chicago Press, 1937), pp. 184–88.

177. Lerner, *The Creation of Patriarchy*, p. 87.

178. Wayne B. Chandler, "The Moor: Light of Europe's Dark Age," in *African Presence in Early Europe*, edited by Ivan Van Sertima (New Brunswick, N.J.: Transaction Publishers, 1985) p.61.

179. Lerner, *The Creation of Patriarchy*, p. 80.

180. Ibid.

181. Lerone Bennett, Jr., *Before the Mayflower* (New York: Penguin Books, 1984), pp.104–105.

182. Ibid., p. 105.

183. G. J. Baker-Benfield, *The Horrors of the Half-Known Life* (New York: Harper & Row, 1976), p. 63.

184. Dr. Robert S. Mendelson, *Male Practice: How Doctors Manipulate Women* (Chicago: Contemporary Books, Inc., 1984), pp. 33–34.

185. Ibid., p. 33.

186. The Human Rights Watch Global Report on Women Rights (New York: Women Human Rights Project, 1995), pp. 9–27.

187. Wayne B. Chandler and Gaynell Catherine, *A Journey Into 365 Days of Black History* (Peteluma, Calif.: Pomegranate Publishers, 1992), p. 1.

188. William Bennett and Joel Gurin, "Science that Frightens Scientists: The Great debate Over DNA," *Atlantic Monthly* (February 1977): 45.

189. Ibid.

190. Peter Duesberg, "HIV is not the Cause of Aids," *Science Journal* 241 (1990):514–16.

191. Robert Strecher, *The Strecher Memorandum* (Los Angeles: Cal-C Publishers, 1987), p. 1.

192. William Campbell Douglas, "WHO Murdered Africa," *Health Freedom News* (September 1987):8.

193. Duesberg, "HIV," p. 514.

194. *NBC Nightly World News*, 31 March, 1994.

195. *Ozone, Making a Killing: How Workers and the Planet Are Disregarded* (Washington, D.C.: Greenpeace Publishers, 1992), p. 9.

196. This data was acquired in an interview with botanist and ecologist Tom Wolf.

197. Ibid.

198. *Cleveland Plain Dealer* (22 February, 1994), p. 5a.

199. Al Gore, Jr., "The Story of the Earth and Us," *Magical Blend Magazine* 42 (April 1994): 47.

200. Associated Press, *Washington Post* (1, April 1994), p. 6.

201. Copenhaver, *Hermetica*, p. 85.

202. H.H. Wilson, *The Vishnu Purana, Vol. II* (London: Kegan Paul, Trench, Trubner, 1864), pp. 45–46. Indian historians are in agreement that the Puranas as well as the Mahabharata are very ancient writings. Many of the historical academicians of India state that the Mahabharatic period was circa 5000 B.C.E., ascribing a much greater antiquity than historians of the West. As the dating of the Indus Valley civilization continues to

reach further into the past of South Asia, the West may eventually discover this date of 5,000 B.C.E., is more accurate.

203. Copenhaver, *Hermetica*, pp. 81–83.

204. Manikkalingam, *The Divine Science*, p. 27.

205. Ibid., p. 170.

206. Joseph Campbell, *Oriental Mythology: The Mask of God* (New York: Viking Penguin, Inc., 1962), p.125.

207. Ibid., p. 113.

208. Daniel Hammerly-Dupuy, "Observations on the Assyro-Babylonian and Sumerian Flood Stories," in *The Flood Myth*, edited by Alan Dundes (Berkeley, Calif.: University of California Press, 1988), pp. 57–58.

209. Ibid., p. 256.

210. Immanuel Velikovsky, *Worlds in Collision*, (New York: Simon & Schuster, 1950), p. 86. Immanuel Velikovsky shocked the Western world with his 1950 release of *Worlds in Collision*. Never before had conventional history or science considered the theories advanced by Velikovsky. Because of his esteemed position in the academic establishment, great controversy was created. Dr. Velikovsky's work crossed so many jurisdictional boundaries in academia, that few experts could check his information against their own competence. Velikovsky described his field of study as "anthropology in the broadest sense within the framework of a single science, concerning itself with the nature of the cosmos and its history." He was born in Russia, in 1895. He went on to study natural sciences at Edinburgh, and law, economics, and history in major Russian universities. Studying medicine at the Moscow Imperial University of Charcow, he would later receive his M.D. and go on to study biology in Berlin. Velikovsky came to America in 1939 with degrees in medicine, biology, psychoanalysis, history, law, and anthropology. Much of what he predicted in 1950 and 1952 is just coming to pass. Science is finding out that what were theories of the 1950s are the realities of the 1990s.

211. Dundes, *The Flood Myth*, p. 190.

212. Ibid., p. 283.

213. Map and translation as viewed by author in the British Museum, May 1993.

214. Dundes, *The Flood Myth*, p. 357. We may assume that at some point in prehistory a great cataclysm occurred, which seems to have taken place just prior to our present era. We find evidence of this event in every culture and civilization on the Earth. Even the Choctaw Indians of Oklahoma relate, "The earth was plunged in darkness for a long time. Finally a bright light appeared in the north, but it was mountain-high waves, rapidly coming nearer" (H.S. Bellamy, *Moons, Myths and Man*, New York: Harper, 1938, p. 277). These "Earth changes" seem to vary in their manifestation — floods, darkness, devastating winds, and tremendous heat. The natives of British Columbia in Canada record in their mythologies that "Great clouds appeared...such a great heat came, that finally the water boiled. People jumped into the streams and lakes to cool themselves and died" (J.A. Teit, "Kaska Tales," *Journal of American Folklore* 1917: 440). On the north Pacific coast of America, Native Americans insist that the oceans boiled, "It grew very hot . . . many animals jumped into the water to save themselves, but the water began to boil" (Stith

Thompson, *Tales of the North American Indians*, Cambridge, MA: Harvard University Press, 1929, p. 255). What we may ascertain from this information is that some form of telluric or astronomic upheaval left its imprint on the record keepers of Earth's past.

215. Alan Cox, *Plate Tectonics and Geomagnetic Reversals* (San Francisco, CA: W.H. Freeman, 1973).

216. John White, *Pole Shift* (Virginia Beach, VA: A.R.E. Press, 1980).

217. Velikovsky, *Worlds in Collision*, pp. 41–42.

218. Ibid.

219. Ibid.

220. John T. Sinkiewicz, "The Planetary Grid: The Cornerstone of Science and Evolution," *Pursuit*, 6(1982):10; Chris Bird, "Planetary Grid," *New Age Journal*, 12(1984):37–39. Though many features of the Earth's grid structure have been researched and substantiated by science, other factors contributed to grid function remain nebulous and unverifiable. One such feature is the grid's ability to respond to increased levels of awareness regarding the planet's human population. This is accomplished through the integration of the human bio-electrical grid with that of the Earth's. Every single species of life on our planet is said to emanate grid patterns. In our case, as a humanoid species, our grid has an integral relationship with mind and genetic activity. When new planes of consciousness are attained by our current human population, the Earth's grid registers and reproduces this new frequency of higher consciousness, creating in time the possibility for a dimensional shift—as from third to fourth or fifth dimensional density, which creates a new global reality indicative of the new mind set for the inhabitants of the planet. Sinkiewicz, who has done exemplary research on grid changes and their relationship to geodetic transformation, feels Earth is at the border of passing into its 4th density stage. There is always an overlapping effect as one grid ceases activity as the third is presently doing, and the incoming grid, the 4th begins to increase steadily in frequency. Many feel this grid because of its unique ratio of vibratory frequency (9 energy nodes per unit instead of 7) will usher in an era of higher or Christ consciousness, elevating the human race to new plateaus in awareness. This will make them full conscious beings. There are probably several types of energy grids surrounding and within our planet. The function of this specific grid is alignment with designs of new and improved awareness capacities. There seems to be inseparable correlations between the Earth's grid, the photon belt, and our own bio-electric grid, as they relate to the story of human evolution. Those who advocate this characteristic via grid analysis, say that without this grid, it would be impossible to evolve into the realms of higher consciousness. Upon the shift from 3rd- to 4th-dimensional reality, the planet is said to undergo total transformation; from chaos and darkness to purity, order and light. One cannot help but recall the passage in the biblical Revelation, book of prophecy, where it states, "Then I saw a new heaven and a new earth; for the first heaven and the first earth had passed away...and I heard a loud voice from the throne saying, 'Behold, the dwelling of God is with man.'"

It must be said for sake of clarity that increase in awareness, that is, to become full conscious beings, does not denote devout spiritual perspective or way of life. If this prophecy is to be fulfilled, we as a race will still have to sacrifice and work for this common end. The human race will still be in the "age of darkness" or Kali Yuga which would have begun a mere 5,000 years ago. 5,000 years of a 432,000 year cycle amounts to little and our prophetic tradition of what the future holds looms conspicuously before us. As a race we will have our work cut out for us and it will not be an easy task. Prophecy speaks of our trials and tribulations in Revelations 20: "I saw an angel coming down from heaven holding in his hand the key to the bottomless pit...and he seized Satan and bound him for a thousand years, and threw him into the pit, and shut it and sealed it over him, that he should deceive the nations no more, till the thousand years were ended. After that he must be loosed for a little while." Many speak and rejoice of the coming "age of enlightenment" but few understand that the human race will have to devote itself to spiritual attainment in order to preserve the pristine quality associated with this new era. Nothing is given for free.

221. Associated Press, "New Antarctic Iceberg May Upset World Climate," *Atlanta Journal* (25 March, 1995).

222. *NBC Evening News*, 28 July, 1997.

223. Associated Press, "New Antarctic Iceberg May Upset World Climate," *Atlanta Journal* (25 March, 1995).

224. Arquelles, *Earth Ascending*, p. 18.

225. Patricia Newton, comments made during lecture "Survival into the 21st Century," Theology Department, University of the District of Columbia, Washington, D.C., Wayne B. Chandler, presenter.

226. Nur Ankh Amen, *The Ankh: The African Origins of Electromagnetism* (Jamaica, N.Y.: Nur Ankh Amen Company, 1993), pp. 28–29. It must be established that the absorption and subsequent functioning of electromagnetism within the human organism has little to do with melanated epidermal skin tissue. There are several types of melanin within the environment as well as in our bodies. Melanin exists in skin, the brain, and fruit, as well as the sky. The exact process of how melanin functions in the body's neural and endocrine glandular systems with respect to brain dynamics and absorption of electromagnetic frequency is an ever-growing field of study. What can be said with absolute certainty is that melanin found in the sky is very different from melanin found in one's brain and glandular body. T. Owens Moore is a psychologist and specialist in brain and behavior relationships at Morehouse College. In his book The Science of Melanin: Dispelling the Myths, Venture Books/Beckham House Publishers, Inc.: Silver Spring, MD, p. xii, 33, & 34. Moore emphatically stated that "it is erroneous to assume that physical attributes of skin pigmentation (melanin) affect a person's mental or brain capacity. Although there are similar bioelectronic properties associated with skin and brain melanin, melanin is synthesized and formed differently in the skin and brain ... levels of skin melanin are not positively correlated with the presence of melanin in the brain. The fact that albinos, who lack skin melanin, have no abnormal change in *substantia nigra* [an important behavioral and motor site in the human brain] pigmentation indicates that there is no direct correlation between the amount of melanin in the skin and the amount of melanin in the brain." Science maintains that internal melanin does affect psychological processes such as extrasensory perception by optimizing the functioning of our physiological systems. Melanin, as stated in the text, also acts as a semiconductor to transform and transfer energy. At present, scientists in

the area of physics are trying to artificially replicate melanin's characteristic of superconductivity because it allows more efficient and practical ways to harness energy. Scientists feel that it is this bioelectronic property of melanin that promotes the functioning of all living organisms that harbor melanin in specific areas of their bodies. As an agent to transform energy, Dr. Moore acknowledges that melanin is strategically placed in bodily locations "to absorb and convert various forms of electromagnetic energy into energy [frequencies] that can be used by the nervous system. Melanin is found in the skin to absorb ultraviolet light, which accounts for the low incidence of skin cancers in melanated individuals. It is found in the retina to increase visual acuity and reaction time, in the midbrain to perform complex motor tasks like those seen in gymnastics and basketball; and the inner ear to perceive rhythm and maintain equilibrium." In all of these examples, melanin acts as an electronic mechanism. In the bioelectronic process involving neuromelanin, melanin is involved in the transformation of one energy form into another by coupling together two different physical states such as vibrational frequency and electricity. Dr. T. Owens Moore's book on melanin research is invaluable for those who want a deeper understanding of their biological interconnectedness universal phenomena and order. It is a book that should be read by all people, no matter what their color. Differences between darker and lighter melanated individuals are also examined; but Moore only cites those differences that are substantiated by science. To conclude, Moore pointedly stated, "We have in no way suggested that melanin can make one 'superior' to those who lack melanin. It is a hollow argument to speak of superiority because people who lack skin melanin could have a biological advantage under specific conditions where the role of skin melanin is not as important." Therefore, with the coming transformation and augmentation of energy, all life forms as we know them will be susceptible to this process of genetic metamorphosis.

227.Tim Friend, "Scientists Eagerly Awaiting Jupiter's Clash with Comet," *USA Today* (8 March, 1994): 5d.

228. Associated Press, ."Severe meteor storms coming this fall," MSNBC (April 27, 1998).

229."Galactic Object Puzzles Astronomers" *TAJ News* [Phoenix, AZ] (June 1996): 1.

230. Kathy Sawyer, "Monstrous Gammaray Spaceburst Pinpointed," *The Washington Post* (11 April, 1997): p.20.

231. Hal Lindsey, *The Late Great Planet Earth* (New York: Bantam Books, 1972), p. 18.

232. Claudia Dreifus, "The Dalai Lama," *The New York Times Magazine* (28 November, 1993):55.

233. Copenhaver, *Hermetica*, p. 85.

234. K.C. Cole, *Sympathetic Vibrations: Reflections on Physics as a Way of Life* (New York: William Morrow and Co., Inc., 1985), p. 132.

235. Frank J. MacHovec, *Nostradamus: His Prophecies for the Future* (New York: Peter Pauper, 1972), pp. 36–45. It must be stated, however, that though prophetic tradition has recorded and predicted these aforementioned events, there seems to be the implementation of a new paradigm. Within the expression of ancient mythological, prophetic, and

scientific sources there is always a pattern one observes to determine when, where, and to what extreme these changes may occur. Because of an absence, as subtle as it may be, of a definitive pattern of events that usually begin twenty-seven years prior to the predicted occurrence on this planet, it is the opinion of the author that maybe, for the first time in the history of the Manvantara, we will undergo this process of transformation without the usual catastrophic upheavals that have always accompanied our spiritual metamorphosis. This is extremely important in that it deviates from the norm, and would be an unprecedented occurrence.

236. Copenhaver, *Hermetica*, p. 91.

237. James Marshall Hendrix, *Band of Gypsys. Machine Gun* (New York: Heaven Research, 1970).

238. Fritjof Capra, *The Tao of Physics* (New York: Bantam Books, 1975), p. 265.

239. Ibid., p. 85.

240. Lin Yutang, *The Wisdom of Lao Tse*. (New York: The Modern Library, 1976), p. 77.

241. Kybalion, *Hermetic Philosophy*, p. 181.

242. Charles Darwin quoted in Wayne B. Chandler, "The Moor: Light of Europe's Dark Age," in *African Presence in Early Europe*, ed. Ivan Van Sertima (New Brunswick, N.J.: Transaction Publishers, 1985)

243. Wayne B. Chandler, *Ebony and Bronze: Race and Ethnicity of the Moors in Spain*. (London: Karnak House, 1994), p. 20. See also Michael Cremo and Richard L. Thompson, *Forbidden Archeology: The Hidden History of the Human Race* (San Diego, CA: Bhaktivedanta Institute, 1993).

Selected Bibliography

Amen, Nur Ankh. *The Ankh: The African Origins of Electromagnetism.* (Jamaica, N.Y.: Nur Ankh Amen Company, 1993).

Amin, Samir. *Eurocentrism.* (New York: Monthy Review Press, 1989).

Aravaanan, K.P. *Anthropological Studies on the Dravidio-Africans.* (Senegal: University of Dakar, 1977).

————.*Dravidians and Africans.* (Senegal: University of Dakar, 1977).

Arguelles, Jose. *Earth Ascending.* (Boulder and London: Shambhala, 1984).

Armatrading, Joan. *The Shouting Stage.* (Hollywood,Calif.: A & M Recordings, 1988).

Assyrian and Babylonian Literature: Selected Translations. (NewYork: D. Appleton & Co., 1901).

Atkinson, William Walker. *Practical Mental Influence.* (Pasadena, Calif.: Walker Publishing, 1971).

Bachofen, J.J. *Myth, Religion and Mother Right.* (Princeton, N.J.: Princeton University Press, 1967).

Baker-Benfield, G. J. *The Horrors of the Half-Known Life.* (New York: Harper & Row, 1976).

Ballentine, Rudolf and Allan Weinstock. *Yoga and Psychotherapy.* (Chicago: Himalayan Institute, 1976).

Becker, Ernest. *The Denial of Death.* (New York: The Free Press, 1973).

Bennett, Lerone, Jr. *Before the Mayflower.* (New York: Penguin Books, 1984).

Bennett, William, and Joel Gurin. "Science that Frightens Scientists: The Great Debate Over DNA." *Atlantic Monthly* (February 1977). 45.

Bernal, Martin. *Black Athena* (2 vols). (New Brunswick, N.J.: Rutgers University Press, 1991).

Bird, Chris. "Planetary Grid." *New Age Journal* (1984): 37–39.

Blavatsky, Helena Petrova. *The Theosophical Glossary.* (Los Angeles: Cunningham Press, Inc., 1982).

Briffault, Robert. *The Mothers* (2 vols). (New York: Macmillan, 1927).

Brunson, James. *Black Jade: African Presence in the Ancient East.* (Dekalb, Illinois: Kara Publishing, 1985).

Budge, Wallis. *Dwellers on the Nile.* (New York: Dover Publications, 1977).

Buhler, G. *The Law of Manu.* (New Delhi, India: Motilal Banarsidas, 1979).

Bullough, Vern L. *The Subordinate Sex.*(Urbana: University of Illinois Press, 1973).

Campbell, Joseph. *Oriental Mythology: The Mask of God.* (New York: Viking Penguin, Inc., 1962).

————. *The Mask of God: Creative Mythology.* (New York: Viking Press, 1970).

Capa, Fritjof. *The Tao of Physics.* (New York: Bantam Books, 1975).

Carus, Paul. *Chinese Thought.* (New York: Open Court Press, 1907).

Chandler, Wayne B., *Ebony and Bronze: Race and Ethnicity of the Moors in Spain.* (London: Karnak House, 1994).

Chandler, Wayne B. and Gaynell Catherine. *A Journey Into 365 Days of Black History.* (Peteluma, Calif.: Pomegranate Publishers, 1992).

Chang, Stephen T. *The Tao of Sexology: The Book of Infinite Wisdom.* (San Francisco: Tao Publishing, 1986).

Chatterji, Bijan Raj. *Indian Cultural Influence in Cambodia.* (Calcutta: University of Calcutta, 1928).

Chia, Mantak. *Cultivating Male Sexual Energy.* (New York: Aurora Press, 1984).

Chissell, John T. *Pyramids of Power! An Ancient African Centered Approach to Optimal Health.* (Baltimore, MD: Positive Perceptions Publications, 1993).

Chopra, Deepak. *Ageless Body, Timeless Mind.* (New York: Harmony Books, 1993).

Cole, K.C. *Sympathetic Vibrations: Reflections on Physics as a Way of Life.* (New York: WilliamMorrow and Co., Inc., 1985).

Coomaraswamy, Ananda K. *The Dance of Shiva.* (New York: Noonday Press, 1957).

Copenhaver, Brian P. *Hermetica.* (London: Cambridge University Press, 1992).

Coulton, G.G. *Inquisition and Liberty.* (Boston: Beacon Press, 1959).

de Lacouperie, Terrien. "The Blackheads of Babylonia and Ancient China." *The Babylonian and Oriental Record* (1891)..

————.*The Language of China Before the Chinese.* (Taipei, China: Che'eng-wen Publishing Company, 1966).

————. *The Yh-King and its Authors.* (London: Davit Nutt, 1892).

D' Estelle, June. *The Illuminated Mind.* (Cotati, Calif.: Alohem Publishing Company, 1988).

de Riencourt, Amaury. *Sex and Power in History.* (New York: Dell Publishing Co., 1974).

Douglas, Emily Taft. *Margaret Sanger: Pioneer of the Future.* (New York: Holt, Rinehart and Winston, 1970).

Douglas, Nik, and Penny Slinger. *Sexual Secrets.* (New York: Destiny Books, 1979).

"The Divine Pymander," *Collectanea Hermetica,* trans. Dr. Everard, ed. William Wynn Westcott (1623; London: Kessinger, 1992), pp. 21–31.

Douglas, William Campbell. "WHO Murdered Africa." *Health Freedom News* (September 1987): 8.

Dreifus, Claudia. "The Dalai Lama." *The New York Times Magazine* (28 November, 1993): 55.

Duesberg, Peter. "HIV is not the Cause of Aids." *Science Journal* 241 (1990).

Dundes, Alan, ed. *The Flood Myth.* (Berkeley, Calif.: University of California Press, 1988).

Eddy, Mary Baker. *Science and Health with Key to the Scriptures.* (Santa Clara, Calif.: Pasadena Press, Inc., 1934).

Ehrenreich, Barbara, and Deirdre English. *For Her Own Good.* (New York; Doubleday, 1978).

————. *Witches, Midwives, and Nurses: A History of Women Healers.* (New York: Feminist Press and SUNY/College at Westbury, 1973).

Evans, Bergen. *The Natural History of Nonsense.* (New York: Alfred A. Knopf, 1965).

Feuerstein, George, David Frawley, and Subhash Kak. "A New View of Ancient India." *Yoga Journal* (1992): 64–69.

Finch, Charles S., III. *Echoes of the Old Darkland.* (Decatur, Ga.: Khenti Publishers, 1991).

Freud, Sigmund. *Civilization and its Discontents.* (London: Hogarth Press, 1949).

Frost, Michael C. *Choosing Life: Guidelines to Avoiding Extinction.* (Silver Spring, MD: American Association of Taoist Studies, 1997).

Gimbutas, Marija. *The Language of the Goddess.* (San Francisco: Harper & Row, 1989).

Gordon, Cyrus. *The Ancient Near East.* (New York: W.W. Norton, 1962).

Gore, Al, Jr. "The Story of the Earth and Us." *Magical Blend Magazine* 42 (April 1994).

Guignebert, Charles. *Ancient, Medieval and Modern Christianity.* (New York: University Books, 1961).

Hazlitt, W. Carew. *Faiths and Folklore of the British Iles* (2 vols). (New York: Benjamin Bloom, Inc., 1965).

Hendrix, James Marshall (Jimi). *Band of Gypsys. Machine Gun.* (New York: Heaven Research, 1970).

Henry, Jules. *Pathways to Madness.* (New York: Random House, 1965).

Hua-Ching Ni, *Mystical Universal Mother.* (San Diego, Calif.: College of Traditional Healing, 1991).

Iyengar, B.K.S. *Light on Pranayama: The Yogic Art of Breathing.* (New York: Crossroad Publishing Co., 1981).

Jairazbhoy, R.A. *Foreign Influence in Ancient India.* (London: Asia Publishing House, 1963).

Johnson, Charles Wsir. *Weight Loss for African Americans: A "Cultural" Lifestyle Change.* (Germantown, Tenn.: Seymour-Smith, Inc., 1994).

Johnson, Kamau R. *Beyond the Watch: A Survey of Human Time Perception* (University of Florida: Unpublished Ph.D. dissertation, 1987).

Jung, Carl, and C. Kerenyi. *Essays on the Science of Mythology.* (New York: Bollingen, 1949).

Kamalu, Chukunyere. *Foundations of African Thought.* (London: Karnak House, 1990).

Keller, Werner. *The Bible as History.* (New York: Bantam Books, 1956).

Kervran, Louis C. *Biological Transmutations.* (Brooklyn, N.Y.: Swan House Publishing, 1972).

Klarwein, Marti. *God Jokes.* (New York: Harmony Books, 1987).

Knaster, Mirka. "Raider of the Lost Goddess." *East West Journal* (1990): 39.

Koch, William F. *The Survival Factor in Neoplastic and Viral Diseases.* (Detroit: Vanderkloot Press, 1961).

Kramer, Heinrich and James Sprenger. *Malleus Malefricarum*. (New York: Dover Publications, 1971).

Kybalion. *Hermetic Philosophy*. (Chicago: The Masonic Publication Society, 1940).

Lattimore, Richmond, ed. *The Iliad of Homer*. (Chicago: University of Chicago Press, 1937).

Lea, Henry Charles. *The Inquisition of the Middle Ages*. (New York: Citadel Press, 1954).

Lederer, Wolfgang. *The Fear of Women*. (New York: Harcourt Brace & Jovanovich, Inc., 1968).

Lentricchia, Frank, and Thomas McLaughlin, ed. *Critical Terms for Literary Study*. (Chicago: University of Chicago Press, 1990).

Lerner, Gerda. *The Creation of Patriarchy*. (New York and London: Oxford University Press, 1986).

Levy, Howard S. *Chinese Footbinding: The History of a Curious Erotic Custom*. (New York: Walton Rawls, 1966).

Lewis, Helen Block. *Psychic War in Men and Women*. (New York: New York University Press, 1976).

Lindsey, Hal, *The Late Great Planet Earth*. (New York: Bantam Books, 1972).

Lin Yutang. *The Wisdom of Lao Tse*. (New York: The Modern Library, 1976).

Maasi, Shaha Mfundishi, and Mfundishi J.H. Hassan K. Salim. *Kupigana Ngumi: Root Symbols of the Ntchru and Ancient Kmt*. Vol. 1. (Orange, N.J.: The Pan-Afrakan Kupigana Ngumi Press and Black Gold Press,1992).

MacHovec, Frank J. *Nostradamus: His Prophecies for the Future*. (New York: Peter Paupe, 1972).

Mallory, J.P. *In Search of the Indo-Europeans*. (London: Thames and Hudson, 1989).

Manikkalingam, P.K. *The Divine Science*. (Madras, India: Paari Nilayam, 1924).

McGill, Ormond. *The Mysticism and Magic of India*. (London: A.S. Barnes and Company, 1977).

Mendelson, Robert S. *Male Practice: How Doctors Manipulate Women*. (Chicago: Contemporary Books, Inc., 1984).

Moore, Marcia and Mark Douglas. *Diet, Sex, and Yoga*. (York, Maine: Arcane Publications, 1966).

Moore, T. Owens. *The Science of Melanin: Dispelling the Myths*. (Silver Spring, Md.: Venture Books-Beckham House Publishers, 1996).

Mumford, Lewis. *Interpretation and Forecasts*. (New York: Harcourt Brace & Jovanovich, Inc., 1973).

Neumann, Erich. *The Origins and History of Consciousness*. (Princeton, N.J.: Princeton University Press, 1973).

Newark, Tim. *Women Warlords*. (London: Karnak House, 1989).

Rashidi, Runoko. *Introduction to the Study of African Classical Civilizations*. (London: Karnak House, 1992).

Rashidi, Runoko, and Ivan Van Sertima, eds. *African Presence in Early Asia*. (New Brunswick, N.J.: Transaction Publishers, 1985).

Reid, Howard, and Michael Croucher. *The Way of the Warrior.* (New York: Simon & Schuster, 1983).

Reinach, Salomon. *Orpheus.* (New York: Horace Liveright, Inc., 1930).

Robbins, Rossell Hope. *Witchcraft and the Inquisition.* (New York: Crown Publishers, 1959).

Scott, Walter. *Letters on Demonology and Witchcraft.* (London: George Routledge & Sons, 1884).

Shankaranarayanan, S. *The Ten Great Cosmic Powers.* (Pondicherry, India: Dipti Publications, 1972).

Shure, Eduard. *The Great Initiates.* (San Francisco: Harper and Row Publishing, 1882).

Sinkiewicz, John T. "The Planetary Grid: The Cornerstone of Science and Evolution." *Pursuit* 6(1982): 10.

Smith, Homer. *Man and His Gods.* (Boston: Little, Brown, & Co., 1952).

Spretnak, Charlene, ed. *The Politics of Women's Spirituality.* (New York: Anchor/Doubleday, 1982).

Stone, Merlin. *When God was a Woman.* (New York: Dial Press, 1976).

Strecher, Robert. *The Strecher Memorandom.* (Los Angeles: Cal-C Publishers, 1987).

Theertha, Dharma. *History of Hindu Imperialism.* (Madras, India: Dalit Educational Literature Center, 1941).

Tuckerman, Barbara. *A Distant Mirror.* (New York: Alfred A. Knopf, 1978).

Van Sertima, Ivan, ed. *African Presence in Early America.* (New Brunswick, N.J.: Transaction Publishers, 1987).

————. *Egypt Revisited.* New Brunswick, (N.J.: Transaction Publishers, 1989).

Velikovsky, Immanuel. *Worlds in Collision.* (New York: Simon & Schuster, 1950).

von Leibniz, Gottfried Wilhelm. *Basic Writings: Discourse on Metaphysics.* (New York: Open Court Classics, 1902).

Walker, Barbara. *The Woman's Dictionary of Symbols & Sacred Objects.* (San Francisco: Harper & Son, 1988).

Weber, Max. *The Protestant Ethic and the Spirit of Capitalism.* (New York: Charles Scribner's Sons, 1930).

Westcott, William Wynn, ed. *Collectanea Hermetica*, trans. Dr. Everard. (1623; London: Kessinger, 1992).

Wheeler, Sir Mortimer. *The Indus Civilization.* (Cambridge: Cambridge University Press, 1960).

Wilhelm, Richard, and C.G. Jung. *The Secret of the Golden Flower.* (London: K. Paul, Trench, & Trubner, 1935).

Wilson, H.H. *The Vishnu Purana, Vol. II.* (London: Kegan Paul, Trench, Trubner, 1864).

Wolf, Geoffrey. *Black Sun.* (New York: Random House, 1976).

Yukteswar, Swami Sri. *The Holy Science.* (Self Realization Fellowship, 1963).

I N D E X

About the Author

Wayne B. Chandler is an anthrophotojournalist specializing in ancient Asian civilization, philosophy and culture. Mr. Chandler is a board member of Afriasia, a national organization dedicated to the historical study of the impact and unition of African and Asian world populations. Mr. Chandler has appeared on numerous television and radio programs and has published widely in his area of expertise domestically and abroad. Mr. Chandler was a visiting lecturer at the University of the District of Columbia from 1982 to 1986. He designed an alternative curriculum for the National Trust School System and was a consultant via W.A.F. for the Portland Oregon schools in their revision of a multicultural curriculum for African Americans. Mr. Chandler helped implement the Genius Transformation Program, which demonstrated successfully that when under-privileged children are exposed to proper historical information and lifestyle, their self-esteem and outlook on life are positively impacted. From 1985 through 1995 Chandler was a regular contributor and co-author to the J.A.C., Journal of African Civilizations, a series of books produced annually, edited by the esteemed professor Ivan Van Sertima and published by Transaction Books, Rutgers University.

Chandler has delved deeply into the Chinese systems of (qi) chi gong or energy enhancement, as it pertains to vitality, physical/mental regeneration (organic alchemy), and longevity. He has studied and practiced these systems with Master Mantak Chia, Dr. Michael Frost and Tao Huang. Chandler is a certified practitioner in Tui Na, one of the four pillars of Chinese medical science.

He has lectured to audiences throughout the continental United States, Canada, Northwestern Europe, Spain, Uganda, Kenya Africa and Great Britain(U.K.). As a researcher Mr. Chandler has traveled extensively to areas related to his field of study.

For sixteen years Mr. Chandler was co-chairman of What's A Face Productions (W.A.F.). A business dedicated to the global dissemination of information on the relations of ancient races and cultures and their effect on current society and civilization. He was also co-founder of the INU Gallery, an intercultural art space for transcultural exchange and co-producer of New World Visions, an award winning cable television program. All establishments were located in the Washington D.C. area.

Chandler's goal is to blend history, science, philosophy and energy practice into one powerful healing modality that can and will lend itself to personal transformation. His studies into alternative medical strategies and systems are on going and continuous. He is currently pursuing certification in medical chi gong from world renown chi gong master, Liang Shou-yu.

For personal appearances and lectures, Mr. Chandler may be contacted at ancient_future81 @hotmail.com